ORGANIZING JAINISM IN INDIA
AND ENGLAND

OXFORD STUDIES IN
SOCIAL AND CULTURAL ANTHROPOLOGY

Oxford Studies in Social and Cultural Anthropology represents the work of authors, new and established, which will set the criteria of excellence in ethnographic description and innovation in analysis. The series serves as an essential source of information about the world and the discipline.

OTHER TITLES IN THIS SERIES

Society and Exchange in Nias
Andrew Beatty

The Female Bridegroom: A Comparative Study of Life-Crisis Rituals in South India and Sri Lanka
Anthony Good

Of Mixed Blood: Kinship and History in Peruvian Amazonia
Peter Gow

Exchange in Oceania: A Graph Theoretic Analysis
Per Hage and Frank Harary

The Arabesk Debate: Music and Musicians in Modern Turkey
Martin Stokes

ORGANIZING JAINISM
IN INDIA AND
ENGLAND

MARCUS BANKS

CLARENDON PRESS · OXFORD

1992

Oxford University Press, Walton Street, Oxford OX2 6DP

Oxford New York Toronto
Delhi Bombay Calcutta Madras Karachi
Petaling Jaya Singapore Hong Kong Tokyo
Nairobi Dar es Salaam Cape Town
Melbourne Auckland
and associated companies in
Berlin Ibadan

Oxford is a trade mark of Oxford University Press

Published in the United States
by Oxford University Press, New York

British Library Cataloguing in Publication Data
Data available

Library of Congress Cataloging in Publication Data
Banks, Marcus.
Organizing Jainism in India and England / Marcus Banks.
p. cm.—(Oxford studies in social and cultural
anthropology)
Revision of thesis (Ph.D.)—University of Cambridge, 1985.
Includes bibliographical references and index.
1. Jainism—India—Jāmnagar. 2. Jainism—England—Leicester.
3. Jāmnagar (India)—Religion. 4. Leicester (England)—Religion.
I. Title. II. Series.
BL1325.9.J35B35 1992 305.6'944—dc20 92-2641
ISBN 0-19-827388-6

Typeset by Pentacor PLC, *High Wycombe, Bucks*
Printed in Great Britain by
Biddles Ltd, Guildford and King's Lynn

In memory of

John Banks
(1912–1987)

Ramesh Gordandhas Shroff
(1934–1989)

(1)

PREFACE

This book is a revised version of a doctoral thesis I submitted to the University of Cambridge in 1985. I have rewritten the text, adding some material and omitting quite a lot. My interests have changed quite substantially since completing the thesis and, while I have updated many of the references, I have not engaged in an extensive discussion of the most recent literature, particularly that on Asian groups in Britain. So little is known about the Jains, however, that I feel any contribution will be worth while.

The material for the thesis and hence for this book was gathered through library research and fieldwork in the English city of Leicester and the Indian city of Jamnagar, Gujarat State. For a variety of reasons it is pointless to try and disguise these locations, given the specificity of the material, although I have used pseudonyms for individuals and have occasionally blurred some of the details. More details of the fieldwork are given in Chapter 1.

People and Places

Individuals in the two cities are linked by ties of kinship and friendship—indeed, some individuals divided their time more or less equally between the two places—but there were no administrative or other links between the organizations I studied in England and those I studied in India. In England, I chose the city of Leicester because I had been informed that it maintained the only functioning immigrant Jain group in the country with any property and structured organization. In the event, this turned out to be not entirely true, but fieldwork was far easier to conduct in Leicester than it would have been in London, for example. While I was in Leicester I chose the city of Jamnagar in Saurashtra (Gujarat) to conduct my parallel study. This decision was partly a result of the size and location of the city, but mostly because of the numerous contacts I could make there through my Leicester informants. Perhaps other towns in Gujarat would have been equally well suited to the study but given the limited amount of time available it seemed wisest to chose one where I could begin work as quickly as possible.

The subjects of my study in both cities were all Gujaratis, and all spoke Gujarati fluently (with the exception of some younger children in Leicester). I met several Rajasthani Jains, both in Leicester and in Rajasthan, who served to broaden my understanding. However, although all my informants were Gujarati by birth or descent, I should stress that Jamnagar is located in the Saurashtran peninsula of Gujarat which differs in several respects (ethnographically and linguistically) from the rest of the State.

For this reason, and because little anthropological research has been conducted in Saurashtra, I have been cautious in the use of ethnographic data from the rest of Gujarat, and throughout the book I have tried to distinguish between the two in general discussions. The majority of my Leicester informants were also born in, or trace their descent to, Saurashtra (either to Jamnagar or to some other town or village). However, the vast majority of these had come to Leicester from East Africa in the late 1960s and early 1970s. Despite residence, and even birth in East Africa, they retain close affective ties with particular towns and villages in Saurashtra or, more rarely, Gujarat. The majority of my informants, especially in Jamnagar, were either unmarried men between twenty and thirty years of age, or male household heads over fifty years. Much of my fieldwork time, however, was spent in households, so I had informal contact with women, children, and young couples and was able to gather specific information from these groups as necessary.

Because I worked alone, without assistants, I did not conduct surveys or use questionnaires as I felt this would be too time-consuming. Some numerical data were, however, gathered from documents compiled by the groups under study. In Leicester, my principle language of communication was English; in Jamnagar it was a mixture of English and Gujarati (often in the same breath!). I am grateful to Shrimati Lilavati Doshi and Shri Manharlal Jhaveri for their help in translating documents and other texts from Gujarati.

Language

Although I used Gujarati for large parts of my fieldwork, I rarely read or wrote the language. Moreover, if I asked my informants for the spelling of a word new to me I could receive several variations depending on the education and background of the informant. In Saurashtra, many Kathiawadi (the alternative name for the region) and Kacchi (the region to the north) terms are used, and local variations in pronunciation make standardization in the text that follows and between it and other works almost impossible. Moreover, there are several specialist terms deriving from Sanskrit or Prakrit. As a result I have been forced to compromise on the transliteration. All indigenous terms are transcribed into Roman letters and italicized, according to standard conventions but with the diacritic marks omitted. I have frequently omitted the final 'a' that would normally come at the end of a word ending in a consonant; in most cases this reflects local pronunciation; the cases where it is retained (for example, *moksa, diksa*) are usually non-Gujarati terms. South Asian specialists should be able to identify terms easily but non-specialists, I hope, should find reading easier. The Glossary at the end of this work gives all the terms with their diacritic marks, allowing the non-specialist reader to work out the 'correct' (that is, learned or standardized) pronunciation. Omitting the diacritic marks does, I confess, allow room for ambiguity in pronunciation if the glossary is not consulted—in particular, aspirated and unaspirated sibillants cannot be distinguished, nor can long and short vowels. The former aspect does, however, reflect local pronunciation, which satisfies one of the conflicting constraints I felt.

Most of the terms in the text are Gujarati in origin and I have not distinguished between them, Kacchi, Kathiawadi, Sanskrit, and Prakrit as all such terms are used only for illustration or authentication (and not as the bases of discussion). Place names, personal names, and some very frequently used or common nouns stand as they are, however, without italicizing. Moreover, rather than confuse the text further with Gujarati, Sanskrit, or Prakrit plurals these are simply denoted with a non-italicized 's' at the end of the word. For my Gujarati spelling I have relied on the excellent English–Gujarati dictionary compiled by Deshpande (1978), while for Sanskrit and Prakrit terms I have used the glossary compiled by P. S. Jaini (1979).

Photographs

This book contains a number of photographs that I took during the main periods of fieldwork. Their purpose is not so much to 'illustrate' the text as to provide a parallel text which complements the written one. I have argued elsewhere (Banks 1989*a*) for the place of photography in anthropological interpretation and against the closure of anthropological meaning that reductive or descriptive captioning brings about. For this reason, the photographs are not captioned, although a descriptive reference for each one is provided below (pp. xiv–xv).

I am grateful to János Tari for all his help in selecting and preparing the photographs and to Éva Bódi for printing them.

Acknowledgements

The research was principally funded with a grant from the Social Science Research Council (now Economic and Social Research Council). For smaller grants, to assist with additional fieldwork, I am grateful to the Managers of the Wyse Fund and the Smuts Memorial Fund (University of Cambridge). Earlier and shorter versions of Chapters 4 and 8 were first published in 1984 (in *Cambridge Anthropology*, 9/3) and in 1991 (in Carrithers and Humphrey 1991) respectively.

In connection with my Leicester fieldwork I would particularly like to thank Drs Valerie and Paul Marett and my numerous non-Jain friends for their support, particularly David Smeaton, and Shobhna and Niranjan Jani. For my Indian fieldwork, I am most deeply indebted to Professor Rameshbhai Shroff of the Gujarat Vidyapith where I was an affiliated student. I would also like to thank his family, and Sharadbhai Jhaveri and his family in Jamnagar, for making me so welcome. Since completing this work Rameshbhai and Sharadbhai (who were related affinally) have both died; I had not even begun to repay my debt to them. Also in Jamnagar, I would like to thank the trustees of the Jain Pravasi Grah as well as all those who made my stay so enjoyable. My thanks are due to Shobhna and Niranjan Jani for their patience in trying to teach me Gujarati in Leicester and to Rameshbhai Patel (Swami Git Govind) in Ahmedabad for admirably continuing the task.

In Cambridge, I must thank my two supervisors, Debby Swallow and Caroline Humphrey, for their continued support and sheer hard work on my part as well as other members of the Department of Social Anthropology at the time. Josephine Reynell proved an invaluable long-distance companion while we were both in the field and a source of help and stimulus while we both grappled with trying to write about the Jains. Outside Cambridge, I must extend my thanks to Maureen Michaelson and Paul Dundas for their valuable comments.

Most of all, however, my thanks must go to all my informants— some of whom became close friends—in Leicester and Jamnagar who provided the information on which this work is based, and for much more besides. They are far too numerous to name, and to single out particular individuals would be unfair for they all helped me in their own ways. I hope they will recognize themselves explicitly or implicitly in the text (I hope equally that others will not). However, while inspiration and guidance have come from others and they must share in any credit, the responsibility for any mistakes or inaccuracies is all mine.

I am not a follower of Jainism (or of any religious tradition): still, for all the Jains in Leicester and Jamnagar it behoves me to say:

Jai Jinendra!

M.B.

Oxford
1991

CONTENTS

PHOTOGRAPHS

FIGURES

MAPS

TABLES

Introduction

On Content

The anthropological study of 'great tradition' religions must of necessity operate on two levels: the study of the people who claim to follow a particular religion together with the institutions and organizations they create and support to this end, and a study of the doctrines and beliefs to which these people adhere. This book proceeds on both levels, but the emphasis rests more on the former than on the latter, simply as a result of my own research interests. But the distinction is not absolute, and is often not perceived by the actors themselves. For example, Baird, in an article on the distinction between 'religion and the secular' in post-independence India, cites numerous cases where, in courts of law, plaintiffs claimed that the administration of temple monies, the appointment of religious specialists, and so on, were an

(2)

integral part of their religious system and not a secular adjunct to their doctrines (1976).

I have tried to adopt a synthetic approach and to deal with belief and behaviour concurrently. I have adopted a similar approach to one of the major issues in the anthropological study of religion, the distinction between precept and practice. To my mind there is an assumption underlying such a distinction that the anthropologist has produced an absolute (be it of doctrine, of historical authenticity, of textual analysis) against which she or he measures the beliefs and actions of the people she or he studies. In the concluding chapter I argue against such a view for the analyst but agree that it has great value for the actor: religious systems are after all primarily concerned with the truth of things, the reality behind the illusion.

Although most, if not all, of the religious systems of south and south-east Asia have been studied by anthropologists, Jainism and the Jains have been curiously ignored. Of course, anthropologists concerned with other issues, especially Indian local economies, have encountered the Jains and occasionally made some comment on their religious beliefs and practices but there has been little rigorous analysis of the group in its own right.[1]

Thus my own work in this book is largely expository rather than analytical, although it is of course impossible to present ethnography without some form of analysis, if for no other reason than that not every last detail can be recorded, and hence a process of selection and elimination must operate. In fact, I have been particularly selective in my choice of data for presentation, preferring to concentrate in detail upon a narrow range of issues and topics, rather than to try to present a comprehensive and all-encompassing picture.

---

[1] In the first category are works such as Bharati (1972), Cottam (1980), Fox (1973), Marriot (1976), and Timberg (1978). The few that deal with the Jains in their own right include Sangave's *Jaina Community* (1980, originally published 1959), and Nevaskar's study of Jains and Quakers, *Capitalists without Capitalism* (1971), but neither of these is based on fieldwork. The only intensive fieldwork was conducted by a missionary, A. M. Stevenson (1910; 1915), which until now has been a major source for most subsequent writers, including Sangave. In addition there are several documentary films which feature the Jains; one was made for the BBC as part of a religious affairs series ('The Frontiers of Peace: Jainism in India', 1985, dir. Paul Kuepferle), another was made on a much more amateur basis by myself and two colleagues ('The Jains. A Religious Community of India', 1985, dir. Marcus Banks, Caroline Humphrey, and James Laidlaw: Rivers Video Unit, University of Cambridge). I have also made a film in Jamnagar ('Raju and His Friends', 1988, dir. Marcus Banks: National Film and Television School/Royal Anthropological Institute) the central character of which is a Jain, although Jainism as such is not discussed.

My aim in this book, therefore, is to present a composite picture of corporate Jain identity, and the meaning of that identity, through an ethnography of Jain institutions and Jain organizations in two countries. Although I do describe certain rituals and ceremonies in Chapters 3 and 7, I do so from the standpoint of their organization and the interpersonal and intergroup relations involved, rather than from the standpoint of their symbolism or doctrinal implications. Nor do I cover aspects of personal and domestic ritual, or the specific content of personal beliefs. All these are worthwhile topics, but I feel they must be preceded by a full understanding of Jain social organization and social identity, hence the subject-matter of this book.

Anthropology or Indology?

Because Indian society has been long and intensively studied by anthropologists, Indian and European, there are a few points of terminology and methodology which are the subject of debate and on which I should perhaps make my own position clear. First, although there is a strong argument for approaching an Indian religion through its texts, this course was not open to me; I do not know Ardhamagadhi or the Prakrits (the language of most of the Jain scriptures) nor Sanskrit. Even those texts which have been translated into European languages I used only occasionally, usually in order to check the accuracy of a point made by a modern author. My justification for this (beyond the fact that I had neither the time nor the resources to support such studies to the point of proficiency in textual analysis) is that few if any of my (lay) informants were familiar with the texts either. The organizational structure of Jainism is such that lay doctrine and belief are derived largely from the ascetics (the 'monks' and 'nuns') who may or may not derive these from the texts. If, in the Leicester community, where there are no 'monks' and 'nuns', or indeed any particularly learned persons, there had been a move back to the texts in search of guidance and direction, I should have been forced to take a greater interest myself. But instead, there was, at worst, a sense of anomie, and, at best, a desire for self-orientation through 'new' forms of Jainism (discussed in Chapter 8) and it was this that I studied. I have therefore been careful in this book not to make any assumptions about what the practice or belief of Jainism 'should' be, unless these are assumptions common in the community in question.

Already I have used the word 'community' and this brings me on to my second point. On the rare occasions I use the word I do so as it is used by Indians themselves, particularly in the overseas context (even when speaking in Gujarati or some other vernacular, the English word may be used). That is, not to denote a group of continuously interacting individuals who may share a common residence location, a common view of life, and who may constitute a faction ('a group organized to deal with a specific but temporary situation'—Morris 1957: 306), but instead to denote a section of Indian society (in India or overseas) that is considered by others in that society to be different from themselves in some way. The basis of difference may be regio-linguistic (the Panjabi community, the Gujarati community), religious (the Muslim community, the Jain community), or it may lie within the Hindu social hierarchy (the Lohana community, the Harijan community). Following Morris (ibid.) I try to preface the word when it is used with an adjective to denote the particular community or level of community that I am discussing at any point; sometimes I place the word in inverted commas to alert the reader to the ambiguous nature of the term. Morris used the word to apply to 'castes and sects' (ibid.: 307), and in a later publication he noted that in Uganda these 'communities' were composed of parts of 'sub-castes or jatis' that had come from different districts in India (1968: 16).

My third point concerns the terminology of caste. In a paper on caste in Gujarat (1982) A. M. Shah has criticized the use of both 'jati' and 'caste' and has instead confined himself for the most part to the term 'division' (of which there are four 'orders') and the use of a group name (Koli, Anavil, etc.) alone, after specifying the order of division. These orders are not the same as the categories of the *varna* hierarchy, but consist of large groups (Brahmans, Kathis, Rajputs) which, amongst other things, limit food transactions to members of the same group. 'Vania' is one of these first-order divisions, of which Srimali and Oswal—the two groups with whom I shall be principally concerned in the chapters that follow—are second-order divisions. Shah is particularly sceptical about the use of prefixes and suffixes to indicate the scale of the group under discussion ('sub-caste', 'caste cluster', 'caste complex', and so forth) (ibid.: 8).

On one level, I agree with him entirely. The terminology of caste has been used carelessly in the literature and has rendered the whole issue impenetrable to many non-Indianists. On another level, however, I find particular terms useful because the relationship between such terms can mirror exactly the relationship between groups. For instance, in my Jamnagar fieldwork I (and, I believe, my informants—see Chapter 2) had a terminological difficulty in distinguishing between members of the same caste or *jati* who lived in the same city but had different origins (urban and rural). The importance attached to the difference varied greatly, but the nature and cause of the difference (although not necessarily the subsequent development) was the same in all cases. Thus in Part I I use the term '*jati*' to refer to endogamous groups composed of individuals bearing the same *jati* name (sometimes referred to as 'sub-castes' in the literature) and the term 'section' to refer to the rural and urban components (or subdivisions) of these *jati*s, although in some cases these sections are now endogamous.[2] I use the word 'caste' sparingly, and only to indicate the ideology and practice of hierarchy and division within Hindu society. Thus I talk about the phenomenon of caste, but not about 'castes', or 'the Srimali caste' (except, of course, when I am quoting from or referring to another author). In Part II of the book, which deals with Jains and other Asians in Britain, I try to avoid any terminology such as 'caste', '*jati*' or 'sub-*jati*', except when referring to a particular issue of Indian ethnography.

Fourthly, although I sometimes refer to the Jains as '*vania*s' ('traders', known in the ethnography of Hindi-speaking areas as '*bania*s') I do not discuss the commonly asserted proposition that Jains are traders and businessmen because of their religious orientation. This idea, that Jains entered the business sphere because their religion debarred them from other types of activity, seems to be the result of a logical but inaccurate deduction by Jacobi (1914: 473) who stated that because of their 'vow' of *ahimsa* (the desire not to cause harm) Jains could not be soldiers or farmers (farming would entail the loss of life through ploughing and reaping) and thus business was the only 'safe' occupation open to them. Yet Jains are and have been farmers, especially in the south of India, and the six professions said to be created by the founder of society and Jainism in the present age, Rishabha, include both farming and the army (Sangave 1980: 278). I

---

[2] The inhabitants of Jamnagar in fact often refer to themselves as members of a '*nat*', a corruption of '*jnati*'. It is, however, more common in the literature to find reference to '*jati*' (or '*jat*') as the local term for what is often called 'caste' or 'sub-caste', and so I have used '*jati*' as my principal term. It should be noted that '*jati*' has a much wider term of reference than simply 'caste', however, and is used to describe the class of any type of thing (i.e. species, kind).

think there are many problems with the Weberian thesis of attitudinal orientation when applied to the Jains, some of which I discuss in the final chapter. My position is that while many of the lay Jain men I worked with in India, and several of those I worked with in Leicester, were businessmen and retailers, I do not consider that their adherence to Jain tenets caused them to behave with a different or superior economic rationality to that of their Hindu neighbours. There is a strong merchant ideology and positive status evaluation of mercantile success in Gujarat and Saurashtra (Shah and Shroff 1959: 63; Tambs-Lyche 1980) to which the Jains also subscribe and their business success is more likely to be related to forms of internal social organization which facilitate the development of rotating credit associations and such like.[3]

Finally, I use the terms 'Buddhism' and 'Hinduism' to make points of comparison with 'Jainism'. If the points were long and rigorous then I would have defined these two religious complexes more accurately, but I believe the labels are adequate for the incidental comparisons I make. By 'Buddhism' I refer either to the religious movement initiated in the fifth century BC by Gotama Buddha, or to Theravada Buddhism, particularly as it is found in Sri Lanka (that is, wherever I refer to the work of Gombrich or Southwold). I use the words 'Hindu' and 'Hinduism' to refer to the majority religious practices of Gujarat: a cluster of beliefs and practices centred around the major deities of Krishna, Rama, Shiva and various forms of the Mother goddess (Shakti, Devi, Mata, etc), and the myths and legends attendant upon them. Specific cults, sects, and beliefs within the Hindu corpus (such as the legends surrounding Jalaram Bapa, and the 'sects' of the Arya Samaj and Sanatan Dharma) are identified and described where necessary.

In the conclusion to the book I argue that Jainism too should not be taken as a single entity, nor can any form of 'pure' or 'original' Jainism be distilled from the mass of ethnographical and historical data I present in the book. Culture (and the cultural aspects of religion) can be seen as the product of myth. Although some of the more nationalistic Indian organizations look back to a 'golden age' of Indian society, when Aryan supremacy was at its height and the ideal form of society, depicted for example in the Mahabharata, and exemplified by

---

[3] Timberg (1971; 1978) gives a convincing account of such developments and a similar approach characterizes Bayly's work (1978; 1983) although Bayly also stresses the need to look beyond the boundaries of caste and sect.

strong personal morality, prevailed, it is equally distant for everyone today. The Jains also have visions of a past 'golden age', enshrined in their texts, and idiosyncratically held by individuals; in this the Leicester Jains are no further from their 'roots' than the Jamnagar Jains. The idea underlying this book is that Jainism (and religion generally) gives meaning and structure to the rag-bag of cultural features that make up Jain, or Indian, society. This is no less true in Jamnagar than it is in Leicester. Hence, I perceive no sharp division between the populations I studied in Leicester and Jamnagar: in both places Jainism holds the pieces of culture together.

Cultural identity, like ethnicity, is emergent, and differences may arise within a religious or cultural group as they may within an ethnic group. My parallel with ethnicity is taken from Yancey et al. (1976: 392), but I differ with them over the necessary causes of such differences. While they argue for external, environmental factors affecting parts of a group in different ways, I argue in this book, particularly in Chapter 8, for the possibility of different perceptions by the members of a group of an abstract phenomenon (Jainism) as the cause of the differences between them.

On Form

The reader, on glancing at the table of contents, may be surprised to find no chapter titled 'Comparisons'. After all, what is the point of conducting parallel fieldwork in two places, bringing the two sets of observations together in one work and then not explicitly comparing them? I state my position on this more clearly in the final chapter, but here would like to point out firstly that a number of low-level comparisons are constantly—almost unavoidably—made in the chapters that follow, and secondly that the architecture or structure of the book itself facilitates comparison.

The book is structured in a symmetrical fashion: this chapter and the final chapter act as book-ends, framing the essentially descriptive chapters between them. Parts I and II, which deal with the Jains in Jamnagar and Leicester respectively, each consist of three chapters, the outer chapters again framing an essentially ethnographic chapter in each case. Chapter 5, on the Jains and others in East Africa, acts as a kind of bridge between the two Parts.

Although the book is essentially a descriptive ethnography of Jain organizations, I found it very difficult to write a transparent narrative of events and description. In the first chapter of each ethnographic Part (Chapters 2 and 6) I try to define the internal structures and external context of the group that I am dealing with, although the essential message of each chapter is that the apparently solid boundaries—both my own analytical categories and those of my informants—are shifting, ephemeral, and fluid. In the second chapter (Chapters 3 and 7) I adopt what one reader of the manuscript referred to as a 'borehole' approach, homing in on a number of group events on the basis that these would seem the most likely place to find some expression of Jain-ness. In the third chapter of each Part (Chapters 4 and 8) I pull back from the borehole and examine in each case a kind of puzzle that worried me while I was conducting the original fieldwork. My answers to these puzzles are not especially novel, but the implications cannot really be understood without the material that precedes these chapters.

Of course, the parallelism is not exact—certain issues receive more prominence in one Part than in the other, and it is most likely that the reading of Part II will be influenced by reading Part I first. Moreover, the differences between the two fieldwork locations were so great that there were very few exact parallels to be found at the organizational level. Briefly put, the Jains of Jamnagar appeared, at least, to have a stable and relatively static set of organizational structures, while those in Leicester were in the process of creating them, but on a much smaller scale. Because this process of creation was—to my mind at least—so novel, I have detailed it fairly closely and tried to be scrupulous in specificities of time and place. Time and space are also important in the discussion of the Jamnagar organizations, but—of necessity—I have had to use slightly broader brush-strokes. The historical depth of the Jain presence in Jamnagar is much greater (and less well documented) and the Jains' spatial and numerical presence is much broader. Thus, for example, the events described in Chapters 3 and 7 are typical of the groups that produced them and the fairly marked contrast between the types of events described is typical of the unique character of the two locations.

Methodology and Related Matters

None of the people I worked with, either in Leicester or Jamnagar, had ever before encountered an anthropologist and thus their thoughts and experiences have never been represented in this way before. Of course, this is a position most anthropologists find themselves in. On a more general level, however, the Jains are a little-known group, especially in this country, and, as mentioned, the anthropological literature on them is sparse. Work on the Jains overseas is even more rare and, apart from passing references in works on Asians in Britain and East Africa, the only fieldwork-based anthropological research is that of Michaelson (1983). On the other hand, literature on Jainism itself is extensive, albeit repetitive, and covers most aspects of philosophy, history, and cosmology.

My problem, then, has been to reconcile a large body of data on the textual religion with my own fieldwork experiences, in the absence of any (or many) other studies or ethnographic data. This, in part, was the reason for conducting fieldwork in two places; that is, to enlarge the scope of the ethnographic data I could draw on. If this were the only reason it would have made better sense to conduct my two studies in the same country, perhaps in adjacent towns, or in a town and a village.

However, I began my fieldwork in Leicester because I was interested in the organization of an immigrant religious group in Britain. Literature on Asian groups in Britain is constantly growing and much of it touches on the groups' religious traditions; studies which focus on these traditions is much scarcer, although again, it is growing.[4] My original aim was simply to see how a religion as complex and little known as Jainism was practised in what was initially a foreign country. Other religious groups from the sub-continent have already been studied in this way (for example, Barot 1973; Jackson 1976) and such studies seem to indicate that while the form of a religious practice or ritual can remain constant, its meaning (to the actors) can change as the context changes. For example, Jackson discusses how the festival of Holi in North India is 'a means of preserving the traditional order with regard to caste status and relations between the sexes' achieved through contained rebellion against the social order (Jackson 1976: 204), while in Coventry the festival gave 'a sense of community identity and fellowship to people of Gujarati language and Hindu religion' (ibid.: 208) irrespective of their birthplace. Moreover, in Coventry the ritual bonfire was used to bless young children in alien (to their

---

[4] See, for example, the collection of essays on Hinduism in Britain, edited by Richard Burghart (1987); Pnina Werbner has also published several articles on the Islam of Manchester Pakistanis and summarized her findings in a single volume (1990). There are also two books on South Asian origin 'new religions': the Hare Krishnas (Knott 1986) and the teachings of Rajneesh (Thompson and Heelas 1986), both of which have substantial followings in Britain. See also Banks 1989*b* for a critique of the latter work.

parents) surroundings—a very minor aspect of the ritual in India. Conversely, the throwing of coloured powder and water—the major element of Holi in India—was not observed in Coventry, partly, suggests Jackson, to avoid giving offence to English neighbours, and partly because Holi in India is an expression of inter-caste rivalry, which is neither possible nor desirable, given the small numbers of Gujaratis in Great Britain at the time (ibid.). I am not concerned here with the validity or accuracy of Jackson's assessment, merely with the methodology. Obviously, such an assessment of the situation requires knowledge of the Indian context and ethnographic observation of the same rituals and practices there. In fact, neither Jackson nor Barot give any account (in the articles cited) of any parallel research conducted in India.

A year after Jackson's article was published, James Watson edited a collection of papers entitled *Between Two Cultures* (1977). Each of the studies in the volume is based on fieldwork conducted with a migrant community in Britain and with members of the same community in the 'home' context. The aim of the studies is not to ascertain religious or organizational changes but, as Watson says, 'to understand the actual processes of immigration and the real meaning of ethnic identity' (ibid.: vii). By and large, the authors each take an issue (loosely defined as 'ethnicity') from their British fieldwork experience, and 'explain' it by reference to factual data from the 'home' community. That is, the emphasis of the analysis is largely restricted to the British 'end' of each study.

While not denying the importance of these studies, such an approach was not really pertinent to the Jain case, or more specifically to the Srimalis, on whom I focused my attention in Leicester. This is partly because the process of migration—from various parts of Gujarat, to three countries in East Africa, to Britain—was more complex than the processes documented in the Watson volume (and more akin to Bhachu's (1985) account of 'twice migrants'), and partly because a study of the transformations of a religious identity was more interesting to me than a study of migration and ethnicity.[5]

Consequently, I decided to adopt the approach of Jackson mentioned earlier: to apply anthropological analysis to both the migrant community and the 'home' community. My aim in doing this

---

[5] Although Schermerhorn devotes a chapter to the Jains in a book entitled *Ethnic Plurality in India* (1978) there seems little justification for regarding them as an ethnic group.

was twofold. First, I wished to know more about organized Jainism in practice, simply to enlarge the ethnography of Jainism. Secondly, I felt that the understanding of a group's behaviour in one place would aid the understanding of the group's behaviour in another location—not merely in a unilateral sense with my Jamnagar ethnography helping to 'explain' my Leicester data, but with each supplying insights into the other. My informants were themselves caught up in this process and often used to ask me what I thought the differences were between the two 'communities', either in the abstract, or with relation to specific issues such as dress, or the respect of children for their parents. This book, however, is not an investigation into fieldwork methodology, hence for the most part such insights are worked through, and not explicitly mentioned in the text.

The final form of the book is, I admit, a result of compromise. While my initial aim was to write about the construction and maintenance of a religious identity, I gradually became more and more involved in presenting the ethnography of organizations. This was partly because I found the ethnographic detail intrinsically interesting, and partly because the Jains are so little known that I felt I could take nothing for granted when considering the reader. As a result factual data and descriptions figure importantly in the finished work, both in the form of whole chapters (3 and 7) and interleaved with the analysis.

Fieldwork

While I include myself in the text from time to time, I have no wish to present a reflexive ethnography. I am aware, however, that knowledge of the fieldwork experience can illuminate the more abstract analyses of anthropologists, grounding them in a known social universe for specialist and non-specialist reader alike (see Ruby 1980: 161).

The original fieldwork for this study was conducted from June 1982 to October 1983 as part of my doctoral research at the University of Cambridge. I spent a total of eight months in Leicester and nine months in India—the first two in Ahmedabad and the rest in Jamnagar —and made several shorter trips to both areas over the next six years.

I had made several day-trips to Leicester before moving there and on these trips I met a number of academics and others involved in the 'race-relations industry'. I had never been in the city before and these contacts were as helpful in orienting me to the human geography of the place as they were in tutoring me in the local ethnic politics. Shortly after I arrived to stay, I was given the telephone number of the President of the local Jain organization; I called, arranged to meet him at the Jain Centre the next day, and so my fieldwork began. Almost all my fieldwork contacts over the next seventeen months can, in a sense, be traced back to that telephone call—through meeting the President I was introduced to other Leicester Jains, who introduced me to others, who wrote to family and friends in India, who received me when I arrived in Jamnagar.

I said, initially, that I had come to 'learn about' the Jains and Jainism. In return, I offered English tuition and administrative help at the Leicester Jain Centre, both of which were taken up, though I fear I was not particularly effective on either front. My own work was slow for the first couple of months: I would attend weekly meetings at the Centre, as well as sitting with a small group of men there most mornings (the 'elders' as I term them later), but hours of each day would stretch emptily before me. I filled them by making studies of what was on sale in 'Asian' shops, gutting the archives of the local newspaper, and taking a lot of photographs. The breakthrough came in August, at Paryushan—the Jains' annual festival of forgiveness—when the frequency of meetings at the Centre was sometimes as high as four a day. I was now in daily contact with several people who had seen me over the previous two months: invitations to their homes began to follow, coming with a flood as word got around that I was apparently serious and reliable. These invitations settled down to a level where I was visiting a handful of households weekly or more and visiting a further ten to fifteen on a more sporadic basis. I continued to attend all the meetings held at the Centre. This is not the place to relate my fieldwork experiences in full but I can mention a few memories that abide to give a sense: sitting for two hours at the very start of my fieldwork, by accident, at a meeting of an entirely different group to whom the Jains had let their main meeting-hall at the Centre while they held their own meeting in another room; the contrast between the hot summer weather and the cold dank interior of the Centre (a disused church, now refurbished and thoroughly bright and dry); taking a 'mystery tour', organized by the local bus company, around Leicestershire, with a group of Asian pensioners; elementary lessons in Gujarati cookery with a woman to whom I was supposed to be teaching English but who taught me far more about what it is to be middle-aged, childless, and yet part of an extensive network of friends and co-religionists.

In January 1983 I arrived in Ahmedabad by way of Cairo and Bombay. I spent the next seven weeks there living at the Gujarat Vidyapith (the Gandhian University to which I was affiliated for my time in India), in the rest house (*dharmasala*) of a large Jain temple, and —most happily and profitably—at the home of Professor Ramesh Shroff, my mentor and friend who died suddenly and tragically in 1989. During this time I had daily language tuition from a homoeopathist and follower of Rajneesh with whom I disagreed constantly but who became a great friend and taught me what little Gujarati I know. I also made several visits to important Jain centres in Gujarat.

Very early one morning, just as the hot season was beginning, I caught a bus at Ahmedabad's central bus station and arrived in Jamnagar eight hours later. I went to stay at a Jain boarding-house of which a friend in Leicester, 'Charandas' as he is known here, was a trustee. It was grand house, formerly in private hands, surrounded by trees and some way from the city centre. I made many attempts over the next few months to leave this house, in order to have a more independent existence and to be closer to the centre, but I never succeeded. Later I was glad of this: I met many people while staying there (who demonstrated the depth of their friendship when I fell ill towards the end of my stay). It was also a wonderful legitimator: if I was staying there, at the invitation of several well-known people, then I had to be trustworthy.

My presence in Jamnagar was entirely due to my contacts in Leicester—I had originally no intention of going to India at all, except perhaps for a brief visit, as is the case with many anthropologists who work with Asian groups in Britain. My Leicester friends and informants thought otherwise; they effectively 'sent' me to India and with their help I selected Jamnagar as a place to work—it had been a home to several of them, it was an area they almost all knew (by reputation if not experience), and it was about the same size as Leicester. Making contacts was no problem—people came to find me at the boarding-house in a continual stream, having been alerted by friends and kin. More by chance than design I found myself spending a month or so with one group of interconnected people (networks of friends, kin, and neighbours), before moving on to another. Clefts and cleavages were deeper here: at one point I received an anonymous letter warning me to drop the company of a particular individual or risk losing my contacts with members of another 'community'. Nevertheless, I kept some contacts constantly throughout the fieldwork period and they acted as a useful sounding-board against which I could gauge findings derived from intense but more short-term contacts elsewhere.

Again, some memories: the sharp white light of the summer sun and the acrid smell of *bidi*s in the air; the continual noise and fumes from the traffic on the streets where most of my work was carried out; losing my footing in swirling flash-floods at the start of the rainy season and sinking deep into one of the open gutters/sewers that line the narrow streets of the old town, while small boys shrieked with delight as their neighbourhood turned into an unexpected swimming-pool; being taken for an albino, overseas Gujarati on more than one occasion (usually by the elderly) until my linguistic incompetence gave me away; a magical evening on the day of Mahavira's birthday (Mahavira Jayanti) when hundreds of candles burned in the city's temples in place of the usual neon strips, their light endlessly reflected in the bejewelled silver ornaments that adorned the idols.

Most of my contacts in Leicester and Jamnagar were men. As a result, I am very aware that some of my observations and my subsequent assessment of them are androcentric. I have tried, therefore, in the text that follows to avoid referring to 'the Jains' when it is clear that a remark is really only applicable to Jain men. Unfortunately, there are a number of occasions (such as in the section on Jainism which follows this) where one can only rely on previous descriptions. Luckily for the reader, a comprehensive study of Jain women has been conducted by my friend and fellow-student, Josephine Reynell, and her work may be consulted to provide a greater balance (Reynell 1985a; 1985b; 1991). Of course, simply having a study of 'men' and a study of 'women', does not necessarily provide an assessment of how these categories are constructed (although Reynell does examine this for 'Jain women') and more work remains to be done on gender relations among the Jains.

The Religion of the Jina

What is the nature of this 'religion' that the Jains profess? In order to make sense of the chapters that follow I need to outline briefly the belief and practice of Jainism while simultaneously reminding the reader of the contingency of such a description. Much of the discussion that follows, especially that of doctrine, I present in a largely ahistorical and a-contextual fashion as befits the information I received

—both from texts and from the Jains themselves. Indeed, to anticipate my conclusions in Chapter 9, it is the very fact that Jainism (and indeed any religious tradition) can be represented in such a fashion that allows it to transcend the contingencies of lived experience. Of course, such a description or representation is inevitably a product of its time and context and it would be difficult, I think, for any of my informants, lay or ascetic, to reproduce this discussion, although all would be acquainted with parts of it. In writing this section I have tried to avoid the style of many of the standard modern works on Jainism, and especially tried to avoid the rather tedious lists (the fifty-three life-cycle rituals, the twenty-eight virtues, the six external austerities, the twenty-two sufferings, and so on) with which these texts are so liberally scattered. However, while some of the details below are open to question and debate, depending on the texts or sources consulted (the discussion on the geography of the universe, for example), I feel that the transcendent (self-) representation of the essence of the religion is adequately conveyed for the purpose of what follows.

Jainism is a religious system based on the insights of twenty-four enlightened *jina*s ('conquerors') who taught the way to salvation. The twenty-four are more commonly known as *tirthankara*s ('ford builders') for they crossed the turbulent ocean of the material world (*samsara*) to reach the safe shore of enlightenment and perfect bliss. Jains hold that other men—and possibly women—can achieve enlightenment, but the twenty-four *tirthankara*s are revered for their special qualities and attributes, most notably their ability to instruct their contemporaries and help them to achieve emancipation (*moksa*).[6] The *tirthankara*s and other worthy beings are praised in the nine-line Namaskar or Naukar (salutation) *mantra*—the core recitation of all Jain religious practices, recitations, and ceremonies. A translation of the *mantra* (which is in Prakrit) is given in P. S. Jaini 1979: 162–3.[7]

At its most abstract, Jainism is nothing more than this—a system of practices for enlightenment; all other aspects (temples, idols, rituals, clothing and food customs, the extensive cosmology) are subsidiary. At this abstract level Jainism is at its most distinctive on two counts: in its

---

[6] The features which distinguish a *tirthankara* from other enlightened souls (*siddha*) are several, although the logic underlying these differences is not always clear. For an enumeration of these features see J. L. Jaini 1916: 129–30. For an example of the sectarian discussions on the nature of the *tirthankara*'s soul see Dundas 1985.

[7] There is also a local etymology, which I met in Jamnagar, based on a variant spelling of 'Navkar' which holds that the meaning is 'agent of nine' (*nav*: nine).

conceptions of the universe and of the soul. Souls for the Jain philosophers are discrete, pure entities, without weight or size but conforming to the shape of the body they inhabit, and are fundamentally immutable. They are all, however, barring those that have achieved emancipation, contaminated by non-soul matter (*karma*) which ties them to the world, to the cycle of life and death. As a result of practising austerities, all *karma*s can be neutralized and the soul can achieve enlightenment (*kevalajnana*); shortly after this the *karma*s drop away and the soul is released, never to be entangled in *karma* again.[8] Jains make a fundamental distinction between soul and non-soul, between living and dead (*jiva* and *ajiva*). All souls are eternal and uncreated, simply existing, like the universe they inhabit. This universe is a physical structure, composed of non-living (*ajiva*) matter and of finite, though immense, size. It is shaped roughly like a man, his legs astride, his hands on his hips. In the centre, at about the 'waist', lies our layer of the universe. In the centre is Mount Meru, and surrounding it are seas and continents arranged in concentric circles. Part of one of these continents is the land we inhabit, Bharata, the land that was home to the Jain cosmologists and into which the twenty-four *tirthankara*s were born. Other *tirthankara*s are born in other continents in such a way that there is always a *tirthankara* preaching in the realms men inhabit: emancipation is always possible, and correct action in Bharata can lead to rebirth in such a place. Some parts of the continents, including Bharata, are subject to fluctuations in the time cycle of the universe, such that the possibility of the birth of a *tirthankara* and the emancipation of men (and, possibly, women) is only possible at a time in which happiness and unhappiness (*susama* and *dusama*) are present in more or less equal proportion: too much of one or the other and the human race is not capable of producing those giants who are able to appreciate both the transience of worldly happiness and the possibility of unalloyed bliss. Other continents, however, perpetually bask in the right balance, and there is always a *tirthankara* there, preaching the message of liberation. (See P. S. Jaini 1979: 29–32, 127–30, for fuller descriptions of the universe.)

---

[8] This is not quite accurate, though the point is rather an obscure one. Of the infinite number of souls in the universe an infinite number are said to be incapable of achieving salvation (see P. S. Jaini 1977). In this case—as opposed to that outlined in n. 6—the logic behind the doctrine is obvious (that is, there must always be a balance of soul and non-soul in the universe and hence in an eternal universe there must be an infinite number of souls), while the details are vague.

Below our part of the universe are seven hells, each more unpleasant than the last, while above are sixteen heavens, full of sensual pleasures (ibid.: 128–9). Gods inhabit the heavens and the first of the hells, while demons inhabit the other six hells. Good or bad actions in this world can lead to rebirth in these realms. Above the highest heaven, at the very top of the universe, lies a crescent-shaped realm, *siddha loka* or *isat pragbharabhumi*, the resting place of emancipated souls. When the soul is freed from *karma* it rises through the universe to inhabit this region. In this way Jainism differs from, for example, Hindu schools of thought which either do not view all souls (of men, gods, animals, demons) as interchangeable (or rather, that one soul can exist in all states serially), or else perceive the universe as an expression of some higher being. That is to say, in doctrinal Jainism there is no distinction made between the mundane and the transcendental: the universe, and everything in it, is knowable and classifiable; even the experience of omniscience and emancipation is described and documented. This is the source and centre of Jain 'atheism'—there is for the Jains no supreme transcendent being in the universe, nor any means of divinely assisted salvation. The *tirthankaras* (and other liberated souls) once emancipated, are unable to intervene in the affairs of men and the universe, for this would involve action and re-entanglement with *karma*.

Emancipation is a state of permanent and unalloyed bliss, repudiation of which is unthinkable. It is also a state of non-action and non-desire, for it is through these qualities that emancipation is realized. Action by the soul (which includes emotion, expressed through desire) attracts *karma*s which stick in a literal and physical sense to the soul, causing it not only to be weighed down and confined to human, divine, or hellish realms, but also to be blinded to its own qualities and, in bodies other than those of men, unable to conceive of the possibility of emancipation. This is the reason that liberation is only possible from a human body. Hellish beings are blinded by their misery, heavenly ones by their happiness, while animals, plants, and other non-human life-forms simply lack sufficient sensory perception or intellect. Only man experiences the right degree of happiness to alert him to the possibility of perfect happiness, balanced with the right degree of unhappiness to warn him that bliss is not to be found in earthly life (and then this is only possible during the right phase of the time-cycle, as mentioned). Jains I met, particularly the ascetics ('monks' and 'nuns'), continually reminded me of the rarity of the circumstances that had led to me being born in a position from which I could begin to tread the Jain path, particularly that out of all the millions in the western world I was one of the very few ever to have sought out the Jains. (In fact my combination of circumstances is not so auspicious. The phase of time (*kala*) that was favourable to the birth of Mahavira and the other twenty-three *tirthankara*s of the present half-cycle (*sarpini*) has passed, and none can now achieve enlightenment directly from our part of the 'continent'.)

Because *karma* is attracted by action, its shedding must be accomplished through inactivity—itself brought about by desirelessness. For the Jains this desirelessness is manifested in the cardinal principle of *ahimsa*—usually translated 'non-violence', but more specifically meaning the lack of desire to inflict harm. With each individual left to work out his or her own salvation, intervention in the life-cycle of another may hinder it from achieving this goal. Moreover, such desires hinder the progress of the perpetrator's soul for they cause more *karma*s to be attracted. While, in principle, the elimination of all desires—good and bad—is necessary for emancipation, Jains in practice stress the need to abstain from the classical 'vices': lust, greed, hatred, and so on. For the Jains *ahimsa* means a respect for life, and the most serious sin is to deprive another creature of its life, or to be more specific, to terminate the residence of a soul in a particular body. Thus Jains are ordained to be strict vegetarians, avoiding any foodstuff which necessitates loss of life; in the rainy season this extends to a prohibition on green leaf vegetables which may harbour small insects (all life is thought to be more prolific in damp conditions). It is difficult in a short space to convey the importance *ahimsa* has for Jains, for it affects every sphere of life and the anthropologist who works with them encounters it a dozen times a day. Just as it is *himsa* to destroy other life-forms, so it is *himsa* to cause them to come into being 'unnecessarily', and Jains for example are forbidden to consume anything involving fermentation and are supposed to be scrupulous in disposing of uneaten food lest bacteria should come into being, grow, and die. Many such prohibitions are multi-faceted, however, and the aetiology is rarely simple. For example, the consumption of alcohol and other intoxicants is forbidden, not only because of the fermentation involved, but also because they cause one to lose self-control which could lead to violence through carelessness and thoughtlessness.

Like any religion, Jainism has, to the non-believer, its inconsistencies and paradoxes, and it is tempting to search for them in the face of claims by some Jains that Jainism is a science, not a religion, entirely logical and consistent, requiring no element of faith or need to believe. This is similar to Southwold's discussion of a similar 'scientific' approach to Buddhism which arose in nineteenth-century Ceylon: a 'Western misinterpretation' embraced by middle-class Sinhalese, seeking to emulate the Europeans, but forced to identify with their own cultural heritage (Southwold 1983: 118–19). I shall return to this issue, with regard to Jainism, in the penultimate and concluding chapters. One inconsistency worth noting here, however, concerns the idea of compassion. Unsophisticated Jains, like their counterparts in other religious traditions, believe that religion (in the general sense) is basically a matter of ethics, and moreover that all religions have the same, or similar, ethical codes: not to lie, steal, cheat, or kill; for younger to respect elder; for men to help each other. All these actions only have meaning in relation to other people of course, and thus it is easy for such people to view *ahimsa* in the same light—that is, one should not hurt others.

On another level, however, *himsa* (the desire to cause violence) is wrong because it engenders (evil) desires in the soul, which attract *karma* matter. Thus one should avoid *himsa*, not only because it damages others but because it damages oneself. However, other religious traditions, especially Buddhism and Christianity, go further than this and stress the idea of compassion; not only should we restrain ourselves from harming others, we should actively seek their good and act benevolently towards them. It is easy to think of some situation in which what appears to be *himsa* is in fact not so. For example, if I crush a tiny insect I may do so in its own best interests, so that the soul (*jiva*) can leave the cramped, perception-lacking body and perhaps be reincarnated in a higher form. No Jain I have met would ever countenance this; indeed, the Jains' concern for the natural preservation of life seems to increase in inverse proportion to the creature's size.[9] (Of course, my own motivation in such a circumstance is morally loaded: what is there to stop me applying the argument one step further and killing those men and women around me whose quality of life I deem to be insufficient for salvation?) Behaviourally too, the orthopraxy engendered by this compassion for life provides a structure which helps bound and define the religion; laity and especially ascetics spend a

---

[9] Lodrick (1981: 19–22) describes in some detail the *jivat-khanas*, or 'insect houses' where pious Jains take the dust swept from their houses and deposit it in a room, together with grain, so that the insects swept up with the dust may live out their natural life spans provided with food.

great deal of time in ritualized attention to removing potential or actual insects from their clothing, seats, bedding, and so forth.

Jainism is not strictly a religion 'of the book', but there is a large textual corpus covering not only doctrine but also mathematics, poetry, astronomy, and so on. Some of these texts are accepted by some sects of Jains as canonical (the *agama*s) but they are not as widely read or quoted (certainly by the laity) as the canonical texts of other traditions. Quite apart from Jain textual sources there is a vast modern literature on the philosophy, cosmology, and principles of Jainism, and beyond the basic outline sketched above I think there is little else needed to introduce what follows in this book. Specific points of doctrine that are relevant to the issues raised are discussed as necessary; the two works I relied on most heavily for my fieldwork preparation, P. S. Jaini's *The Jaina Path of Purification* (1979) and V. A. Sangave's *Jaina Community* (1980) both contain extensive bibliographies and it is from these works that much of my doctrinal information derives, supplemented with data gathered during fieldwork.

A Brief History

While the intention of this book is to provide an ethnographic introduction to the organization of modern Jainism, there are some points concerning the origins and early development of the religion which need to be made, either to clarify later arguments or to demonstrate earlier parallels with some of the issues I shall go on to discuss. This section is of necessity somewhat detailed and the reader may for the present wish to skip over it, perhaps returning to it later. The next section, which gives some general details of Jainism in practice, begins on page 28.

Any historical approach to Jainism must consider the founders of the religion and the issues that gave rise to the new movement. The Jains' own attitude to the origin of their religion has two aspects. The first is that Jainism has no 'origin', and hence no founder; just as the universe is eternal, so is the religion. Indeed, in this view Jainism is not a religion at all. The nature of the universe, including its geography, is as fixed and absolute as its eternity, though there is a regular fluctuation in the relationship between the universe and the souls (*jiva*) that inhabit it—the 'dark' and 'light' halves of the time-cycle. The religion we call Jainism is, at its most basic, simply a method for the soul to traverse the universe and reach the highest heaven (*isat-*

pragbharabhumi—the 'slightly bending place', P. S. Jaini 1979: 270). Although most Jain writers stress the absolute disjunction between emancipation and entanglement in the world (*samsara*), the cosmologists clearly perceived of the universe as a whole: *isat-pragbharabhumi* is only locationally disjoined from the world men and women inhabit. It is the nature of the souls inhabiting the two regions that render them qualitatively different.

Jaini cites a story concerning Rishabha, the first *tirthankara* of the most recent series (P. S. Jaini 1979: 203). The members of the community in which he lived did not know how to help the *tirthankara* break a severe fast until one, a prince named Sreyamsa, dreamed of a previous life in which he had offered food to a Jain ascetic. With this information he was able to make the appropriate offerings. To the Jains, the story demonstrates the existence of the Jain path in ages before the present cycle.

The second aspect concerns the form of the religion we see in the present age. This, it is generally agreed, reflects the lives, teachings, and examples of the twenty-third and twenty-fourth *tirthankaras*, Parsvanath and Mahavira. Although stories concerning the lives and deeds of all the *tirthankaras* are found in the canonical literature, the emphasis is overwhelmingly on Mahavira, and large sections of the canon are given over to his preachings and to replies to his disciples' questions (for example the *mulasutra*, Uttaradhyayana, and the fifth *anga*, Vyakhyaprajnapti. Details of the canonical texts can be found in P. S. Jaini 1979: 47–87).

Parsvanath's successor, Vardhaman, also known as Mahavira, was born in the city of Vaisali, near Patna in modern Bihar, some time in the sixth century BC (dates of 599 BC, 569 BC and 539 BC have all been advanced).[10] Most of the details of Mahavira's biography come from the canonical and extra-canonical texts of the Jains themselves; certain details of his later life, especially as an ascetic leader, are also corroborated by Buddhist texts.

Like the other *tirthankaras*, Mahavira is ascribed to a royal lineage, his father Siddhartha being a Kshatriya chieftain, while on his mother's side he was descended from Cetaka, chief of Vaisali, one of the confederate states of the Virji republic. Jain tradition makes two

[10] The dating of Mahavira's birth is calculated by some scholars from the dating of his death and emancipation, which are in turn calculated from the dates of Buddha's birth and death. Bechert argues that the date of Buddha's death should be placed much later, around 350 BC, instead of the more commonly accepted 480 BC (Bechert 1983).

significant statements about his conception. The first is that the embryo was in fact conceived in the womb of a Brahman woman and transferred to Siddhartha's wife, Trisala, by Harinegamesi, an antelope-headed demi-god, at the instruction of Indra, king of the gods. Indra felt it improper that one who was to be a great leader (spiritual or temporal) should be born in 'a minor clan or fringe clan or a lowly, destitute or miserly clan, a clan of beggars or of brahmanas' (Kalpa Sutra 17; Vinayasagar and Lath 1977: 33). Some authors (for example, Chatterjee 1978: 19) have pointed out the similarities between this episode and the adoption of the infant Krishna in the Vaishnavite tradition.

It should be noted that the embryo swapping episode belongs to the Svetambara tradition alone (see below); the Digambaras consider Trisala and Siddartha to be the natural and only parents of Mahavira. They also deny other events in the *tirthankara*'s biography as recorded in the Kalpa Sutra, particularly his marriage (and hence pre-renunciation sexual activity).

The second tradition relating to the pre-birth period concerns fourteen (or sixteen according to the Digambaras) dreams that both mothers had when carrying the embryo. These dreams are still commemorated today during the festival of Paryushan and together with the story of the embryo transfer form an important part of the corpus of myths and beliefs that surround the historical figure of Mahavira and enshrine him as a figurehead and focal point for the Jains.

Mahavira was not the first-born son and as such was not destined to assume whatever leadership position his father occupied. At the time of his renunciation (aged thirty) his parents were dead and he was considered to have discharged his duties as a son (according to Digambara tradition) or as a householder (according to Svetambara tradition). He then wandered from place to place until, after 13 years, he achieved enlightenment (*kevaljnana*). From then until his death, thirty years later, he preached the message of enlightenment to all beings (the *samavasarana*—an idea which will be taken up in Chapter 3). In particular, he gathered around himself eleven learned Brahman disciples (*ganadharas*) who became convinced of the truth of the Jain path after hearing the *tirthankara* preach and renounced the world at once. Mahavira's death occurred almost at the end of the *dusama-susama* period (equally balanced happiness and unhappiness) of the current *avasarpini* half-cycle, and although many people attained omniscience after him, they all did so within a period of less than three years after his death (P. S. Jaini 1979: 34). After this the *dusama*, or fifth and unhappy stage of the *avasarpini*, began, in which we live today and during which enlightenment is not possible.

Two quotations from the Kalpa Sutra will serve to describe the enlightenment of the *tirthankara* and the circumstances of his death:

He sat with heels together, crouching in the posture of milking a cow, exposing himself to the heat of the sun . . . And thus Bhagavan Mahavira became an Arhat, a Jina possessed of the all-knowing, all-seeing kevala-vision. He knew and saw the minds and conditions of gods, men and demons . . . For to an Arhat nothing is hidden. He knows and can perceive all beings in all the worlds. (*Kalpa Sutra* 120, 121; Vinayasagar and Lath 1977: 185, 187).

Annihilating the bonds of birth, decay and death, he passed away from this world into the state beyond karma and reached the ultimate state of perfection, enlightenment and liberation: a state beyond all pain. He breathed his last early at dawn while sitting in the yogic posture called samparyanka . . . meditating on the chapter [of his final discourse] called pradhana (the most important of all). (*Kalpa Sutra* 146; Vinayasagar and Lath 1977: 205).

A lengthier and more critical account of the life of Mahavira is to be found in P. S. Jaini 1979: 1–41 (see also Chatterjee 1978: 17–34). Aside from the career of Mahavira himself, what can we learn of the structure of the earliest Jain 'community'? Jainism arose not alone, but as one of several renunciatory movements (the Sramana schools) the best known of which today is Buddhism. According to some authors, the changes that mark the end of the Vedic period and usher in the Sramana renunciatory movements are characterized by a new economic order, which culminated in a new monied class, known (loosely) as the Vaishyas. The development of a money economy, paralleled by the development of trade and industry, led to an increased potential for capital accumulation, and the concentration of power and resources in the hands of a few. This coincided with the growth of cities and towns and the organization of traders and artisans into guilds. The causes of this economic shift can only be guessed at: one author who propounds this theory, R. S. Sharma, attributes it to the introduction of iron implements (cited in N. N. Bhattacharya 1976: 60). Other authors (for example, S. Bhattacharya 1973) feel that it was the natural outcome of the assimilation of the indigenous mode of sedentary agriculturalism by the pastoralist 'Aryans'. In either case, the result was capital accumulation by both the state and private individuals.

As for Jainism itself, the general picture outlined by some scholars contains some or all of the following elements: that Jainism, with its stress on *ahimsa*, arose as a reaction to Brahmanical animal sacrifices; that the notion of rebirth—and consequently of escape from rebirth— was a Jain innovation prompted by the massive social and political upheavals that were taking place in the fifth and sixth centuries BC; that renunciation was a new idea and the only solution to this upheaval; that Jainism developed as a 'Kshatriya rebellion' against the prevailing Brahmanical hegemony; that the strength and consequent survival of Jain doctrines rested on the cohesion of the fourfold *sangha* ('community': in this case, the male and female ascetics and the male and female laity) and, when Jainism was adopted by the trading community, on the fact that Jains were enjoined to be honest people in all their dealings (and hence respected).[11]

This picture rests on an essential dichotomy of Vedic religion (and social order) versus non- or 'post'-Vedic—a notion which is attractive —but too simplistic.[12] There is no sense in which the Sramana schools 'took over' from the Brahmanical Hindu order, for this itself was not a homogeneous entity and both must have been evolving and adapting to each other at the same time. While Vedic Brahmanism emphasized ritual and the integration of society, the Sramana movements stressed the inherent sterility and emptiness of the world. Sramana philosophers asserted that while man's goal was happiness, it could never be achieved in one lifetime, where the lot of the individual was so unpredictable. The various theories of rebirth and *karma* they advocated served to explain suffering and apparent injustice within the bounds of one's own understanding, without the need of recourse to transcendental mysteries and priestly interpreters.

In discussing the Sramana movements, several authors have advanced the idea—as mentioned above—that the Sramanas were part of a 'Kshatriya rebellion' against increasingly powerful Brahmans who were usurping state control through ritual authority—a view which presupposes the coincidence of opposed interest groups or factions with hereditary or occupational social groupings.[13] Such a

---

[11] For these views see, for example, Guseva 1971; J. C. Jain 1947; Pande 1978*a*; 1978*c*.

[12] See, for example, Deo 1956: 48–56; Majumdar *et al.* 1963.

[13] See, for example, the views outlined in Deo 1956: 48–56. Horsch writes of the 'Ksatriya Revolution' and states that the Kshatriyas made a substantial contribution to the transformation of ideas in the Upanishads (Horsch 1966, cited in Tsuj 1970: 33). Tsuj, however, notes that 'it is very difficult to answer the question why just the ksatriyas

view is too vague and imprecise to be of any help, given that it is not clear that 'Brahmanism' and 'Sramanism' were diametrically opposed, nor that the agents of each were clearly identified with the Brahmans and the Kshatriyas (however these groups may have been composed). What is clear is that the Sramana movements were not an exclusively Kshatriya phenomenon, nor were their members exclusively Kshatriya by status. Members of almost all communities were admitted to the Jain *sangha* initially, and some kind of caste distinctions were maintained within the *sangha* (Deo 1956: 49), emphasizing reliance on it as a structuring principle. Moreover, the eleven *ganadharas*—or chief disciples—of Mahavira are all said by the texts to be Brahmans and it is they who are largely (perhaps exclusively) responsible for the organization of the *sangha* given that Mahavira, after attaining omniscience, performed no organizational or administrative function (P. S. Jaini 1979: 44–6). In some respects the Jain *sangha* presented in microcosm the later Hindu ideal—the divine king, surrounded by and 'interpreted' by a Brahman élite, and ruling over a large mixed population.

Even if the founders and followers of the renunciatory movements were not Kshatriyas, or members of the ruling élite, many of their patrons were. Both Jainism and Buddhism achieved the status of state religion in the pre-Moghul period and both sets of scriptures abound with stories of ascetics or pious laymen influencing the affairs of state through their advice or conduct. P. S. Jaini advocates the view that the Sramanas (as a body, rather than as individual groups) created an entirely new society, running parallel to the post-Vedic majority society and recruiting from it at all levels (1979: 275). Thus kings and other rulers were quick to patronize them in view of the power such a social movement might have.

However, if the difficulties of mapping out the founders and patrons of early Jainism are great, they increase dramatically when we try to discover who the early laity might have been. This 'problem' of the laity is most simply—and radically—dealt with by Williams. In his introduction to *Jaina Yoga*, a work describing the medieval (fifth to thirteenth centuries AD) Jain texts on lay discipline—the *sravakacaras* —he states: ' . . . the essential change in Jainism during the medieval

played a leading part in that age of mental fermentation' (Tsuj 1970: 33 n. 16). Moreover, the difficulty of dating some of the Upanishads by no means makes it clear that they all were written prior to Horsch's 'Revolution'; nor is it by any means certain that 'just the ksatriyas' were involved in this 'Revolution'.

period is its transformation from a philosophy, a *darsana*, to a religion.' (R. H. B. Williams 1963: xx). Implicit in his introduction is the idea that prior to the medieval period the laity had minimal significance for the ascetic Jains, the propounders of orthodoxy and orthopraxy for whom Jainism represented a practical means of salvation, based on a scientific assessment of the nature of the universe.

Actually, Williams had been anticipated by Max Weber, some forty years previously, who wrote: 'The Jains are from the outset not a community of individual wise men who, as old men or temporary students, devoted themselves to ascetic life. Nor were they individual virtuosi of life-long asceticism; nor did they represent a plurality of schools and monasteries. Rather they were a special order of "professional monks"' (Weber 1958: 196). The point of this argument is not that the laity did not exist before the medieval period—clearly they did if for no other reason that the wandering ascetics had to be fed —but simply that they may have had little religious significance for the ascetics and may not have had a fixed self-identity as 'Jains', simply seeing themselves as pious householders supporting (a variety of) wandering holy men.[14]

Weber goes on to discuss the existence of the laity as the cause of the ascetics' professionalism (ibid.). Williams, however, points out that Jainism is not as changeless as some authors suppose (for example, Sangave 1980: 377) and that the solid fourfold *sangha* we see today is not necessarily the reason for the 'survival' of Jainism (though it may, in part, explain the relatively unchanged doctrine. R. H. B. Williams 1963: ix). Instead, in the medieval period 'the ritual changes and assumes an astonishing complexity and richness of symbolism. From implying merely the feeding of religious mendicants the duty of *dan* [giving] comes to mean the provision of rich ecclesiastical endowments . . . And all the time more and more stress is being laid on the individual's duties to the community' (ibid.: xx).

The main propounder of *darsana* to *dharma* (philosophy to religion) shift is the Digambara scholar-ascetic, Jinasena, who was active in the late ninth century AD. In his Adi-purana, he rewrites much of Indian mythical history from a Jain point of view: indeed, Williams remarks

---

[14] The Buddhist position is even more extreme: today the Buddhist *sangha* encompasses only ascetics and not laity (Gombrich 1971: *passim*). P. S. Jaini points out that while Williams lists over 40 *sravakacaras* (texts on lay discipline), Theravada Buddhists produced only one such work and Mahayana Buddhists produced none (1979: 285 n. 20).

that the work was intended to rival the Hindu Mahabharata (ibid.: 20). It is to Jinasena that we owe almost all of Jain thought on society and a recognition of a Jain life within the world. Jinasena created the notion of a Jain 'caste system' which he legitimated as an institution of Rishabha's. Rishabha was similarly accredited with structuring civilization by instituting occupations, arts, and the idea of kingship. All these things therefore preceded the Hindu world view, and any expression of them in Hindu society is to be seen as a result of Jain influence. The story, mentioned earlier, of Rishabha's first fast-breaking, and the involvement of the laity in this, was popularized in the medieval period: this time the author is the twelfth-century Svetambara writer, Hemachandra (although he was in fact using earlier, canonical, sources). The *sravakacaras* are dealt with in admirable detail in R. H. B. Williams 1963, and Jinasena's Adi-purana is discussed at length in P. S. Jaini 1979: 288–304. Unfortunately no translation of the Adipurana exists.

Why did the *sravakacaras* appear so late in Jain history, a millenium after the death of Mahavira? For the purposes of this discussion, a distinction might be made between patronage and lay affiliation, and the realization made that the *sravakacaras* were written for the benefit of the laity, not the patrons. During the first millenium after Mahavira's death the Jain ascetics, Weber's 'professional monks', had actively sought the patronage and protection of various royal houses, moving slowly westwards and southwards from the north-eastern homeland. In doing this they were in competition with both Buddhists and Hindus, and whilst some rulers, such as Ashoka, showed liberal impartiality, others were more partisan. However, the resurgence of Hindu identity and power through the *bhakti* movement of the sixth century AD, followed by the Muslim invasions and Hindu renaissance of the twelfth century, threatened both Jainism and Buddhism. Buddhism was unable to survive and seems to have died out in India around the fourteenth century (P. S. Jaini 1979: 274).

The Jain reaction was to 'Hindu-ize'. Jinasena not only rewrote Hindu mythological history, he also included all the major Hindu *samskaras* (life-cycle rituals) within the Jain ritual system by giving them a Jain gloss (ibid.: 288–304). Jaini sees Jinasena's Hinduization as a purely religious reform (ibid.: 291–2) but its political overtones cannot be ignored.

As the Jain ascetics acquired more power and influence through their royal patrons, we find the presence of influential lay Jains as prime ministers and other officials in the courts of many northern and southern kings (see, for example, P. S. Jaini 1979: 275–84; Chatterjee 1978: *passim*; C. B. Sheth 1953: *passim*; Sangave 1980: 362–8). The period of the *sravakacara*s marked the consolidation of this tendency by elaborating the roles of lay participation and especially of lay patronage (R. H. B. Williams 1963: xx). Thus, we have a model of the dual strands of Kshatriya (or ruling group) patronage and Vaishya (and other) lay participation continuing together. In this model, the Jain ascetics devote themselves to their royal patrons initially—even Jinasena describes and praises the qualities of Kshatriyas—but after weathering the first wave of Hindu reformism in the sixth century AD (during which much of the laity must have adopted Hindu practices) they turn increasingly to their lay devotees, and naturally towards the wealthy Vaishya followers (Renou 1953: 122). Of course, ascetic interest in the laity must extend further back, and we should perhaps see the writing down of the *sravakacara*s as the culmination of this interest and not the beginning of it. In this they were wise. After the reign of Ashoka, state patronage of Jainism declined, although some lay Jains retained ministerial positions, for example in Rajasthan (Tod 1920: ii. 603–5). From the *sravakacara*s and beyond Jainism became a religion, with an elaborate ritual structure and a fourfold *sangha*.

Following the Jina's Way

Although several of the following chapters deal with specific instances of Jainism in practice, there are some general points that can usefully be made at the outset. The normative set of organizational divisions often referred to in the literature are those between *sadhu*s, *sadhvi*s, *sravak*s and *sravika*s—'monks', 'nuns', lay men and lay women. Although there are parallels with Christian tradition I hesitate to use the words 'monk' and 'nun', precisely because the parallels are not complete (there is no concept among the Jains for example of contemplative monks and nuns devoted to prayer for the good of the world). Burghart (1983) uses the term 'Renouncer' to describe the Ramanandi 'monks' he studied, but here I shall use the term 'ascetic', as I feel it more applicable to the Jains' doctrinal position. Of course, the laity also practise asceticism but I shall confine the use of the term, and related terms, to those who have taken *diksa*—the ceremony of renouncing the world and becoming a chaste, homeless, and possessionless *sadhu* or *sadhvi*. The ascetics are enjoined to wander (*vihar*), though they may use no means of transport, in order that they may preach to the laity and also in order that they may not form attachments to any particular place or group of people. In practice, however, the wanderings of the *vihar* are generally fairly confined and scripted, and are planned weeks or even months in advance. The ascetics I encountered in Saurashtra only left the province to travel to Ahmedabad, Bombay, or occasionally to Rajasthan.

The laity can and do travel by vehicle, though they may if they wish take temporary or permanent vows not to travel beyond a certain distance (as a means of self-discipline). Some laity form attachments to particular ascetics and will follow them in their *vihar* where possible, and encourage them to visit their home town as often as possible. In some cases this may result in the lay person taking *diksa* him- or herself and adopting the ascetic he or she respects as his or her *guru*. (This can only happen between same-sex lay and ascetic. Ascetics are forbidden to touch or be in close proximity to laity or ascetics of the opposite sex. A male ascetic, for example, wishing to pass a book or other object to a lay woman, will throw it to the ground to be picked up. Lay and ascetic women may touch each other, as may lay and ascetic men, but they do so rarely.) Others act as emissaries for their favourite ascetics: one informant and close friend of mine in Jamnagar spends a large part of his time travelling around Saurashtra and Gujarat on behalf of a certain *acarya* (head of an ascetic order), carrying messages, preparing Jains in other towns for his arrival, and arranging the details of ceremonies at which the *acarya* will have some role to play when he finally arrives at the place on foot.

Another normative division often noted is that of the two major sects: the Digambaras and the Svetambaras, the two terms meaning 'sky-clothed' and 'white-clothed' respectively. Historically, the division is actually a division of ascetics, but as the ascetics demand slightly different behaviour (especially ritual behaviour) from the laity, the laity is also thus divided. As a result of the schism two distinct ritual traditions have developed, each of which constrains the lay Jain devotee to a certain mode of ritual behaviour. Separate temples for each sect exist all over India (often side by side) and disputes, occasionally resulting in physical violence, over the ownership of a temple are not unknown.[15]

[15] Three related articles, Nahar 1929, K. P. Jain 1930, and Nahar 1932 neatly illustrate the rivalry between the two sects from a partisan perspective. Carrithers (1988) provides a detailed account of a modern conflict—the 'Bahubali affair'—and mentions that there are over 130 similar conflicts to be found in India today; see also *India Today* (1984) for a journalistic account of the same 'affair'.

Doctrinally, Digambaras consider that nudity is an essential prerequisite for salvation (members of the highest ascetic grade, which is exclusively male, go naked or 'sky-clothed'), and that women are incapable of achieving salvation (largely because they cannot, for reasons of modesty, discard their clothing). They do not deny, however, as is sometimes claimed, that women can perform meritorious acts in this life which will lead to a male birth and emancipation at some time in the future, and there are some *sadhvi*s in the lower Digambara ascetic grades (*ksullak* and *ailak*). There are few, if any, Digambaras of the unreformed sects in Saurashtra and my work was confined to Svetambara ascetics and laity. A neo-Digambara movement, the Kanji Panth, has its major stronghold in Saurashtra, however, and I discuss this movement in Chapter 5. Svetambara ascetics wear plain white unstitched robes (hence their name) and believe in the possibility of women achieving salvation. They hold that one of the *tirthankara*s (Mallinath, the nineteenth) was in fact a woman, although she is portrayed in a fashion identical to the rest of the *tirthankara*s in all paintings, idols, book illustrations, and such like that I have seen. *Sadhvi*s, or female ascetics, by far outnumber *sadhu*s in most if not all Svetambara orders (although numbers are very difficult to come by), although I never came across any evidence that they hold Mallinath particularly dear.

In the fifteenth and seventeenth centuries AD there arose, in both the Svetambara and Digambara sects, reform movements (the Svetambara Sthanakavasi, and Digambara Terapanthi and Tarana-panthi), which condemned ascetic laxity and, more importantly, idol- and image-worship. Unreformed Digamabaras and Svetambaras maintain temples, and idol-worship (*puja*), akin to Hindu practices, is an important aspect of the religion for the laity. Indeed, installing idols and building or restoring temples come into the seven 'fields of merit' (*punya ksetra*) by which a lay man or woman can earn great merit[16] and possibly future *tirthankara*-hood. The reformed sects, by contrast, place greater emphasis on austerities; their members simply meditate and attend, or give, preachings in bare halls.

Figure 1.1 represents in diagrammatic form the 'lineage' of the

---

[16] Merit (*punya*) in this context appears to mean 'good *karma*' which, while it may bring about worldly benefits (such as a good rebirth), should ultimately be eschewed as all *karma*—good or bad—binds the soul and prevents it achieving liberation. Jains I have spoken to, however, also believe that merit may serve to 'burn off' bad *karma*, thereby being helpful in the process of achieving liberation.

major Jain schisms. For the sake of comparison I have included the major Digambara sect under its common name in Rajasthan (a Digambara stronghold), 'Bisapanthi', and shown the point of departure of the two important reformatory Digambara sects. The Digambara Terapanthis arose as a reaction to the office of *bhattarakas* or lay administrators, which dominated Bisapanthi organization. The Terana-panthis arose, like the Sthanakavasis, as a non-idolatrous movement. Unlike the Svetambara Terapanth, numbers of Digambara Terapanthis are thought to be few today. However, the Digamabara sects are listed

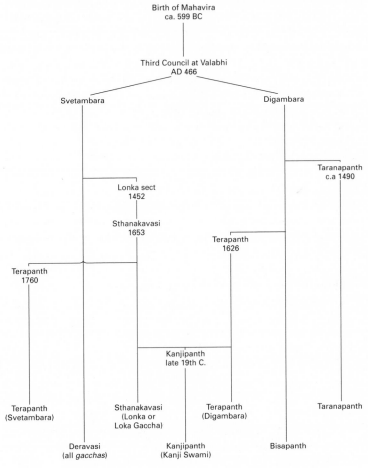

FIG. 1.1. The 'Lineage' of Jain Sects. *After Sangare 1980: Chapter 2*

here only for the sake of completeness and will not be referred to again by name in this work. In Figure 1.1 I have also referred to the unreformed Svetambara sect as 'Deravasi'. This is a term (meaning 'dwellers in temples') that is used generally in Gujarat and Saurashtra to refer to idol-worshipping Svetambaras and which therefore matches neatly with Sthanakavasi (meaning 'dwellers in halls'). Indeed, this division between Deravasi and Sthanakavasi is the only one of all those given in the Figure that has any real salience in the Jamnagar context and even that diminishes by the time we come to Leicester.

While idol-worshipping ascetics may take *darsana* in temples (that is, they 'behold' the idols), they may not touch or make offerings to the idols. The laity by contrast can and do touch the idols (after purifying themselves by bathing). Indeed, once an idol has been consecrated *puja* must be performed before it daily. Sandalwood and other pastes are used to anoint parts of the idol's body and flowers to adorn it. (Only Svetambara laity do this; lay Digambaras do not actually touch their idols.) Flowers and other objects such as rice, sweets, and coins are placed before the idol by both sects, while incense and lamps are lit and waved. A discussion of offerings used by Jains in *puja* and an interpretation of their meaning can be found in Humphrey 1985. The principal idol in a Jain temple always represents one of the *tirthankaras*. Except for Parsvanath, the twenty-third, who has the hood of a cobra behind his head, the idols of all the other *tirthankaras* are identical, including, as noted, those (in Svetambara temples) representing Mallinath. The idols are identified by a symbol of the particular *tirthankara* carved as a cartouche on the pedestal. Mahavira, the twenty-fourth and last *tirthankara* is represented by a lion, for example, Rishabha, the first, by a bull. The main idol is usually surrounded by many smaller idols, also of *tirthankaras*. Idols of some of the attendant goddesses (*sasana devis*), and occasionally of Hindu deities (Hanuman or Ganesh, for example), are sometimes found near the doorway, or within the temple precincts. The temples also act as a focus for many rituals that take place annually or sporadically, although these may in fact take place anywhere: small idols can be transported and set up under awnings on open land if many people are expected to attend. (This, of course, like much of the preceding discussion, is applicable only to India. The particular circumstances pertaining to Leicester are presented in Part II, particularly in Chapter 7.)

Tithi *and* gaccha

The strict vegetarianism of the Jains is regulated by calendrical calculations which ordain that green foodstuffs be avoided on certain days in the lunar month, known as *tithi*. The idol-worshipping part of the Svetambara sect is divided into a number of sub-sects known as *gaccha*s (the non-idol-worshipping component, the Sthanakavasi sect, constitutes a *gaccha* in its own right). Again, strictly speaking, these are ascetic divisions but, because each *gaccha* maintains a separate calendar (*pancang*), the laity are also so divided. As a result of the separate calendars the *tithi* may fall on different days for different *gaccha*s. Not everyone that I knew in India, by any means, and almost no one in Leicester, fully abided by the *tithi* observances but enough did to bring it to my attention and placed enough stress on it for me to investigate further.

There are other contexts in which *gaccha* divisions have salience for the laity (for example, those described in Chapter 4) and it is worth saying a little more about *gaccha* here. *Gaccha* affiliation is inherited (and changed on marriage by a woman, if necessary) but has little day-to-day significance for most laity. It determines the dates of the *tithi* as mentioned above (and one or two calendrical festivals) and there are some minor differences in ritual practice among the different *gaccha*s. These differences are more pronounced among the ascetics (who must be ordained into a particular *gaccha*—usually, but not always, that of their birth). Certain small visual clues (the colour of their food bowls, the presence or absence of a red border to a garment) allow one to identify the *gaccha* of an ascetic, which is not the case with the laity. Probably the largest Svetambara *gaccha* in India (as well as in Jamnagar) is the Tapa Gaccha; two others that will be encountered in Chapters 2 and 4 are the Anchala and Kharatara Gacchas. The Lonka or Sthanakavasi sect (the non-idolatrous Svetambara sect) is some-times, as mentioned above, also considered as a *gaccha* (the Loka or Lonka Gaccha), although the differences in practice (both lay and ascetic) between this *gaccha* and any of the other Svetamabara *gaccha*s (all others of which are idol-worshipping and collectively known as Deravasi) are very great.

While the literature on lay Jain practice is not as extensive as that on doctrine, belief, and ascetic practice, useful additional information can be found in Sangave's work (1980), the work of the missionary, A. M. Stevenson (1910; 1915), and the introduction to Fischer and Jain's book on Jain art and rituals (1977). As before, I discuss particular aspects of practice where necessary in the book, and the two major descriptive chapters on Jamnagar and Leicester (Chapters 3 and 7) describe certain practices in some detail. As I mentioned above, this brief synopsis of Jainism is a composite picture, gathered from books and observation, and represents rather an idealized and sterile view. As an anthropologist, I am concerned with what Jainism is, not what it should be, and the remainder of the book is devoted to exploring this from a contemporary perspective (a brief historical sketch of the difficulties earlier writers encountered can be found in Banks 1986).

Which Path is the Best Path?

However, while many Jains I met (both in Jamnagar and in Leicester) rarely thought about their religion in an analytical way, there were one or two 'natural philosophers' among my informants—a joy to every anthropologist—who supplied me with many insights. I therefore end this chapter with a brief example to show how the tenets of Jainism may or may not be used by a Jain.

When I returned to Jamnagar briefly in 1984, Jagjivandas Mehta, an elderly shopkeeper and one of my closest contacts, asked me whether, in the year since completing my fieldwork, I had come to any major conclusions about my findings. I told him that I was still working on them, but that I was intrigued by the diversity of belief in and attitudes towards the religion. I mentioned particularly that several of the Jains I had studied in Leicester seemed to find the religion of their birth inadequate in some way and often visited Hindu temples as well (see Chapter 8). He agreed with me, saying that Jains were not all equal in their depth of piety or in their commitment to their religion. Unlike others, however, he did not consider this to be a fault but as an example of alternative ways of looking at the world. For example, he said, take the case of his daughter Hina. Hina had extremely poor eyesight and had from a very early age worn heavy spectacles. When she was of the right age Jagjivandas had tried to find her a husband, but all the families he approached had been put off by the disfiguring spectacles and had either refused to negotiate, or demanded an absurdly high dowry to compensate. Some of his family and friends, pious Jains all of them, had said that Hina's misfortune was a result of (bad) *karma* brought from a previous life; she would just have to suffer until that particular *karma* (for weak eyesight) expired (in this life or the next). Perhaps *tapasya*s (austerities, penances) would extirpate the *karma* more quickly. Others, less pious Jains, advised Jagjivandas to consult an astrologer.[17] He should take guidance from 'fate' and the movement of the planets to determine the time, place, and circumstances under which the offer of his daughter would be most readily accepted. As a modern-thinking man he found neither of these courses of action satisfactory. Instead, he invested Rs 500 (about £35 at the time) in a pair of contact lenses for his daughter, threw away her spectacles, and had her married within six months.

Aside from being an amusing anecdote, this story contains in essence a key theme of this book and one which is developed most fully in Chapter 8 and touched on again in the conclusions: how the individual—or group—situates him- or herself in relation to the abstract corpus that is reified by them as 'Jainism'.

[17] There is, strictly, nothing wrong with astrology for Jains, given that they are committed to predestination. However, the ethos is such that one should suffer or accept, rather than try and 'cheat' fate by foreguessing it.

PART I
INDIA

(3)

(4)

2

The City of Jamnagar:
Its Jain Inhabitants

A Sense of Place

Jamnagar is a small city with a population of some 277,000 (1981 Census), situated on the northern coast of the peninsular part of Gujarat State—a region known as Saurashtra or Kathiawad. The name derives from the title, *jam*, of its royal family. The city was originally the capital of a princely state both of which were known in the years leading up to Independence as Navanagar ('new city'), although the names were changed afterwards. Navanagar State was one of the larger, Class I, states and was ruled over in the latter part of the British period by Jam Saheb Ranjitsinhji (1907–33), who was known to the British public as a fine cricketer and to the British administration as a model ruler. Ranjitsinhji was responsible for trying to turn his city into the 'Paris of Saurashtra' (Gazetteer 1970: 501) by widening the major streets into boulevards and by building sweeping parades and majestic façades. The city still retains something of his vision, though much has been neglected or buried under new development.

Navanagar was founded in AD 1540 by Jam Raval, a Jadeja Rajput from Kaccha, who exploited the peace wrought by Emperor Humayun and Sultan Bahadur of Gujarat (Gazetteer 1884: 566). The fortunes of the Jam Sahebs over the ensuing 400 years are described in the State Gazetteers, as well as in British works (e.g. Wilberforce-Bell 1916; Kincaid 1931), Indian works of the period (e.g. Dumasia 1927) and recent local works (e.g. Mankad 1972; Joshi 1988), but the records are usually confined to the political and romantic vicissitudes of the ruling family and tell us little about the town, the region, or the people who lived there. At one point, around 1662, the city was briefly known as Islamnagar when rival Jadeja factions lost it to Kutab-ud-din, Fauzdar of Sorath and acting Viceroy of Gujarat (Wilberforce-Bell 1916: 118). Otherwise, the city and region have largely been under Hindu influence, and the political climate has been such that the Jains have also been able to thrive.

The city expanded considerably under Jam Ranmalji (reigned 1820–52) causing the orientalist Burgess, some thirty years later, some disappointment, there being 'not much of antiquarian interest about it' (1876: 188), although he conceded that the large Jain temples 'may possibly be somewhat older' (ibid.). Under indirect Mogul rule, the state had largely stagnated: reinstating the Jadeja rulers after Kutab-ud-din's direct rule had been costly, and skirmishes with itinerant bands of Koli and Kathi bandits in the eighteenth century left little money for internal development. By Jam Ranmalji's time, however, stability in the peninsula and the more liberal views of the British towards the inhabitants of the Native States brought about greater home development, the peak of which was reached in Jam Ranjitsinhji's reign. In 1916 Ranjitsinhji dispensed with his diwan and created a secretariat system, designed to ensure greater administrative efficiency. The newly created Department of Commerce and Industries transformed Navanagar's port, Bedi, extended the railway system and made many concessions to traders and merchants. Imports and exports moving through Bedi doubled during the 1920s and the revenue of the state increased proportionally. On the eve of Indian independence in 1947 Navanagar, under Rajitsinhji's successor, Digvijaysinhji, was considered to be one of the most progressive and well-administered states in Saurashtra.

In 1948 the 222 States and Estates of Saurashtra (having had a brief existence from 1947 as the Western India States Agency) merged into the United State of Saurashtra and thus into independent India, a movement led by Jam Digvijaysinhji. In 1956 Saurashtra became part of the State of Bombay and finally achieved its present position as part of Gujarat State in 1960. At this time, Jamnagar *taluka* (district) and *jilla* (sub-district) came into being, the latter conforming roughly to the boundaries of the old princely state. Map 2.1 shows Jamnagar within Gujarat State.

Beyond the need for some context, the historical details given above (which I have gleaned almost exclusively from the works mentioned) alert us to two features: firstly, that Jamnagar was in some respects a created city, not one that evolved in any 'natural' or organic fashion; and secondly, that over the past century it was renowned as a home of successful commerce and trade. Both of these features are significant in understanding the lives of the city's Jains, as I shall discuss below. A

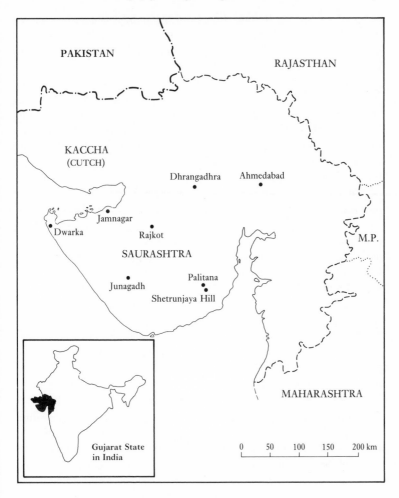

MAP 2.1. Gujarat State

further point should be noted—although I do not have the space to go into it in any detail—that it is clear that the evolution of both Jamnagar State and city (and therefore the place and role of the Jains within them) should be considered within a broader context of the interaction of several complex polities throughout the centuries. The rapid formation and reformation of administrative and governing units in the middle of the present century should be viewed as a series of attempts to accommodate the shifting patterns of hierarchy and interdependence which appear to characterize Saurashtran political life in previous centuries to the centre-dominated federal model which came into existence with Indian independence.

Today, Jamnagar city occupies a strategic position for India's defence, Karachi being only twelve minutes distant by fighter jet according to many of the residents. Permanent forces of the Army, Navy, and Air Force are stationed just outside the city; these are seen as putting Jamnagar at risk by many (the city suffered slight bombing during the last Indo-Pakistan war) and no large industry is located there. Instead, Rajkot, 80 kilometres to the east, has become the largest and most important city of Saurashtra, a fact resented by many Jamnagar residents. There is also a ban on multi-storeyed structures in the city, to allow flight paths for low-flying aircraft; a seven-storeyed residential building under construction in 1982 was being knocked down again when I returned in 1984, the builders having gone ahead before the planning application was processed.

In the mid-1970s, however, the Gujarat Industrial Development Corporation established a small-scale industrial area, Udyognagar, south-west of the city centre. Jamnagar, long famed as the home of *bandhani* tie-and-dye textiles, is now famous as the home of small-scale brass parts—spectacle hinges, bicycle-tube valves and the like—produced in small workshops in Udyognagar. (The 1981 Census of India lists brass parts, *bandhani*, and plastic buttons as the most important items manufactured in the city.) In addition, the cultivation, storage, and processing of groundnuts which takes place in and around Jamnagar, constitutes an important sector of the city's economy; groundnut oil is the most important commodity manufactured in the whole of Jamnagar district (1981 Census). Chicory, maize, and millet are also important crops in the region and are processed or sold in the city's grain market—a trade that is largely dominated by Jain middle-men.

The city is oriented along the main Rajkot to Dwarka highway; expansion to the east is blocked by the Nagmati and Rangmati Rivers, but housing has proliferated in the south-west, creating a distinctly 'bottom-heavy' impression (see Map 2.2). Dwarka has been a centre of Vaisnavite pilgrimage for centuries and Jamnagar acted as a convenient resting-place before the railway was developed. In the centre of the city is the Lakhota Tank, the *talav* as it is known, in the middle of which is a fortress (now a museum) and an equestrian statue of Jam

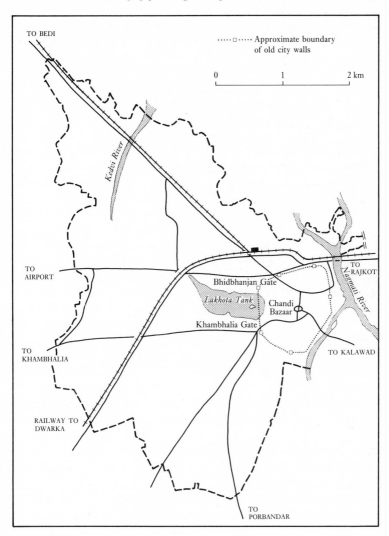

MAP 2.2. Jamnagar City

Raval. The lake is almost purely ornamental, although its importance as a water source became apparent during the drought of 1985–8. East of the lake is Chandi Bazaar, the centre of the old walled city. (All towns and many villages in Saurashtra were once walled.) Some of Jamnagar's gates still stand, but little remains of the walls. The centre of Chandi Bazaar is dominated by cloth retailers and general provisions stores, the silver shops which give it its name (*candi*) being located in narrow side streets radiating off from the central bazaar.

Two large 'islands' in the centre of Chandi Bazaar are the situation of the city's three principal Jain temples (*derasar*s) and much of my time in Jamnagar was spent in close proximity to them, for many of the shops situated along the outside walls of the temples are owned by Jain *vania*s. To the north-east of Chandi Bazaar lies the Darbar Gadh, one of the principal palaces of the Jam Sahebs, although today it stands empty, majestically crumbling above and behind a busy commercial street. Burgess, despite his disappointment in Jamnagar's antiquities, reproduces a fine photograph of the palace revealing the delicate nineteenth-century Hindu carving (Burgess 1876: plate LIV). The area around the Darbar Gadh is the traditional residence area of the Visa Srimalis, the main Jain *jati* to be discussed in this work. To the west of Chandi Bazaar lies the residence area of the Jamnagar Visa Oswals—the other large Jain *jati* traditionally found in Jamnagar. Further west again, beyond the remains of the old city wall, lies the Lal Bungalow, another of the Jam Sahebs' palaces and now the offices of the municipal corporation and the *taluka* and *jilla* headquarters. Due east and south of the lake lies an area of land recently settled—that is, within this century—which has become the residence area of the city's newest Jain *jati*, the Halari Visa Oswals. This is known as Digvijay Plot, after the last Jam Saheb before Indian independence, Jam Digvijaysinghji. The most recently developed part of this land is called Oswal Colony, because of the high presence of the Halari Visa Oswals.

Such a wealth of detail might seem superfluous, but I quickly learned that apparently idle questions about where I had been and the route I had taken from one place to another required the manipulation of a complex social geography. I obtained a map of the city early on in my stay but found that few if any of my informants could read it; instead, I quickly became adept at orienting myself according to widely recognized landmarks—this school, that bank, the such-and-such temple—and to knowing the characteristics of each area—Muslims live here, so meat is on sale, so never drink tea in that tea house, for example. Jains and other *vania*s knew the economic worth of each area, not by the grandeur of the buildings (as I might have attempted to gauge it), but by the price of land per square foot. The social use and division of space is well documented for both ancient and modern India (see, for example, Galey 1985; 1986; Noble 1987), but only recently have anthropologists begun to look beyond the symbolic ordering of space towards more pragmatic and experiential manipulations of folk models of the environment (see, for example, Holy and Stuchlik 1981).

The Jains of Jamnagar

Jains seem to have been in Jamnagar city since its foundation. Indeed, two groups of Jains claim to have been 'invited' over from Kaccha by Jam Raval: one, the Jamnagar Visa Oswals, to develop commerce and trade in the city; the other, the Halari Visa Oswals, to promote agriculture in Halar, the area around the city which formed the territory of the old Navanagar State and which nowadays comprises most of Jamnagar *jilla*. I will return to this 'invitation' later.

The oldest Jain temple standing today was erected in AD 1564, although it has been much altered in the intervening four centuries (Sompura 1968: 222). The temple, known as 'Shethji's temple' (*Shethji no derasar*) because it was built by one Shethji Tejasinha, is now controlled by the Jamnagar Visa Oswal *jati*; the Visa Srimali *jati*, the other major Jain *jati* in the city, had erected a temple for themselves (Adeshwar, in Chandi Bazaar) by 1577 (Gazetteer 1970: 625). I will discuss all the city's *derasar*s more fully in Chapter 4.

The 1981 Census of India recorded the distribution of Jains, Hindus, and Muslims in Jamnagar city and the remainder of the district as listed in Table 2.1.

TABLE 2.1. *Jain Populations in the Jamnagar Region*

	Jamnagar Municipality		Jamnagar District	
	No.	%	No.	%
Hindu	207,246	74.65	984,341	88.24
Muslim	54,995	19.80	116,216	10.41
Jain	12,315	4.43	14,424	1.29
Other	3,059	1.10	480	0.04
Total population	277,615	100.00	1,115,461	100.00

Source: Census of India 1981: Series 5, Gujarat, Paper 4, Table HH-15.

Roughly equal numbers of Jains live in Jamnagar city and in the immediate area, which contrasts noticeably with the Hindu population, for example. Of the 14,000 or so non-Jamnagar Jains in the district, some are to be found in small towns (almost 900 in Kalawad, a town of some 17,000 inhabitants about forty km. to the south-east of Jamnagar, for example) but most are in small villages. The Jains are often characterized as an urban population, an observation supported more broadly by the census figures; for example, in 1981 Jains accounted for 1.37 per cent of the total population of Gujarat, but they formed 3.09 per cent of the total urban population and only 0.59 per cent of the total rural population. In Jamnagar district, however, the figures show that while the percentages hold roughly true the absolute numbers are nearer equivalence, reflecting the Jains' local involvement in agriculture and the rural economy (see also n. 8, below).

It is not entirely clear when the religion of the *jina* first came to Gujarat, and to Saurashtra in particular. Deo cites literary tradition and says that Jainism had spread into Saurashtra by the second century BC. He also points out the link between Krishna and Neminath, the 22nd *tirthankara*, in the region (1974: 27). Canonical tradition holds that Neminath, who achieved enlightenment on the sacred hills of Girnar, near Junaghad, was Krishna's maternal uncle. P. S. Jaini, citing Renou and Jacobi, thinks there is historical evidence to support this, or at least to support Neminath's existence as a contemporary of Krishna (1979: 33) although, of course, the historical evidence to prove the existence of either is dubious in the extreme. More convincing are an inscription at Junaghad referring to *kevaljnana* or enlightenment (a specifically Jain term), and some *tirthankara* idols found in Rajkot district, both of which date from the early Christian era (Deo 1974: 29). Furthermore, the fact that Valabhi (near modern Bhavnagar) in Saurashtra was chosen for the meeting place of the canonical council (see Fig. 1.1), some time in the fifth century AD, would indicate that the region was by then an important political and administrative centre for the Jains.

Later Jain influence in the region is undeniable. In the thirteenth century AD construction of the magnificent hill-top temple complexes of Shetrunjaya and Girnar (near Palitana and Junaghad respectively) was begun, and Jains were occupying important ministerial posts as a result of newly established 'Jain Kingdoms' (or certainly kingdoms where those in power were sympathetic to the Jains). The earliest of these may have been established in the first century of the Christian era (P. S. Jaini 1979: 283), although the 'golden age' came in the mid-twelfth century when the Svetambara *acarya* (monastic leader) and author, Hemachandra, arranged for his protégé Kumarapala (who had taken the minor vows—*anuvrata*s—of a Jain layman) to ascend the throne of the kingdom of Anhilvad in northern Gujarat, a kingdom which Kumarapala's predecessor, Siddharaja, had extended through the conquest of the Saurashtran kingdom of Girnar (Commissariat 1938: pp. lxv–lxx).

There is some evidence too that a specifically regional character was developing: Sheth remarks for example that from the fourteenth century many Jain texts were composed in Gujarati, because of the Muslim dislike of Sanskrit and Prakrit (1953: 187). Certainly Saurashtra and Gujarat were regarded as Svetambara strongholds. By the fifth or sixth century AD Digambaras were largely to be found in southern parts of India (Maharashtra and Karnataka) while the Svetambaras were concentrated in the north and west (P. S. Jaini 1979: 279). Majmudar cites a legend that a public debate was held between Digambaras and Svetambaras in Gujarat during the reign of Siddharaja (Kumarapala's predecessor) on the condition that the losing side—the Digambaras as it turned out—would leave the region (1965: 200; Deo 1974: 31). In the fifteenth century AD the Lonka, non-idolatrous, reform movement began in Ahmedabad, and quickly spread through western India.

Today Gujarat is regarded as an important centre for Svetambara Jains. Leading *acarya*s often spend long periods of time in Ahmedabad (the largest city) where they can be easily visited from other parts of the country, and where they have easy access to publishing houses and communications networks. The Lalbhai Dalpatbhai Institute of Indology in Ahmedabad was established by a leading Jain industrialist earlier this century; until recently Jain historical and textual studies formed the major research interest of the Institute, and it is common to see Jain ascetics studying in the library there. For Jamnagar residents (including the Jains) Bombay has always been the more important city, however, largely for commercial reasons, and the flow of permanent migration has mostly been one-way. Saurashtra, however, is the location of the two sacred hill sites, as mentioned, and Jamnagar Jains consider themselves fortunate to be in such close proximity to these holy places.

I shall have more to say at the end of this chapter about the lives of individual Jamnagar Jains. First, however, I would like to turn to the main issue of the chapter—the complex divisions and groupings by which the Jamnagar Jains organize themselves corporately.

Srimali and Oswal

The two '*jati*-clusters' with which I was concerned in Jamnagar were those known as the Srimali and the Oswal.[1] Both these groups are said to be of the Vaishya *varna* by the classical scheme, although as I said in Chapter 1, I prefer to confine myself to the discussion of *jati*s. Throughout Gujarat and Rajasthan there are many *jati*s named either Srimali or Oswal and there has been speculation that both *jati*s may have had a common origin (Russell 1916: 161). Whether this suspicion is correct or not, I chose the two *jati*s because they were the largest among Jamnagar Jain *jati*s and because I had already worked with them in Leicester (see Part II). Of course, if they do have a common origin, the subsequent fission only confirms the processes of division described in this chapter. These '*jati*-cluster' populations (for want of a better term, but analogous to Fox's idea (1969a) of 'supra-local caste clusters') are not totally endogamous, nor do the component like-named parts necessarily recognize any similarity or parity between themselves, although they may have similar or identical origin myths.

For example, within and around Jamnagar I encountered two distinct groups calling themselves Oswal—Jamnagar Visa Oswals and Halari Visa Oswals. Halari Oswals and Visa Srimalis referred to the Jamnagar Visa Oswals as 'Jamnagaris' (who referred to themselves simply as 'Oswals'), while the Halari Oswals were known to themselves and others (Jain and non-Jain) as 'Mahajans'. All Mahajans have a surname (surname exogamy is practised) but use 'Shah' as an additional surname; several Jamnagari Oswals are also surnamed 'Shah'.

Halari Visa Oswals (Halar is a local name for the region around Jamnagar city) are mostly to be found in villages surrounding the city, although since the late nineteenth century they have been settling within the city (but outside the old city walls), as well as migrating overseas (see Part II). More recently, the Halari Visa Oswals have been establishing themselves in Bombay and nearby Thana district. I was told that there are now some 15,000 individuals there, although I have no documentary evidence for this. Jamnagar Visa Oswals, on the other hand, are to be found exclusively within the city and in Bombay (where they have been settling for the past century); more than half the household heads (of the endogamous *jati*) are now settled there (354 in

[1] Technically, I should spell these names 'Shrimali' and 'Oshwal', but my spelling in the text follows local pronounciation.

Bombay as against 292 in Jamnagar, in 1980), although there is frequent movement between the two places and many Bombay-settled families have (unused) houses in Jamnagar.[2]

Both Halari and Jamnagar groups claim to have been 'invited' to the region from Kaccha by Jam Raval. There may well be some truth in this—after all, other commercial centres were established this way. For example, Rowe, citing Kane, notes that the scriptural (Dharmasastra) duties of a king included 'arranging to have the proper complement of economic and ritually necessary functional castes in the capital' (Rowe 1973: 213). Fox's work on 'Tezibazaar' (1969b: 77 and *passim*), provides an actual example from eastern Uttar Pradesh. Equally, the Oswals may well have left the notoriously dry desert region for the wetter land across the Gulf of Kaccha.

The Jamnagar Visa Oswals are, on the whole, involved in trade within the city, while the Halaris are known as agriculturalists. Halaris, including those now settled in the city and even those abroad retain very strong links with the villages where they initially settled (referred to today as the *covisi khambhalio*—the 'Khambhalia twenty-four'); later, Oswals moved into other villages in the kingdom, and today give the number of villages in the region where they have settled as fifty-two (the *bavangami*), although in fact fifty-six are named in their *jati* directories.[3]

However, both the Jamnagar-based Oswals (the Jamnagaris, as I refer to them, following local practice) and the Halari Oswals who had settled in the surrounding villages (Mahajans) deny any previous link or intermarriage between the two groups, claiming that the common term 'Oswal' in their *jati* names is a mere coincidence. (This may of course be merely a case of 'genealogical amnesia'.) This, for a number of reasons strikes me as unlikely, and, although Jamnagaris and Halaris

[2] All figures for Jamnagar Visa Oswals, and for Halari Visa Oswals living in Jamnagar, are taken from their '*jati* directories' (*vastipatrak*). As these are not freely available, even to visiting anthropologists, I have not included them in my bibliography.

[3] In addition to the Halari and Jamnagari Oswals, there are also one or two families of Oswals in Jamnagar known as 'Kacchi Oswals'; those that I met were extensions of families based in Kaccha, who had come to Jamnagar for business purposes and did not marry there. As Oswals resident in Jamnagar, they have cordial relations with 'Jamnagari' Oswals and each group has relatively free access to the other group's religious property—discussed more fully in Chapter 4. Elsewhere in Saurashtra and Gujarat there are Oswals referred to in the literature as 'Gurjar Oswals', although I personally never encountered any of these. Thus we have a typical example of one of Fox's 'clusters'—several endogamous groups all carrying a shared name element (Oswal) and yet not necessarily recognizing any links between them.

(5)

claim to have been separate groups in Kaccha 400 years ago and thus to have migrated separately, I find it more plausible that one group migrated over a period of time, gradually fissioning through occupational difference. Space does not permit a full account of this migration and the reasons for my conjecture but I have discussed the issue elsewhere (Banks forthcoming).

Open and Concealed

One could speculate that fission within a *jati*, such as that which has apparently taken place between Halari and Jamnagari Oswals, could be either along pre-existing lines of division, especially if hypergamy were involved (and there is evidence that this occurred between the two Oswal groups—see Zarwan 1974: 135), or realized through more arbitrary channels (that is to say, circumstances such as differential geographical mobility, which are largely 'accidental' and not necessarily culturally structured). We might call the former a 'concealed' type of division, as I will discuss below, while the latter, in the example I wish to present now, is 'open', in that the two parts recognize a common link (unlike some Halari and Jamnagari Oswals who did not) which they may or may not activate.

Above, I mentioned that the Oswals coming from Kaccha were Visa Oswals (literally, 'twenty Oswals'—that is to say, 'full' Oswals). In Jamnagar I encountered only Visa Oswals, while among the Srimalis there were both Visa and Dasa (literally, 'ten'—that is, 'half'). Such a division is not confined to Srimali and Oswal: A. M. Shah notes, 'among almost every Vania division [in Gujarat] there was a dual division into Visa and Dasa' (1982: 7). Russell, citing the Bombay Gazetteer, notes that as Visa means twenty and Dasa means ten, the implication is that the Dasa group is 'worth' half the Visa (the subdivision beyond Dasa is Pancha—'five') (Russell 1916: 157). The Srimalis, like other *jati*s so divided have several stories which describe the event or circumstances that led to the division. The sources I used for these stories relate to Srimalis generally and not specifically to the Jamnagar group. In fact I met few in Jamnagar who knew the stories, though many were aware of the origin of the *jati* in the town of Srimala. One story, cited by Russell, relates that the name Srimali derives from the holy garland (*sri mala*) worn by the goddess Lakshmi. She created 90,000 *vania*s from her garland to be the clients of 90,000 Brahmans who served her: the Visa Srimalis were those who came from the right side of her garland, the Dasas from the left (ibid.: 161). Sangave cites another story, less fanciful but equally vague, to the effect that the Visa Srimalis were those who wandered through *vidisa* (which he translates as 'the four quarters'), while the Dasas were those who wandered through *disa* (which he translates as 'the four directions'). The names are therefore corruptions of these terms (Sangave 1980: 87). In fact, the prefix *vi*- denotes separation, or the idea of otherness, outsideness (for example, *videsi*—a foreigner, someone not from one's country), so the idea, if it is valid at all, denotes not so much wandering in different places (before settling), as staying within, instead of going out (of a known territory).

An alternative—and more common—set of explanations hold that the Visa/Dasa division (within whatever group) denotes the degree of purity or legitimacy of ancestral blood and, while I encountered no such explanations for the Srimalis, it seems unlikely that an entirely separate etymology (such as given above) would be uniquely applicable to the Srimalis. For the Oswals, for example, the myth explaining the Visa/Dasa division refers to a feast given by two illegitimate brothers for their *jati*-mates. Those Oswals who attended and ate the food were (ritually) polluted as a result (because of the brothers' illegitimacy) and became the Dasa subsection, while those who cautiously abstained became the 'purer' Visas (Bombay Gazetteer, cited in Sangave 1980:

85). Russell says of the Agrawals (a largely Hindu *jati* found in northern India) that legitimate offspring of the founding ancestor (one King Agra Sena) became the ancestors of the Visa Agrawals, while those from his wives' servants became the ancestors of the Dasas (Russell 1916: 137). It seems that such tales have been interpreted literally; for example, J. N. Bhattacharya suggests that all illegitimate offspring of such *jati*s, implying also those born at the time he was writing (1896), automatically form the Dasa subsection, by a process of continual recruitment, as though babies were taken from their mothers at birth and assigned to one or other category (1973: 168).

In Jamnagar there is no marriage between the Visa and Dasa Srimalis and little contact, but the distinction is still an important one. This form of division, however, may be conflated with other kinds. Some Jamnagari Oswals, for example, claimed that while they were the Visa Oswals, the Halari Oswals were Dasa (thus asserting the 'open' division over the 'concealed' one). Similarly, in Leicester I occasionally heard Halari Oswals referring to the Srimalis there as 'Dasas'. (Indeed, some of the Srimalis in Leicester are in fact Dasa Srimalis, but the Halaris were implying that as the 'Visa' half of the local Jain population, the Srimalis must be the corresponding 'Dasa'. See the following example of the Navnat, and Part II.) That is to say, a known and common form of division with a strong historical/mythological underpinning (Visa/Dasa) is used to describe various other forms of division which may be entirely contingent or accidental, in a sense that is almost—to borrow a term from Sahlins—'mytho-praxic' (Sahlins 1987: 120, 144 and *passim*). Before assessing any further the implications of these divisions it would be wise to discuss the Jains' own attitude to caste and *jati*.

It is my experience that, in the urban centres of north-west India at least, the mid-section of the *jati* hierarchy (i.e. that which encompasses the *vania* grouping) has transmuted into what Morris calls 'competitive communities' (1968: 48). That is to say, a hierarchy of *jati*s ranked according to notions of ritual purity has been replaced by a fluid set of endogamous status groups which provide an arena for individual or group action and competition. Concepts of purity and hierarchy still persist, of course, but vary according to the education and experience of the individual. Purity, for example, is often rationalized in a western framework—that one would hesitate to associate too closely with a street-sweeper because, by the nature of the occupation, he or she would be physically dirty. Most Jains see themselves as superior to

Brahmans, simply because they believe Jainism to be a superior religion to Hinduism (particularly Shaivism with its stress on sacrifice) and because they consider themselves better traders than Brahmans who have entered into trade and with whom they come into closest contact. Vaishnavism is generally seen as a religion of equivalent worth, perhaps because the Jains have always had a very close association with Vaishnavites in this part of India; several *jati*s (the Dasa Srimalis, for example) have both Hindu and Jain members, although the association in this instance of Srimali with Jain is the stronger one (see also Sangave 1980: 148–9 and *passim*).

Discussions of the *varna* hierarchy do not, in my experience, constitute part of the day-to-day discourse and I rarely heard anyone using terms from the schema apart from 'Brahman'. The word *nat* is used, with its variants *nati* and *jnati*, as is the English word 'community', but on the whole *jati* names are used, by the Jains at least, as nouns standing alone—'He's a Visa', 'Those Oswals . . . ', 'Where's that Khatri friend of yours?', etc. This means that other, non-Hindu, groups can be talked of in the same way—'Bohoras', 'Jains', 'Parsis', etc.

Non-Jains regard the Jains as a single group when describing behaviour, or making value-judgements, although some may be aware of the internal divisions between Jains. Jains are usually assigned to the status category '*vania*', although if the speaker is himself a Hindu *vania* he will point out that they are 'Jain *vanias*'. It is interesting to note that the early Census compilers classified the *vania*s as a 'caste', divided into two 'sects'—Shravacs (Jains) and Meshris (Vaishnavas) (see, for example, Gazetteer 1884: 148). A nineteenth-century visitor to the area wrote: 'Only till 1839 the Misri [Meshri]—pure Vanias, who are disciples of Gosaji Maharaj [a Vaishnavite leader]—and the Sarawak [Shravac] indiscriminately mixed in their social entertainments, and partook of meals at each other's hands' (Briggs 1849: 336). Discussing themselves, individual Jains are cognizant of most, if not all, the divisions within their community, but to the anthropologist they seem unable or unwilling to distinguish between *jati* groups and sect groups. That is, to distinguish between a form of social classification endemic to all Indian society and which, in a modern urban locale, seems stripped of its religious-philosophical base,[4] on the one hand, and on the other, a form of sectarian social and religious organization

---

[4] I have no wish to enter the complexities of the debate on caste, although I have little sympathy with Dumont's structuralist interpretations. Apart from the argument

predicated upon the particular tenets of Jainism and their interpretation; in short, the old sect versus caste debate. A good illustration of this are the responses I received when I asked about the Navnat.

The Navnat

The Navnat is a group of *vania jati*s (ideally nine—*navnat* means 'nine *jnati*s') which are allied for trading purposes and, to some extent, marriage and which used to follow the normal practices of commensality (inter-dining for example). To my knowledge it does not exist, in a formally constituted sense, in Saurashtra any more although it was reconstituted in East Africa (see Chapter 5) and a transformation of it exists in Britain (see Chapter 6). Parallel, like-named, organizations existed elsewhere (for example, in Kaccha—see Khakhar 1876) but there were not necessarily marriage relations between such groupings. There is nothing inherently Jain about the Navnat, but from my own observations it is clear that Saurashtran Jains at least feel it to be an important part of their identity.

Most Jains I spoke to in Jamnagar volunteered the information at some point that Jains are divided into nine parts or groups, although they meant very different things by this. There was no common word used for these groups. Informants speaking in English used the word 'part' or some non-specialized synonym such as 'kind'. Gujarati speakers used the words '*nat*', '*paks*', '*panth*', or occasionally, '*sampra-daya*'. These last two have religious overtones in Gujarati and especially for Jains. The lack of a common term and the general vagueness with which my questions were answered suggests that divisions of this type, while recognized, were not assessed. Further questioning could sometimes, but not always, elicit the names of these nine parts. If the speaker was of the older generation he might correct himself and say that not all the parts were Jain but that Jains by far outweighed the Vaishnavas. He would then make it clear that he was referring to the Navnat, mentioning it by name in most cases, as well as trying to list the nine members. Younger speakers, who would have no experience of the Navnat, and who would perhaps only be dimly aware of its existence, would none the less still know that nine was an important number when discussing divisions that relate to Jains, and

contained in *Homo Hierarchicus* (Dumont 1980), those interested—particularly in the notion of the 'substantialization' of caste—could consult Inden (1986) and Quigley (1988) as a neatly matched pair of articles.

would try to list nine groups that had (for the most part) Jain members. In almost all cases, however, the lists would contain *jati*, *gaccha*, and sect names, which resulted in groups being listed that had overlapping membership or which could be wholly subsumed within another group.[5] In the discussion that follows, the reader may find it helpful to refer to Figure 2.1.

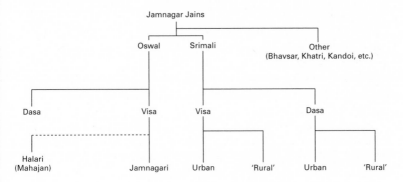

FIG. 2.1. Jamnagar Jains: *Jati* divisions

For example, here is a written list prepared for me by Anil, a Jamnagar Visa Oswal in his mid-forties, which refers to the Navnat and was identified by him as such:

1. Visa Srimali Tapagaccha (Murti Pujaka)
2. Visa Srimali Sthanakavasi
3. Visa Oswal
4. Visa Oswal (Halari) (Mahajan)
5. Dasa Srimali Sthanakavasi
6. Digambar
7. Dasa Srimali Tapagaccha
8. Sorathiya Vania (Kandoi)
9. Achalgaccha
10. Poravad Vania

Without going into great detail it should be noted that groups 1–5, 7, 8, and 10 are *jati* groups or subgroups, some of which (the *gacchas*) are

---

[5] *Gacchas*, it will be remembered, are subdivisions of ascetic orders which are reproduced among the laity. They were discussed briefly at the end of Chapter 1 and will be dealt with more fully in Chapter 4.

also religious groups that have influenced lay thinking about social organization, while 6 and 9 are purely sectarian terms as they stand (although in the local context they carry *jati* implications). Moreover 8 and 10 are exclusively Vaishnavite *jati*s while all other groups are Jain; further notes on groups 1–7 and 9 are to be found below. Sorathiya (8) is actually a subdivision of the Poravad *jati* (10) according to Sangave (1980: 88) and Kandoi, a group of sweet-makers, can be a Dasa Srimali subdivision: see below.

Anil included himself in group 3. He originally wrote 'Jamnagar' after 'Visa Oswal' but then deleted it; an example to my mind of an old rivalry over which (of 3 and 4) is the 'purer' group. That is, to refer to 'Jamnagari Oswal' and 'Halari Oswal', would indicate that both are members of some higher category, 'Oswal'. Instead, he chose to make his own the primary category, which contains a sub-member, 'Halari'.

By contrast, here is a list given by Bipin, a Visa Srimali Tapa Gaccha man of twenty-three (I discuss *gaccha* labels more fully in Chapter 4). He was unable to complete the list to give a total of nine and told me to go and consult someone more knowledgeable:

1. Visa
2. Dasa
3. Deravasi
4. Sthanakavasi
5. Mahajan
6. Oswal
7. Digambar

Here, all the groups are Jain by implication but again there is a mixture of *jati* and sect names. Bipin included himself in group 1. 'Visa' and 'Dasa' could, of course, refer to any Jain, Hindu, or mixed Jain/Hindu *jati*, but he named individuals known to us who I know to be Visa and Dasa Srimali.

Thus as far as I understand it, Jains perceive groups within and without their community (and which thus serve to bound and define that 'community') but are unwilling or unable to categorize these according to a consistent set of differentiating criteria. This inability is not confined to the young, uneducated, or socially marginal. None of the elected leaders of the groups I asked could classify in the way I wished them to classify and, for the most part were unwilling to discuss the subject at all, perhaps for fear of committing themselves, in view of the authority they held, to something that might be repeated or reproduced.

As a final example let us take the list given to me by Jagjivandas, a highly articulate Visa Srimali Tapa Gaccha man of seventy who I mentioned briefly at the end of Chapter 1 and whose story is told at the end of this chapter. Jagjivandas had, for personal reasons, taken a great interest in local Jain history and the relations between various Jain groups.

1. Visa Srimali (all *gacchas*)
2. Dasa Srimali (all *gacchas*)
3. Oswal – Jamnagar
4. Visa Oswal – Mahajan
5. Nagori
6. Sorathia
7. Modh Bania
8. Kandoi
9. Soni

These are all *jati* names and include Jain *jati*, Hindu *jati*, as well as mixed ones. On a subsequent occasion Jagjivandas wished to include another *jati*, Porvad, but could not leave the list with ten members. Eventually he claimed that Kandoi was merely a subdivision of the Dasa Srimali *jati* and so merged these two categories. The 1884 Kathiawar Gazetteer repeats this merging, though it mentions there are no marriage relations between the two, and thus they would not have been amalgamated in the Navnat (Gazetteer 1884: 148).

In fact, all my informants seemed convinced of the necessity to have nine castes, although my own findings and those of Michaelson (1983: 101) in Leicester suggest that nine is not a fixed number in East Africa or England; the general vagueness I encountered in Jamnagar when I discussed it makes me think that the same was true there also. I must stress that Jagjivandas was an exception, however. His interest stemmed from the fact that although he was born into a Tapa Gaccha family and therefore should have been an idol-worshipper, he rejected this and followed an exclusively Sthanakavasi religious path. However, and this is a point of importance that I shall return to in Chapter 5, his daughters were married at the Visa Srimali Tapa Gaccha *vadi* (meeting-hall), not at the Loka Gaccha one which Srimali Sthanakavasis would use. Furthermore, he followed Tapa Gaccha *tithi* (days of abstinence, prescribed by calendars issued by various pan-Indian Jain organizations) during the year and at Paryushan (the annual Jain festival of confession and forgiveness), and he made his annual gifts to charity at the Visa Srimali Tapa Gaccha *pathsala* (teaching-hall—part of an *upasraya*).[6]

No Jain I spoke to knew that hereditary *jati* groups and status ranking were proscribed by the canonical Jain writers,[7] though they were perfectly willing to believe me. However, almost all said that *jati* wasn't really important, that religion overrode petty social divisions, and would occasionally use this as an excuse for ignorance in matters of caste and sect.

Concealed and Open

The discussion of the Navnat above has introduced the *gaccha* division, mentioned in Chapter 1 as a form of ascetic division. Chapter 4 will analyse the penetration of *gaccha* into the lay community, but for the moment I wish to return to the idea of 'open' and 'concealed' divisions among the Jamnagar Jains. The 'open' division I said, was that between Visa and Dasa, and it could be operationalized by all Jains, albeit unconsciously (the use of the terms 'Visa' and 'Dasa' in the Navnat lists, for example). Similarly, it could be used to articulate the 'concealed' division, between rural and urban (see below), in a more acceptable (and possibly euphemistic) way, as, for example, with Jamnagari Oswals referring to the Halari Oswals as 'Dasas'.

The concealed division I wish to focus on now is between urban and rural members of the same group. I have been at a loss to find suitable terms for this division: Visa Srimalis living in Khambhalia (a town of over 26,000 inhabitants), for example, can hardly be said to be 'rural'. However, as my urban, Jamnagar, informants referred to such people as *desi* ('county', 'rustic'—with the slightly pejorative implication of 'hick') and thus unconsciously articulated the old 'rural versus urban' debates of earlier anthropological writing (see P. Mayer 1961, for example), I decided to 'clean up' 'rustic' into 'rural' and leave it stand as an example of the indigenous model mimicking (probably, in fact,

---

[6] All Jains make some kind of financial gifts to charity on samvatsari, the last day of the annual festival of Paryushan. The gifts are made at special booths set up within the temple or upasraya precincts.

[7] For example, the Adi-purana of the eighth-century Digambara writer Jinasena, discussed by P. S. Jaini (1979: 290). Also the Svetambara Uttaradhyayana dating from the Council of Valabhi in AD 453 or 466 (ibid.: 74–5).

giving rise to) the anthropological model. Of course, the deconstruction of the rural–urban dichotomy is now well advanced—see Cottam 1980 and A. M. Shah 1988 for India-based examples.

To return: Visa Srimalis, Visa Oswals, and Dasa Srimalis are to be found in most of the villages and small towns surrounding Jamnagar, especially to the west, in Jamnagar, Lalpur, and Khambhalia *taluka*s (sub-districts). For the Visa and Dasa Srimalis there is no bar to marriage between urban and rural *jati*-mates—that is, between a Visa Srimali man from Lalpur and a Visa Srimali woman from Jamnagar, for example. However, since the turn of the century, and especially after independence, migrants from the villages have been coming to Jamnagar in search of employment and educational opportunities. Once settled in the city these migrants regard it as their home and wish to celebrate marriages and other functions there, for which they need facilities such as a *vadi* (large enclosed courtyard with cooking pits, storage rooms, and, occasionally, some kind of temporary residential accommodation), enough utensils to prepare and serve food to a marriage party, etc. Quite naturally they expect to share the facilities of their urban *jati*-fellows with whom they have been accustomed to intermarry and inter-dine. With relation to the Jain groups that I studied, however, this degree of co-operation between urban- and rural-origin *jati*-fellows was only met with in one instance, as I shall discuss below.

In all the cases I studied, the rural migrants to the town outnumbered (or were thought to outnumber, as in many cases accurate figures were not available) the urban element. This was particularly true in the case of the Halari Visa Oswals or Mahajans. (Note that below I use the term 'rural' to refer only to those individuals of rural origin now settled in Jamnagar, and not to those still living in rural areas). Rural Visa Oswals (Halaris) now living in Jamnagar trace their origin as mentioned, in the first instance, to fifty-six villages in the district. They often have close kin there, having left only one or two generations previously themselves. Most of the Halari Oswals in the villages are farmers (as indeed are some of those now living in Jamnagar if their ancestral village is not too distant),[8] and may wear

---

[8] 'Farming', of course, can mean a variety of things. My contact with Halari Oswals still living in the *bavangami* was infrequent and I had no time to make any systematic study of them. Those I knew managed small- to medium-sized landholdings which they worked themselves with hired labour. Those I knew in Jamnagar who continued to hold land in their ancestral village rented it out to share-croppers or had it managed by kin still resident in the village. Of course, a whole panoply of occupational strategies is

easily identifiable farmer's clothing, and eat a standard rural diet of millet, *khicadi* (rice and pulse cooked together), and milk or yoghurt—items which are seen as rustic and coarse by urbanites. Both clothing and food customs have changed little among the older generation of Mahajans now resident in Jamnagar, and serve to mark them off from the urban Visa Oswals (Jamnagaris).

Both the rural and urban Oswal sections (that is, the Halaris and Jamnagaris) are subdivided on the basis of religious affiliation, although these differences are not of great importance to the majority of the members. The urban section is divided into three *gacchas*, all Deravasi, or idol-worshipping: the Anchala, Kharatara, and Tapa Gacchas. For the layman *gaccha* affiliation dictates the dates of the *tihi* (days for abstinence and austerities) and the *upasraya* one goes to to attend *vyakhyan* (religious discourse) or to seek ascetic advice. These three *gaccha* groups are formally constituted in the sense of having a president and committee and in appointing trustees to manage *gaccha*-owned property. In addition there are, in the urban section, some 60 families who are Sthanakavasi—all descendants of an original Sthanakavasi 'convert'; they are not organized into a *gaccha* and own no property.[9]

The divisions in the rural section—that is, the Halari Visa Oswal—resemble *gaccha* divisions, but the term is deliberately not used. The majority of household heads are Deravasi—I would estimate about 75 per cent, though I have no figures. The remaining 25 per cent or so of households are equally divided between followers of the Sthanakavasi tradition and followers of Kanji Swami, the neo-Digambara reformer. Some Halari Visa Oswals outside Jamnagar are not Jain at all but Hindu—Vaishnavites and Swaminarayans. There were reported to be one or two such families in Jamnagar but I never encountered them. As a result of the urban/rural division there are no formal contacts between Jamnagar Visa Oswals and Halari Visa Oswals residing in

revealed when one considers the household as a whole: several village-based households I knew might have one son and the father engaged in managing the family farm, while other sons would commute to Jamnagar or other nearby towns to speculate on the futures market, engage in retail trade, or enter 'service' occupations (working for the Municipal Corporation, school-teaching, etc.)

[9] Of the 292 Jamnagar Visa Oswal families residing in Jamnagar in 1980, approximately 20% were Sthanakavasi, 20% Anchala Gaccha, 20% Kharatara Gaccha, and the remaining 40% Tapa Gaccha. *Gaccha* affiliation is not listed in their *jati* directory, so these percentages represent my own assessment on the basis of verbal and surname evidence.

Jamnagar (both of which refer to themselves as a '*jnati*' in their respective *jati* directories), and very few contacts of any other kind that I could discover. Some worked together at the Satta Bazaar, a commodity speculation or futures market (technically illegal) that operated in the narrow streets and small offices of the city's Grain Market, but the numbers involved are small. The two groups represent the urban/rural division at its most extreme.

Among the Srimalis the situation is less marked. Urban and rural sections of both Visa and Dasa groups intermarry and have some degree of social intercourse. The urban Dasa Srimalis, however, excluded the rural members from using *jati* property when the latter first began to come to Jamnagar, and, after some years of acrimony, the rural section now owns its own property and has its own internal organization. Dasa Srimalis may be either Jain or Hindu but this does not seem to be a significant division and is not a bar to marriage. The Jain Dasa Srimalis are all Sthanakavasi.

The Visa Srimalis are divided by religious affiliation, however, about half of them being Sthanakavasis and the other half being idol-worshippers, or Deravasis. These groups, although originally sharing a common organization and property, now form two separate groups which are formally identified by *gaccha* names, the Sthanakavasis being the Loka Gaccha, whilst the Deravasis are members of the Tapa Gaccha. The sectarian term (Sthanakavasi, Deravasi) is generally used when discussing specifically religious issues or practices ('Deravasis cut flowers and offer them to their idols, but we Sthanakavasis say that is violence [*himsa*].') while the *gaccha* term (Tapa, Loka) is used when discussing property or social organization. There is no hard and fast rule of usage, however. These *gaccha* designations are really ascetic divisions as mentioned in Chapter 1 but are reproduced in the lay community to designate which ascetics they show their allegiance to. Visa Srimalis have only the two *gaccha*s mentioned. In addition, however, there are a few families which follow the neo-Digambara Kanji Panth, but for the present they must retain their family *gaccha* affiliation. This is because *gaccha* affiliation (which, as I shall show in Chapter 4, is effectively a *jati* subdivision) is important in providing access to property which is needed at times of marriage, etc.

Thus we have a fourfold division within the Visa Srimali community in Jamnagar—urban versus rural, Tapa versus Loka. The rural and urban Tapa Gaccha sections have a joint organization and hold property which was originally restricted to the urban section only. I was told that the two sections merged about ten years ago, but on the condition that the ratio of rural members to urban would never rise above 40:60. The 'merging' consisted of adding 'rural' names on to the list of urban members—which I was never allowed to see—thus allowing them access to *jati* property (such as *vadi*s and other meeting-halls), in exchange for which they paid a nominal annual subscription. In view of the greater number of individuals in the rural section and hence the difficulty of keeping to the 40:60 ratio, I was told that groups of related household heads are represented on the list by only one name, the eldest brother, or even the name of a deceased male ancestor. Each entry on the list, of course, has only one vote, regardless of how many individuals it may represent. This merger relates, of course, only to Visa Srimali Tapa Gaccha members resident in Jamnagar, and does not include those living in nearby villages, although these are still accepted as marriage partners.

A merger did not take place, however, between the urban and rural sections of the Visa Srimali Loka Gaccha, despite the desire for this by the rural section. At present the urban section allows members of the rural section to hire its *vadi* and other facilities, but charges them double what it charges its own members (in 1983, Rs 200 instead of Rs 100 for the hire of the *vadi*, for example) which is greatly resented, quite apart from the resentment at being excluded. The presidents of both the Visa Srimali Tapa Gaccha and the Visa Srimali Loka Gaccha (urban section, the rural section has no formal organization as yet) told me that any Visa Srimali whose father was born in Jamnagar counted as a 'Jamnagari'—i.e. was entitled to membership of the urban section. In the Tapa Gaccha case this is, of course, now irrelevant, but it is a burning issue for the Loka Gaccha as, by this definition, the vast majority of the rural section would be considered urbanites. As a consequence the urban section has deliberately not updated its membership list for the last thirty years or so and most of the 221 household heads listed are dead. A further 142 heads of household are listed as being 'outside' Jamnagar (but of Jamnagar origin) although no place is specified. The descendants of most of these will probably be in Bombay and some may even be overseas. The opinion of the urban section is that the rural section (which numbers some 500 households) should cease clamouring for membership and should set up its own organization as the rural section of the Dasa Srimali *jati* has done.

Why did I refer to this urban/rural division as 'concealed'? I did so firstly because the division was concealed from me as an anthropologist when I first arrived in Jamnagar. This was so partly because my informants thought I would not be interested (in their eyes I was there to study Jainism in practice, which was to them a totally unrelated issue), and partly because some found it rather embarrassing: an interview with an official of the Visa Srimali Loka Gaccha (urban section) committee was rather abruptly terminated when I began to press the point, for example. Secondly, it was concealed because it was an event in process and few people were able to distance themselves sufficiently to see it in perspective (unlike the Visa/Dasa division which was an event from the mythological past, although still of contemporary significance). Moreover, the circumstances surrounding the example in which the division had been fully realized—between the Halari and Jamnagari Oswals—led to forgetfulness on the whole issue; hence my being told that both groups had migrated separately from Kaccha 400 years ago.

Given that the division had been completed among the Oswals, are there any grounds to suppose that the process will also move to completion amongst the Visa Srimalis? I think the answer is no. For one thing, the urban and rural sections of the Visa Srimali Tapa Gaccha have already merged, which means we are considering only the Loka Gaccha, and among the Jamnagar Sthanakavasis (of which the Loka Gaccha is a part), as I shall describe in Chapter 4, there are other linking factors. Secondly, as both Michaelson (1983) and Zarwan (1974; 1975) point out, the basis of division among the Visa Oswals was not solely geographical and temporal, but occupational also. That is to say, Halari Visa Oswals had an exclusively agricultural background, unlike the trading Jamnagaris. As far as I can establish, Visa Srimalis living in villages, while they may own and farm land, are also involved in local trade, and thus closer in occupation to their urban *jati*-fellows. (Between 1540 and 1900 the Jamnagari section of the Oswal *jati* emerged as the more dominant economic force. But from 1920 or so Halari business success outside the region, in East Africa, began to turn the tables.) Finally, caste ideology and *jati* practice in India have changed in form and content considerably since the 1540–1900 period of Oswal division: the nineteenth- and twentieth-century development of 'caste associations' in urban centres, the 'abolition' of caste after independence, the separation of the judicial process from the internal organization of the *jati*, and so on. There is also the factor of scale: the world-wide population of Halari Visa Oswals is some 61,000 (informants' estimates), a population which is theoretically endogamous,[10] while that of the Jamnagar Visa Oswals is a mere 3,700 (in 1980 there were 1,546 Jamnagari Oswals in Jamnagar, 1,913 in Bombay, 202 elsewhere in India, and 33 abroad). Even considering only those Halari Oswals and Jamnagari Oswals resident in Jamnagar the ratio is still roughly 3:1 (4,385 Halaris in 1979 to 1,546 Jamnagaris in 1980). An accurate comparison of the Loka Gaccha Visa Srimalis is not possible, as figures are not available, but the ratio could not be greater than 2:1 (rural:urban) in or out of Jamnagar.

In this sense, then, the 'concealed division' within the Visa Srimali *jati* is perhaps less significant than I have made it appear. Indeed, one could look at it the other way round and say that there is no division at all, merely that some of Jamnagar's Visa Srimali Sthanakavasis are not members of a particular property-owning organization, for whatever reasons. My work on the Visa Oswals leads me to think otherwise, however. They reveal one manifestation of a particular pattern, the details being contingent upon the intersection of a variety of factors: *jati* ideology, occupation, residence, population size. What is clear is that the ideology of Jainism plays a small or irrelevant part in all this. In the following two chapters I shall try to gauge the extent to which being Jain is important.

Jains as People

So far I have said a lot concerning the Visa Srimali, Jamnagar Visa Oswal, and Halari Visa Oswal *jati*s in the abstract, but relatively little concerning the lives and experiences of contemporary Jamnagar Jains. I therefore wish to conclude this chapter by sketching in a few details that will put some flesh on these rather dry bones. As I mentioned at the start of the chapter, the city of Jamnagar consists of a central 'core' —the old city, still bounded by the remains of its walls and marked by its gates—which is surrounded by a periphery of newer development. The Visa Srimalis and Jamnagar Visa Oswals both have 'traditional' residence areas within the old city, while the Halari Visa Oswals—as newer arrivals—have settled on land beyond the city walls. Many Visa Srimalis and Jamnagar Visa Oswals have, however, moved out of the crowded city centre in recent years and have begun building more

---

[10] Michaelson claims that another division is developing, through marriage strategies, between village-dwelling Halari Oswals on the one hand, and urban-dwelling Halaris in India, East Africa, and the UK on the other (Michaelson 1983: 134–5).

spacious bungalows in the suburbs—usually to the north and west. Most continue to work in the city centre, wherever their residence, and most are involved in some way with trade and commerce. The densest concentrations of working Jains are to be found in the Chandi Bazaar area, where they own or run many of the retail outlets, particularly cloth shops, and in the Grain Market. My impression is that Jamnagar and Halari Visa Oswals by far outweigh Visa Srimalis in the Grain Market, the Visa Srimalis tending more towards retail sale. Occupations in the Grain Market vary, but very commonly men choose to be dealers (*dalal*s) or speculators in the (illegal) commodity futures market.

Most Jains, in common with most other settled Jamnagar residents, tend towards a joint family form of domestic arrangement. In general this tends to be of the 'stem' type—three generations with usually only one married couple in the two senior generations. There are numerous exceptions, however, ranging from households containing a single individual to households of twenty or more persons. Households occupying flats and apartments outside the city centre are frequently nuclear in form; for example, many Visa Halari Oswal households in the Digvijay Plot consist of a husband, wife, and their children, with the husband and wife's parents remaining in their village of origin, living alone or with younger, possibly unmarried children. Women from all three *jati*s rarely work outside the home, though some may take in sewing or other minor homeworking occupations. While some women remain at home almost all the time (their husbands buying daily provisions at the market), emerging only to attend weddings and rituals, others move around quite freely within the town, going shopping or visiting friends and relatives. One woman I knew, who had spent the first few years of her married life in Kenya, frequently made long bus journeys alone, to other parts of Saurashtra and Gujarat, often meeting up with her husband who had gone on ahead for business or religious reasons.

Most children attend the state schools in the city, although one or two from wealthier families are sent to private school. The two most prestigious of these—St Xaviour's and St Anne's—are both 'English medium' (of instruction); the parents I knew who sent their sons and daughters to these schools had hopes of their entering the professions (particularly the medical profession), rather than simple commerce.

The Visa Srimalis—the group with whom I am most concerned— have, as mentioned, a traditional residence area within the city walls and also corporately own a number of religious properties (these are

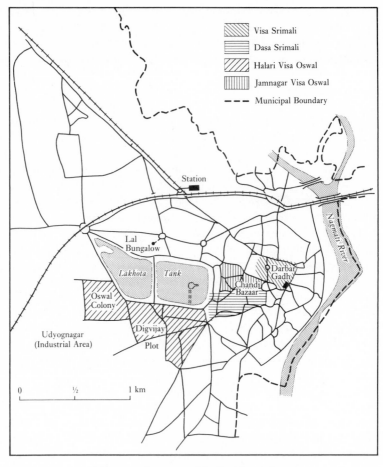

MAP. 2.3. Jamnagar: Jain Residence Areas

discussed in Chapter 4). Many of them are well established in the city, running family businesses that were set up generations earlier.

Jagjivandas Mehta has already been mentioned, at the end of Chapter 1 where I told the story of his attempts to find a husband for his short-sighted daughter, Hina, and earlier in this chapter in my discussion of the Navnat. He is also one of the most prominent businessmen in Jamnagar and claims that his success is largely due to his patriarchal style of management. Jagjivandas was one of my main informants and acted as a kind of father-figure to me—much as

Charandas Sanghvi (who I discuss in Chapter 5) had done while I was in Leicester—advising me on correct behaviour at ritual events, introducing me to his many friends and fellow-shopkeepers, and taking me into his family as a near-member.

Even before I knew him well, many people I met would ask me if I had met him yet. This was usually for one of the following reasons: first, he was thought by many to be very knowledgeable about many aspects of Jain belief and practice; secondly, he was a successful and respected businessman; thirdly, he and his family were often cited as a prime example of the 'traditional' joint family. All these claims contained some element of truth, but the fact that I was referred to Jagjivandas on many occasions when I enquired about these topics— all potential constituents in an ideal Jain identity—in some senses only served to emphasize the (perceived) lack of such qualities elsewhere in Jamnagar.

Jagjivandas is one of the older generation of Visa Srimali Tapa Gaccha Jains and had been educated under the British *raj*. Consequently, he was a pronounced anglophile while still being a loyal Indian nationalist and Gandhian. He takes a daily English-language news-paper, follows the national political scene closely, and has ensured that all his sons are fluent English speakers. One of only two sons, he and his brother had inherited their father's grain business, which they later divided. By the time I met him he maintained a store-front and wholesale warehouse in Jamnagar's Grain Market, and two other shops in the area which sold grain directly to the public. He lives, together with his wife, their five sons, four of the sons' wives, two unmarried daughters, six grandchildren, and his wife's mother, in a large house in the traditional residential area of the Visa Srimalis (see Map 2.3). Four of the sons run the two retail stores, while the youngest sits with his father at the wholesale store; they return home in shifts to eat lunch. For taxation purposes, Jagjivandas retains the entire business in his own name, paying his sons a small salary each month (about Rs 1,000) for personal spending, while a portion of the business profits maintains the joint household (some Rs 6,000 per month).

Jagjivandas's reputation for Jain knowledge stems from the fact that, while born and brought up a Deravasi (worshipper of idols) in the Tapa Gaccha tradition he had, in mid-adulthood, rejected this *panth* (path) in favour of the Sthanakavasi *panth*. During this period he had 'researched' (as he put it) both traditions and found the Sthanakavasi to be the more in accordance with what he took to be the teachings of

(6)

Mahavira. Consequently he is highly knowledgeable about the beliefs and practices of both and has himself acquired a certain distance from the religion of his birth. His 'conversion' was a highly personal affair, however, and the rest of his family remain Deravasi. He also sought brides for his sons amongst the Visa Srimali Tapa Gaccha and not the Loka Gaccha. While he no longer visits Deravasi temples and attends only Sthanakavasi *vyakhyan*s (morning sessions of instruction by *sadhu*s and *sadhvi*s) he is familiar with all the Deravasi *sadhu*s and *sadhvi*s who pass through Jamnagar and knows of all Deravasi ritual events that are to take place.

He is also inordinately proud of his 'joint family', and invited me to his home often to demonstrate and discuss with me the details and practicalities of such an arrangement. He also acknowledges its comparative rarity (although I know of many examples of 'stem'-type joint families among the Jamnagar Jains). One of the problems which mitigates against such an arrangement was the availability of suitable housing. Often the joint family house is part of the post-mortem property and effects to be divided among the sons together with business premises, smallholdings, and other non-movable property. In cases where the brothers wish to divide, or see it to be financially advantageous to do so, the house will go to one brother alone, who will promptly demolish it and build two smaller houses on the site or divide the property in some other way. Either way, the stock of suitable buildings within the densely packed streets of the old city of Jamnagar appears to be diminishing. One solution—of which there is a very well-known Jain example in Jamnagar—is to reconstitute the joint family outside the old town, by building a large bungalow in one of the suburbs. Jagjivandas acknowledged to me the good fortune which had allowed him to maintain the large house, especially during the early years of his marriage when both family and business were small, and said that he felt it to be preferable to the suburban bungalow option.

He also described on one occasion the ingenious inheritance arrangement he had devised for his children. His married daughter receives a small but not insignificant amount of grain from the family business three times a year; this will be extended to the other two when they marry and will continue after his death through the agency of his sons. The sons meanwhile will inherit the joint house, the three commercial properties, and a variable percentage of the liquid assets, such that each son will receive Rs 5,000 more than the next one junior to him. The logic for such an arrangement is that the older sons will need to arrange their daughters' weddings before the younger (all the sons having been married in order of seniority) and will thus need access to cash more quickly. The younger sons meanwhile can be investing and increasing their inheritance while their daughters mature. The youngest son of all, however, will inherit an additional

Rs 5,000 as he is not yet married and will need to buy jewellery and gifts for his wife and her kin.

Jagjivandas therefore combines within his person qualities and attributes that are to be found in lesser degree or in less satisfying combination amongst many of the Jamnagar Jains—Visa Srimalis, Jamnagar Visa Oswals, and Halari Visa Oswals alike. While family firms such as Jagjivandas's may achieve great success, this is not always guaranteed. The case of Bharat Shah which now follows is an example of a Visa Oswal household that once appeared to have had the potential fulfilled by Jagjivandas.

Like Jagjivandas Mehta, mentioned above, Bharat Shah also lives in a large house in a traditional residence area, this time in the Jamnagar Visa Oswal quarter (see Map 2.3). As with Jagjivandas's family, members of Bharat's family once owned the entire *gali* (small cul-de-sac which can be completely sealed off with massive wooden gates) in which Bharat's house is situated. The house itself is large, three storeys high with a basement, but is all that remains of a once large and thriving business concern. Bharat's paternal grandfather, Jhaverchand Jagjivandas, was a Jamnagar grain speculator who joined with a distant cousin and established a textile importing and distribution business, in the early years of this century. They imported fine Swiss cottons and other luxury textiles from Europe and supplied them to dealers in Jamnagar, Ahmedabad, and Bombay, who sold them to the British and to upper-class Indian households. The business grew rapidly and with the profits Jhaverchand began buying land in the centre of the city and erecting luxurious houses, furnished with European fittings and Indian marble floors. The houses were given to his sons and the sons of his brothers until by the 1920s the whole *gali* was occupied by one extended family. Jhaverchand became an amiable patriarch, driving around in imported cars and attending the social functions of Jamnagar's mercantile élite. Sheth Popat Dharshi (mentioned again in Chapter 3) was a close friend and together they held meetings with the Jam Saheb, Ranjitsinhji, to discuss ways of improving Jamnagar's commercial strength.

The next generation, however, including Bharat's father, Nagindas, proved not to be so astute. Nagindas, the eldest son of the eldest son, never worked at all in his lifetime (according to Bharat) and left the management of the business (which was now largely located in Bombay) to his brothers. While he lived a life of relative ease in Jamnagar, trading on his father's reputation, his brothers were

effectively asset-stripping in Bombay, moving the financial under-
pinnings of the family business across into privately owned concerns.
On Jhaverchand's death, in the early 1960s, Nagindas's wife,
Pannaben, demanded a partition of the family and thus of the family
wealth. Jhaverchand's brothers and their children had moved to
Bombay, as had Nagindas's brothers, leaving their Jamnagar houses
empty or tenanted by caretaker families. At partition each son or son's
son received a house in Jamnagar and a small amount of money, the
rest having been effectively pre-partitioned. Nagindas died shortly
afterwards leaving Bharat, the sole son, to care for his mother and to
maintain their house.

Bharat himself, while born in Jamnagar, had spent much of his early
life in Bombay and Ahmedabad and was enrolled at a prestigious
private school in Bombay when the partition happened. He was
allowed to finish his studies, but returned to Jamnagar shortly
afterwards, instead of going on to university as planned. Immediately
on his return, Nagindas tried to set him up in business in a small shop
that the family had rented in the centre of Jamnagar, which was at the
time sub-let to another cloth merchant. But neither Nagindas nor
Bharat had any commercial experience and found it impossible to
maintain the shop without the rest of the family business to supply it.
On Nagindas's death a few months later, Bharat sold up the remaining
stock, gave up the shop lease, and became a clerk in a local bank. The
small amount of cash from the stock sale helped to pay for his marriage
a year later and the remainder was invested to pay for the marriages of
his own children.

Bharat is now in the incongruous position of living in one of the
finest houses of Jamnagar's old city and earning a wage equivalent to
that which his grandfather would have paid one of his business
employees. The fine furniture and drapes are becoming worn and
threadbare, while cracks are appearing in the inlaid marble floors. All
but one of the houses in the *gali* are shuttered and empty or inhabited
by a transient population of tenants (as, it must be said, are many such
houses in the centre of Jamnagar—their owners are now settled in
Bombay or abroad, but while the city's planning restrictions (mentioned
at the start of this chapter) remain in force there is little point in selling
them). Perhaps as a result of the family misfortunes Bharat has become
exceedingly pious, attending all the rituals and functions organized by
the Jamnagar Visa Oswals, and many others besides. His children all
receive a strict religious education at the Jamnagar Visa Oswal *pathsala*

('religious school') in addition to their normal studies and his hopes for them are that they will remain pious but gain a good education and move into the professions. He sees no future in commerce in the modern India, an India of fragmented nucleated families like his own, claiming that only a strong extended family can maintain the necessary division of labour and pooling of capital required.

With Jhaverchand, Bharat's grandfather, we can see the traits that were supposed to be responsible for the Jains' initial presence in Jamnagar—a sound business sense, coupled with a close liaison with the city's ruler. Jhaverchand was typical of a whole generation of Jamnagar Visa Oswals, who preferred to stay in Jamnagar and develop strong—if localized—business interests under the pax Britannica, in contrast to the Visa Srimalis who utilized the British presence to seek their fortunes overseas.[11] However, while the British were favourably disposed towards the Jamnagar Jams, seeing them as an example of an enlightened Indian monarchy, Jamnagar's fortunes under British rule were transient and no amount of investment in Bedi, Jamnagar's port, could disguise the fact that Bombay was emerging as the premier port of western India. Even were it not for the shady dealings of Bharat's paternal uncles (of which I have only Bharat's account, corroborated by statements from one of the uncles who subsequently lost his business and returned to Jamnagar), it seems likely that Jhaverchand's business could only have survived in Bombay. The migration of Bharat's senior kin to Bombay was paralleled many times over, so that today over 50 per cent of Jamnagar Visa Oswals have their primary residence there.

The final example I would like to give is that of an Halari Visa Oswal and his family. The example I give is fairly typical. There are some Halari Oswal families who have amassed comparatively large fortunes over the last 100 years or so and now either reside permanently overseas, or live in large and palatial houses in the Oswal Colony. On the other hand, there are many Halari Visa Oswals who have never left their native village and continue to be petty landowners and cash-crop farmers. The example given here is illuminating in that it combines several of the options taken by the Halari Visa Oswals in recent years.

As mentioned earlier, while the Jamnagar Visa Oswals took

---

[11] A Bombay-produced book of the period (Dumasia 1927) captures the mood of Jamnagar's energetic entry into the twentieth century and contains several pages of plates of 'Merchants who have helped build up Jamnagar's revived trade'. One of these is of Jhaverchand Jagjivandas, under his real name.

advantage of British rule to consolidate their entrepreneurial activities in Jamnagar and the Visa Srimalis took the chance to emigrate to other parts of the Empire, the Halari Visa Oswals began to raise their status from an agricultural *jati* to that of a trading *jati*. In the case of Rajesh Shah and his family, this involved both a move into the city of Jamnagar (both residential and occupational) and a move to East Africa. Rajesh's brother, Mansukh, later moved on to Leicester and his story is told in Chapter 6.

Rajesh was born just before Indian independence in the village of Changa, some 15 km. south of Jamnagar. He is the youngest of five brothers (the eldest now dead) and his early years were spent in the village, apart from a period spent at school in Jamnagar. The family owned a fairly large farm and played an active role in local politics and —to a lesser extent—in local Jain affairs (the Jain temple in the village, with accompanying *upasraya* (rest hall for ascetics) was not built until the 1960s). On their father's death, however, the brothers sold a large part of the land and the family effectively partitioned, although entirely amicably. Rajesh, now aged 15 or so, stayed in the care of his eldest brother, Ramniklal, while the three middle brothers migrated to East Africa and set up in business there.

Ramniklal used his and Rajesh's share of the land sale money to buy a small warehouse in Jamnagar and began a business selling fertilizer and other agricultural requirements. He moved his family—including Rajesh—into the city, first renting and later building a house in the newly established Digvijay Plot. This is a piece of land immediately outside the city's Khambhalia gate (and thus outside the old city and its traditional Jain residence areas—see Map 2.3) which was given over to the city administration for residential use by the last Jam, Digvijay-sinhji, at independence. Rajesh worked alongside Ramniklal, following his studies intermittently, and then left for Kenya, having been 'called' by Mahesh, to help in the brothers' enterprise there. The enterprise, however, was not thriving and Rajesh returned home shortly after-wards and continued working with Ramniklal. He later made a couple of shorter visits to Kenya but always returned without making any significant investment of time, labour, or money; he said that he enjoyed the life there, but missed India and—in particular—the family home and farm in Changa.

As mentioned above, the tie of the Halari Visa Oswals to their village of origin is strong and enduring. Rajesh's family was not unusual in retaining part of the family farm, even though the rest was sold off to finance urban-based ventures. The farm, of which only some 4 acres remain, is situated some little way outside Changa and is tended by share-croppers from the village. (The family home is lived in and maintained by distant relatives of the brothers' father.) On the land, Rajesh—who takes the most interest in agriculture—grows mainly groundnuts (one of the region's principal crops) and millet, together with a small supply of vegetables for domestic consumption. Rajesh tends to favour a fairly simple life-style, returning to Changa several times a week to see friends and relatives and to keep an eye on the land. When in Jamnagar, he runs small errands for the family business (which Ramniklal's son Jitu has now joined and effectively manages) and keeps the books, but he leaves the major decisions to Ramniklal and Jitu. The business has diversified into supplying parts for agricultural machinery and, during the major drought in the region which began in 1983, into selling pumps for tube wells.

Rajesh, perhaps more so than his brothers, is meticulous in his Jain observances, never eating root vegetables and observing most of the calendrical austerities. Due to his prompting, the business has made several donations to temple funds in Jamnagar and in Changa, and he regularly visits any ascetics staying at the *upasraya*s attached to the Halari Visa Oswals' temples in the city (both of which are located outside the Khambhalia gate). Following what seems to be a common pattern, Rajesh and his brothers have maintained a link with their agricultural past, while taking full advantage of the opportunities which came, first under the joint rule of the British and the later Jams and then under the new democracy which was trumpeted in with Indian independence. The Halari Visa Oswals' relationship with organizational Jainism is best seen as symbiotic, each being of service to the other over the past century.

3

Coming Together in Jamnagar

This chapter expands the ethnography presented in the last chapter and prepares the main argument of the next—religious property as a focus of division for the Jamnagar Jains. In this chapter I concentrate on events—'functions' as they are known—which bring the Jamnagar Jains together; events which, like ritual, can be seen as a possible locus for that which makes the Jains Jain. As I hinted in Chapter 1, in my discussion of Jinasena's 'Hindu-ization' of Jain orthopraxy, there are many ways in which it is hard to see any distinctive traits among the Jains: they wear the same day-to-day clothing as their Hindu *vania* neighbours, eat largely the same food, live in the same kind of housing, follow the same kinds of occupational and educational careers. In short, they inhabit the same moral universe, or one that is so broadly contiguous that the points of variance seem to recede in importance, overshadowed by the points of similarity. The fact that there are many

*jati*s in northern India with both Hindu and Jain members means that even marriage strategies may not be a singular defining feature (Cottam (1980) discusses such strategies, without of course claiming that these are uniquely Jain).

One possible area of distinctiveness may lie in the experience of women and a peculiarly Jain construction of gender relations, in which women take on the role of renunciant within a marriage in a paralleling of the relations between lay and ascetic. If such a parallel exists, however, is it fragile and uni-dimensional: again, the contiguity of the *vania* Hindu moral world is too close to permit radical divergence.[1] Another area of distinctiveness may lie in the ritual transition from lay to ascetic status, where, although the passage between such statuses is common enough in India (and apparently very similar among such reformed Hindu groups as the Swaminarayan *satsang*; see R. B. Williams 1984: 95–7), a peculiarly Jain symbolic order is invoked.

Below I discuss a number of events—including two provoked by ascetic initiation and several which involve women as major participants —as revelatory of principles of division and cohesion, rather than as constellations of Jain symbols or arenas where specifically Jain meaning is invoked and negotiated, which is in keeping with the largely ethnographic tone of this chapter and its Leicester parallel, Chapter 7.

These events—processions, ceremonies of honour and respect, fasts, and feasts—all occur regularly, and together they form items on a 'menu' from which communal gatherings can be constructed. Structuring this 'menu' are certain ground rules which one might refer to as those of 'social collocation'—that is, that certain types of event are best marked in combination with other types of event (processions and feasts, for example, 'go together', while processions and communal dietary austerities do not). As we shall see in Part II, these 'social collocations' are not always appropriate or possible in Leicester and the Jains there are in the process of finding new arrangements. This chapter concludes with a discussion of a new form of coming together, the Jain Social Group, which dispenses with these standard items and which therefore also marks a break with the rules of social collocation. I witnessed, or heard about, all the events discussed below, but I preface the discussion with a description of a mythological event, the *samavsarana* (the coming together), which I refer to as an archetype, a

---

[1] Jain women's religiosity and the construction of Jain gender relations is thoroughly dealt with by Reynell (1985*a*; 1985*b*; 1991).

form of symbolic patterning and religious legitimator for all the events that follow it.

There are, of course, many other ways for Jains to come together in Jamnagar beyond those that I describe. For example, there are many regular *puja*s (acts of worship) performed for special purposes, or to mark anniversaries, as well as religious camps (*sibir*s) and other educational events organized by visiting ascetics. Informally, Jains meet for business or pleasure, or, for those living in the old city, to share water and other facilities. Below, however, I present only particular aspects of formal events which have an overtly religious or Jain content, and which have been organized by the groups discussed in the previous chapter. It would take more than the space available in the book —let alone this chapter—to describe the entire range of Jain rituals and festivals. The selection I have chosen to describe in detail both typifies the Jain communal life of Jamnagar and exemplifies certain themes that run through the preceding and ensuing chapters, most especially the expression of *jati* solidarity (or part-*jati*, that is the 'sections' I discussed in the previous chapter).[2] I make only fleeting references to the ascetics in what follows; a discussion of ascetic practices and rituals is to be found in Deo 1956; Fischer and Jain 1977; Tatia and Kumar 1981.

The samavsarana *as archetype*

For all Jains the archetypal form of gathering is the *samavsarana*—the 'holy assembly of the Jina' (P. S. Jaini 1979: 350). Jaini, describing Mahavira after his enlightenment describes the *samavsarana* as follows:

Thus he sat in the lotus posture, maintaining constant omniscient trance, housed in an assembly hall which had been miraculously created by the gods. His body, free from all impurities, shone like a crystal on all sides. Above his head was hoisted the royal insignia of a white umbrella, signifying that nothing could be higher or holier than he. A divine sound (*divyadhvani*) emanated from his person for the benefit of the audience. As this audience consisted of gods, demi-gods, human beings, and animals, the entire assembly was called *samavsarana*, a place of resort for all. (ibid.: 35)

---

[2] I am aware that one glaring omission in this chapter is a discussion of the festival of Paryushan, the major annual event for all Jains, at which the sins of the previous year are confessed and the forgiveness of one's fellow men and women sought. Misfortune prevented me from attending the ceremonies during my time in Jamnagar: I do, however, discuss in Chapter 7 the ceremonies that I witnessed in Leicester.

Thus the basis for coming together is to hear the *tirthankara*'s teaching and to gain knowledge of the truth which will lead to one's own enlightenment. At the *samavsarana* differences in caste and kind are forgotten, for all attention is turned to the omniscient *tirthankara*. By means of a miraculous illusion the *tirthankara* seems to be facing in four directions (corresponding to the cardinal points), so that all the beings, assembled about him in concentric circles, may see his face. In Gujarat today, as in the rest of India, the *samavsarana* is represented as a three-dimensional model, worked in silver, and some three or four feet tall. It consists of a series of circular slabs, each representing an enclosure of the 'assembly-hall', arranged on top of each other and decreasing in size towards the top. The side of each slab is marked with animals, men, and gods in bas relief; a shallowly incised flight of steps leads up to the next enclosure. Placed at the top is a small statue of a *tirthankara* (often Mahavira, but it varies with the occasion) seated in meditation. This representation (itself called a *samavsarana*) is a centre, the object and focus of attention at many temple rituals and ceremonies. It is also a tempting repository for the vision of the anthropologist (take, for example, the title of Carrithers' and Humphrey's (1991) edited collection on the Jains: *The Assembly of Listeners*); it concretizes our assumptions that the 'community' must have some locus, some central point around which it is organized.

Processions

All the Jamnagar Jain sections and *jati*s hold processions (generally '*varghodo*', though this refers specifically to wedding processions), through the city on various occasions, either to celebrate an event in the calendar, such as the birth of Mahavira, or to mark a special ceremony, such as a *diksa* (religious initiation). In addition, an individual may organize a procession to celebrate a major religious event in his or her own family, such as a major fast. Families, of course, organize the wedding processions of their children, but in this section I wish to concentrate on processions with some overtly religious (Jain) purpose.[3]

---

[3] Jain writers maintain that marriage and other life-cycle events (*samskara*s) are purely secular affairs. While it is a moot point whether the Jamnagar Jains view the status of marriage any differently from their Hindu neighbours, their marriages are contracted according to the Hindu rite. Attendance at a marriage may be entirely Jain by default (that is, only Jains are invited) but, although there is rumoured to be a Jain marriage rite, I never came across anyone who had used it.

There is no fixed course that a procession may make through the city, and the city is too large to be completely encircled. Instead, the course is determined by the point of departure, the residence location of the group organizing the procession, places that must be visited or passed *en route*, and the termination-point of the procession. Other practical considerations are to take into account the course of suitable roads—wide enough to accommodate the carriages, chariots, elephants (if used), bands, and crowds that make up the procession, yet not so busy that the city's traffic circulation would be disrupted. Processions almost always lead up to some event or ceremony, so they generally last no more than an hour or so. A common pattern would be to have a procession from 8.30 a.m. until 10.00 a.m., followed by a ceremony lasting until noon, followed by a meal or feast.

A procession is one of the few occasions on which the Jains manifestly demonstrate their existence—and more importantly, their corporate existence—to the rest of the city, and it is significant that all sections according to the fourfold scheme (men, women—and children—male and female ascetics) take part. Processions are never exclusively composed of Jains—certain skilled persons are needed such as bandsmen, elephant drivers, and dancers—and there is nothing to stop others joining the procession as it passes through the streets. Jains themselves perform several functions within the procession. Women, who are always at the rear, often sing religious songs, for example, and it is a custom that six men, barefoot and attired in *dhoti* and *khes* (loin and shoulder cloths, the clothing worn in the temple) should pull the chariot bearing the image of the *tirthankara*. In addition, small boys, also wearing *dhoti* and *khes*, carry lamps and dribble a milk and water mixture (in which the idol has previously been bathed) in front of the chariot bearing the *tirthankara*.[4] The procession is headed by any resident male ascetics of the same sect or *gaccha* as the organizing group (that is to say, an ascetic who is resident in the organizing group's property), followed by male laity, the chariots, and carriages. Bringing up the rear are the female ascetics and the female laity.

The processions are noisy, colourful affairs, often preceded by pipe and drum bands playing arrangements of the latest film songs. People lean out of their doors and windows to watch, small children run along

---

[4] This bathing ceremony, *snatra puja*, is made in memory of the holy bath given to the new-born *tirthankara* by the king of the gods, on Mt. Meru, the mountain at the centre of the world in Jain cosmology.

side. Although women will generally wear a best sari, men not involved
in the ritual proceedings dress in their everyday clothes. People chatter
happily about topics totally unconnected with the day's events, and
men may even stop off at their favourite tea-stall or -shop for a cup of
tea and a *bidi*, before taking a short cut through the streets and
rejoining the procession further on.

Varsi dan

(Lit. 'yearly giving' or, according to another interpretation, 'year of
giving'.) Although this event should, as the name implies, take place
yearly, it is in fact only performed on the occasion of a *diksa*. The
diksarthi or initiate in this case was a girl of twenty, Nita, who told me
she had decided to renounce the world after her father died when she
realized the transience of worldly happiness. Usually on such an
occasion the *varsi dan* procession would be organized by the family of
the *diksarthi*, but in this case, as the family were not rich, it was paid for
by her *jati*—the Jamnagar Visa Oswals (JVO).

Nita, the *diksarthi*, was not one of my regular informants; indeed, I
only met her because she was taking *diksa* and friends thought it
important that I should interview her. It is thus difficult for me to say
what it was that prompted her to take such a radical step. At other
times and in other places I heard stories of women who had become
*sadhvi*s to escape marriage or who had physical disabilities (withered
arms, hare lips) that would have made finding a spouse difficult. In
Nita's case—without, of course, wishing to belittle her own explanation
—it is possible that the family's financial circumstances were a factor.

The procession begins from Nita's house, in the old city (and in the
heart of her *jati*'s residence area) at about 8.30 a.m. I arrive at the
advertised time, 8.00 a.m. and stand around drinking tea from a
nearby stall with friends until all the preparations are complete.
When it finally gets under way, the procession is led by a hired band
playing film music, and a horse-drawn carriage full of small children
—relatives of the *diksarthi*—who are laughing and singing. Then
comes another band, leading the male ascetics (including an *acarya*
of the Tapa Gaccha: Nita is in fact of the Anchala Gaccha but as
there are very few ascetics in this *gaccha* the proceedings are being
conducted by Tapa Gaccha ascetics). One of the ascetics—the
right-hand man of the *acarya* and soon to become an *acarya* himself,
is himself of JVO origin and had followed this same route at his own

varsi dan procession some twenty years previously.[5] The ascetics are
followed by male laity—mostly JVOs, but also others—who are very
few at first, but gradually increase in number until they are sixty or
seventy strong by the time we arrive at the destination.

After the male laity comes the *diksarthi*'s chariot. This is a large,
silver-clad affair, strapped to the top of a Land Rover, raising Nita
high above the heads of the crowds. Adorned with jewellery, and
wearing an ornate red silk and gold brocade sari, she stands behind
a large silver bowl full of rice, coins, a few currency notes, and some
fruit. On her carefully oiled hair, which for once hangs free (all
Gujarati women past puberty tie or braid their hair), she wears a
small diadem of paste jewels. As the carriage moves she dips both
hands into the bowl and with a smooth and stylized gesture flings
them up and out, showering the crowd with rice and coins. Small
boys scramble for these amongst our feet as we try to negotiate our
way through the narrow streets. At times, Nita lets a small quantity
of rice fall directly into someone's outstretched hands, simultaneously
bestowing on them a triumphant smile.

Following Nita's chariot comes a bullock-drawn carriage bearing
her mother, sister, and other female relatives. These women are
seated around a small brass image of Mahavira, adorned with
flowers and silver leaf. Later this image will be placed on top of the
samavsarana for the final ceremony. The carriage, like the chariot, is
of silver-cladding and ornately carved and decorated. Bringing up
the rear of the procession are the Tapa Gaccha *sadhvi*s and the lay
women, two of whom bear baskets on their heads containing the
plain white clothes Nita will wear as a *sadhvi*.

The procession moves slowly from Nita's home, around Chandi
Bazaar, east through to the residential area of the Visa Srimalis, then
along the main road of the city which leads eventually to Bedi,
Jamnagar's port, for some way before doubling back at the edge of
the old town and finishing at a privately owned *upasraya* where the
final ceremonies will take place. Although the procession does not
stop at any particular place *en route* there are occasions when it

---

[5] Numbers are hard to estimate, but the 1980 Jamnagar Visa Oswal *jnati vastipatrak*
lists the numbers of *sadhu*s and *sadhvi*s (currently living) from the *jati* as follows: 6
Deravasi *sadhu*s (no *gaccha* given) and 23 *sadhvi*s. The Halari Visa Oswal *vastipatrak*
claims that up until 1979 the current (i.e. living) numbers of Halari Visa Oswals who had
taken *diksa* were: Deravasi (no *gaccha* given)—14 *sadhu*s, 23 *sadhvi*s; Sthanakavasi—15
*sadhvi*s (no *sadhu*s); Kanji Panth—1 *sadhu* (unknown status); Swaminarayan (ie. Hindu)
—2 *sadhu*s.

pauses so that Nita can distribute her *dan* or gifts more effectively. At these times, the procession—which may have become drawn-out —can reformulate, allowing the various groups involved to regroup and reorganize themselves.

The Jains I spoke to said the *diksa varsi dan* procession discharged the *diksarthi*'s duty as a lay woman to give alms unconditionally and without restraint; it also demonstrated to the world at large the status she could have had as a lay woman, yet which she had chosen to renounce in favour of asceticism. To the anthropologist looking on, the elevated position can be seen as a metaphor for rank, for prestige, and honour: the jewellery indicates riches, the red and gold sari—a wedding sari—shows the possibility of marriage and fulfilment in family life, the diadem is a symbol of the princely or kingly rank renounced by the *tirthankara*s and renounced (albeit in its absence) by the *diksarthi*.

Mahavira Jayanti

(The birthday of Mahavira.) This festival is celebrated on Chaitra *sud* 13 by the Vikram calendar, a date which in 1983 fell in April. The procession was organized by the Visa Srimali Tapa Gaccha (VSTG). At the same, or at other times in the day, processions were held by the Jamnagar Sthanakavasi Jain Sangh (a cross-*jati* organization, discussed in the next chapter), the Jamnagar Visa Oswals and the Halari Visa Oswals.

The VSTG procession, which I joined, set off eastwards from their temple in Chandi Bazaar, moved round the south side of the old city to the Khambhalia Gate, and continued up past the eastern end of the lake, past the western gate of the old city (Bhidbhanjan Gate—now no longer standing), before swinging east down the main arterial highway and back into Chandi Bazaar.

This procession is led by half a dozen small girls bearing water pots (*loto*) on their heads, filled with a milk and water mixture in which the small idol of Mahavira, travelling in a carriage further back in the procession, had been bathed earlier that morning. Then come the Tapa Gaccha *sadhu*s, including the *acarya* (this procession takes place about a month before the *diksa* ceremony, described above and below, for which the *acarya* has come to Jamnagar: one cannot normally count on having an *acarya* in residence for Mahavira

Jayanti), and the male laity. Behind them walk some small boys, dressed in *dhoti* and *khes*, who precede the two main chariots drawn by bullocks wearing cloths of gold brocade; the boys beat gongs, carry lamps and sprinkle more milk and water in the path of the chariots. The first of these is empty of people but contains a 'photo' (that is, an oleograph) of the *siddhacakra* (lit. wheel of the enlightened souls), while the second carries the brass image of Mahavira, surrounded by members of a VSTG family who are keeping the image cool with palm-leaf fans.[6] This family had earlier won the 'auction' of this privilege and the right to perform *arti* (the lamp waving ceremony) at the evening *puja*.

It is a peculiarly Jain practice to auction privileges such as this. Interested parties gather in the temple beforehand and bid against each other to perform *arti*, to ride in a chariot, to represent a god in a religious drama, and other such things. The process of bidding for *arti* is briefly described in Chapter 7, when it occurs in the Leicester context, and discussed in much fuller detail in Banks 1991.

The two men in the chariot wear *dhoti* and *khes*, while the women wear magnificent saris. All four wear paste diadems on their heads and knotted handkerchiefs as *muh patti* or mouth protectors. Generally, while lay and ascetic Sthanakavasis wear specially stitched *muh patti*, lay Deravasis knot a handkerchief about their faces when entering the inner sanctum of a Jain temple (*garbha grha*) or when coming into close contact with an idol, as in this instance. In both cases the *muh patti* prevents damage (*himsa*) being done to air-living creatures and other tiny beings (*nigoda*, though most Gujaratis would simply say '*nana jiva*': small lives) by the heat and force of one's breath. The diadems are supposed to indicate the status of the wearers as gods, paying respect to the new-born *jina*. Bringing up the rear of the procession come the Tapa Gaccha *sadhvis* and the lay women.

Halfway along the route, by Bhidbhanjan Gate, the procession stops for *darsana* ('beholding' or taking the sight of an idol) at a privately owned *derasar* (temple) on the edge of the old city. The

---

[6] The *siddhacakra* is a diagrammatic representation of the Jain faith. It depicts the five beings worthy of worship (*panca paramesthin*)—*arihant* (*tirthankara*), *siddha* (other enlightened souls), *acarya*, *upadhyaya* (teaching ascetic), and other ascetics. Between the five are written the 'three jewels' of Jainism (true insight, true knowledge, and correct conduct) and the word '*tapas*' (austerities).

derasar is situated within a compound and is dedicated to Mahavira. The pause allows the stragglers to catch up while the cool interior of the temple provides a brief but welcome respite from the blazing summer sun. After some fifteen minutes or so, the procession continues on its way, finishing at the VSTG *pathsala* (teaching hall) which is part of one of the *upasraya*s.

Again there are two ways to see the procession. For the Jains I spoke to it re-enacted the events at Mahavira's birth when he was taken to Mt. Meru and adored by the gods—this is the overtly recognized purpose. Secondly, it makes the re-enactment of these events a public act, demonstrating a number of status oppositions—between the *tirthankara* and the gods of heaven (who may be seen as the Hindu pantheon) and between the 'winning' family and the rest of the Jamnagar Jains.

Both the processions described above were organized by Deravasis, as indeed are most of the Jain processions in Jamnagar. While Sthanakavasis do hold processions, they have a saying, *dhamalman dharam na hoy*: 'the religious way is not to be found in hubbub'—which means that their celebrations are more sober and serious. In Jamnagar at least, Sthanakavasi ascetics do not join processions, silver chariots are forbidden (by the Jamnagar Sthanakavasi Jain Sangh) although ordinary motor-cars are permissible, as are wooden chariots; real flowers are also never used for garlands. Of course, being non-idolatrous, they do not take out an idol or any other image.

Ceremonies of Honour and Respect

Although ascetics do praise specific lay individuals from time to time—either in private conversation or in *vyakhyan* (the religious discourses held each morning)—on the whole they are wary of encouraging too much pride (*mad*) for fear of the damage this may cause the soul.

Nevertheless, the laity frequently take advantage of a noble action by one of their number to offer that person honour and respect (*man*). This at the same time provides for the possibility of bringing all lay Jains together and provides recognition of religiosity. In a religion such as Jainism, where the role of the deity is eliminated, or at least minimalized, a response to one's meritorious acts is looked for amongst one's co-religionists. The two occasions described below formed part of larger celebrations: each for example was preceded by a procession. I justify my isolation of these incidents from their

(8)

contexts on the grounds that informants, both during and after the events, similarly isolated them and viewed them as a chance to 'reply' to the initial act of piety.

Both examples involve women receiving gifts from their co-religionists; although men do perform the *varsitap* fast and become ascetics (the two cases detailed below), these, and many more meritorious acts, are much more commonly made by women.

Honouring the *tapasvi*

Central to the religious life of lay and ascetic Jains alike is the performance of *upvas*, fasting. One who fasts or undertakes austerities (*tapasya*s) generally is known as a *tapasvi* (female) or a *tapasi* (male). The Jains probably have more varieties of fast and dietary austerity than any other religious group, and it would be an insurmountable task to try and record all the local variants (several for Rajasthan are detailed in Reynell 1985*a* and 1985*b*). The fast of *varsitap* (austerity of a year), however, is one of the principal fasts (although rarely performed), fixed calendrically and thought to be extremely effective in destroying *karma*s.

The fast is made in memory of Rishabha, the first *tirthankara*, who took no food for an entire year. Jains realize that few, if any, are capable of such a feat today and have instead instituted a fast, beginning on Chaitra *sud* 2 (April–May), which alternates a day of complete fasting with a day of normal eating for a year (or, according to some, for two years so that a complete year's fast is achieved). A year later, on Chaitra *sud* 2, the fast is broken by drinking sugar-cane juice in a ceremony known as *parana* (this is a common term for any fast-breaking).

On this occasion, Madhuben, the wife of a rich Visa Srimali of the Tapa Gaccha, is being honoured by the VSTG at her *parana* after a procession organized by her husband has carried her around the city. The procession finishes at the VSTG *pathsala* where two other *varsitap* fasters (both VSTG women) are waiting; coming from less well-off families they have not had a procession. The hall has been decked out with streamers and bunting and each of the fasters takes her place under a canopy, Madhuben's being the grandest. For 90 minutes or so (from 10.30 am until noon) the people who have been in the procession, plus friends, relatives, and *jati*-fellows (mostly women, but some men) take it in turns to approach Madhuben and offer her the sugar-cane juice (*seradino ras*). The juice is presented to the well-wisher in a tiny silver pot (*loti*) by an attendant, and then poured by the well-wisher into a *thali* (flat steel dish) from which Madhuben drinks, or rather—given the large number of people— touches her lips to, in a gesture of drinking. The well-wishers also make a monetary gift—Rs 10–20 generally—which is taken by Madhuben and passed to another attendant who records the name of the giver and the amount. A photographer, hired by Madhuben's husband, is on hand to take photographs of more important friends and relatives as they help Madhuben break her fast. At the same time, friends and relatives are queuing before the other two women and feeding them the juice. Ideally, I was later told, the *parana* should take place at Shetrunjaya Hill, near Palitana—a place particularly associated with Rishabha—but for reasons of convenience, it rarely does. Also, short of providing transport for half the Jamnagar Jains, the *parana* proceedings would be on a far more modest scale.

At one point three Tapa Gaccha *sadhvi*s and a *sadhu* enter the *pathsala*. They approach each *tapasvi* in turn and are given large glassfuls of the juice, which they pour into their water pots. The ascetics, who are out on their daily food-gathering trip around the old city's Jain households, have been specially invited by Madhuben, who has herself been attending *vyakhyan* at their *upasraya*s for the past few weeks. Here, then, is a reversal: Madhuben and the other women who have been receiving the juice as a sign of respect all morning now give some of it to those who transcend them in (religious) status; the juice—which, in the context of the *parana*, is emblematic of the specialness of the occasion—briefly reverts to its more usual and mundane state—a sweet and slightly nutritious way of obtaining one's fluid requirements. No lay person can ordinarily hope to set him- or herself up higher than an ascetic, but the action of giving to the ascetics increases the merit earned by the *varsitap* fast (or any other austerity). It is common to invite an ascetic to collect food at one's home on the occasion of some special celebration, such as a wedding, although the ascetics are careful never to commit themselves to such arrangements: to favour one household over another would demonstrate the very kind of attachments that they are supposed to have renounced. This morning the ascetics smile and nod at all those they know and exchange a few words with Madhuben and the other women. They leave quickly and the process of offering the *thali* to the fasters continues. Gradually the line of those waiting diminishes, although most of those who have made the offering remain in the *pathsala*, talking in small groups. After the fast-breaking is finally over, all of us at the *pathsala*, plus others, make our way to the VSTG *vadi* where Madhuben's husband has provided a feast.

Relations between lay and ascetic over such matters are not always so smooth. Prior to Paryushan 1983 (which fell in September) a Jamnagar woman of the VSTG fasted totally for forty-five days, timing her fast to conclude on the last day of Paryushan, *samvatsari*. The next day she broke her fast in a *parana* ceremony similar to the one described above, but shortly afterwards had some kind of seizure and died. One of the *sadhu*s invited to Jamnagar by the VSTG for the monsoon period (in which Paryushan falls) publicly praised the woman during the next day's *vyakhyan*, saying that she had earned herself even more honour, that her soul had conquered the body, and that she would achieve liberation quickly (i.e. after very few rebirths).[7] Members of the VSTG considered these remarks in poor taste, however, and attributed the woman's death to a lack of due care and attention on the part of her family (the implication being that during the period of fasting she had been overstrained with domestic tasks). Although no lay criticism was publicly expressed, it was felt that the ascetic concerned had appropriated an exclusively lay matter, shifting it unwarrantably from one realm of moral discourse to another. The unexpected death of the woman indicated a failure, not a triumph; it should have been an occasion for sorrow and recrimination, not further respect.

Honouring the *diksarthi*

This function, which preceded the *varsi dan* procession described above by two or three days, was held during the course of the morning *vyakhyan* (religious discourse). The discourse, given by a *sadhu* (originally from a Jamnagar Visa Oswal family), was held in a privately owned *upasraya* and concerned the importance and worthiness of renunciation.

> After the *vyakhyan* discourse has concluded, Nita, the *diksarthi*, who has been sitting with her *guru*, an Anchala Gaccha *sadhvi*, comes to the front and salutes the *sadhu*s and their *acarya*. In turn they 'bless' her by anointing her head with the sandalwood powder (*candan*) that all male ascetics carry. Nita has dressed specially for the occasion in

---

[7] From what I can tell, the *sadhu* was making some kind of allusion to *sallekhana* (ritual death by fasting). This is a strictly controlled form of austerity and is only meritorious (in the sense of bringing liberation within very few rebirths) when properly initiated and directed. One of the fundamental criteria is that the faster chooses to enter this final austerity and makes a request of an ascetic before embarking upon it. (See P. S. Jaini 1979: 227–33; R. H. B. Williams 1963: 166–72). There was no evidence in this case that the woman desired such an end.

a beautiful gold and purple sari, and wears many gold ornaments. She herself is a Jamnagar Visa Oswal of the Anchala Gaccha and is to join that *gaccha* as an ascetic (although, as mentioned above, the ceremony will be performed by a Tapa Gaccha *acarya*, in the absence of an Anchala Gaccha *acarya*).

Short speeches are given by the lay president of the JVO Anchala Gaccha, a representative of the JVO Sthanakavasis, and the president of all the JVOs. These speeches praise the qualities in Nita which have led her to take this step and at the same time stress the pride the Oswal *jati* feels in her. After each speech small children present Nita with gifts of money, jewellery, coconuts and a type of engraved plaque depicting Mahavira and other *tirthankaras*.

This was simply a public enactment of events that had been happening daily. For a period of about two weeks before her *diksa* Nita had been visiting many of the JVO homes where her forehead was marked by the household head with a *tilak* of *kanku* (a mark of red turmeric paste) into which were pressed rice grains—a mark of the highest respect—while a sum of money—usually some Rs 10–20—was pressed into her hands. (These gifts were later distributed by the *diksarthi* at the *varsi dan* procession (described above) and by donation to charities.) This short ritual, repeated many times over a few days, was in fact the final stages of a process that had been going on for the past seven years. After her father's death, Nita—who told me she had previously had no interest in religion (although, in truth, she was only thirteen at the time)—began to attend *vyakhyan* and formed an attachment to a *sadhvi* who became her *guru*. After studying religious texts with her *guru* and accompanying her on her *vihar* (mendicant journeys), Nita felt she was ready to take *diksa* herself and sought her *guru*'s permission. The *guru* in turn sought the permission of Nita's family and the family in turn sought permission of their *jati*. The bestowal of the *kanku tilak* at the JVO households she visited were the sign that the *jati* members (represented by heads of households) assented to her desire for *diksa*.

On one of these occasions Nita has arranged to come to the home of some friends of mine and I have been quickly summoned and presented to her. While the family and visitors bustle around and offer or accept cups of tea and bottles of lemonade, Nita sits aloof, refusing all refreshment and keeping her eyes fixed modestly on the ground.

After the money and *tilak* have been given to her—offerings that
she does accept—I have a chance to ask both Nita and Anil, a JVO
leader who has accompanied her, about these expressions of
respect: is it not paradoxical to shower praise and wealth on one who
has expressed a desire to renounce such things? Nita sits quietly,
shaking her head, while Anil tells me I am misinterpreting the
situation. The tributes are not made to Nita as a person but to the
monastic path itself—the riches are appropriate to the richness and
nobleness of the path Nita has undertaken. It is also more generally
a tribute to the qualities of mankind, which, being equally poised
between good and bad, between happiness and unhappiness, can
see and appreciate the ultimate happiness and fulfilment of *moksa*
and, more importantly, can have the strength of will to attain this
goal.

Yet it would be impossible to deny the pride a *jati* feels when one of its
members takes *diksa*. All the *jati* directories or 'census books'
(*vastipatrak*) I have seen of Jain *jati*s record the names (lay and ascetic)
of members who have taken this step, together with details of when
and where the ceremony took place; similarly, the *jati* background of
many popular ascetics is well known. Moreover, *jati* identity, although
renounced at *diksa*, can be reactivated. I was told of an elderly Tapa
Gaccha *sadhu* who, some years ago, quarrelled with the leaders of his
gaccha sub-section (*sangharo*) and left the small band of monks (*gana*)
with which he was travelling. He was of Jamnagar Visa Srimali origin
and, on hearing of his circumstances, the VSTG invited him to stay in
their *upasraya*, where he resided for two years until he settled his
differences with his *sangharo*. Nita then became a representative of her
jati in the spiritually higher world of the ascetics. The *jati* as a whole
benefited from her action and it honoured her accordingly.

Fasts and Feasts: Austerity and Celebration

At any form of Jain communal gathering in Jamnagar it is rare not to
find food in some form or other. All major temple rituals, for example,
involve the offering of large, sometimes vast, quantities of food—
mostly sweets and fruit—to the *tirthankara*. All the items are
beautifully arranged in pyramids or two-dimensional designs, much of
it adorned with silver leaf. Similarly, most processions, festivals, fasts,
and other communal celebrations culminate in a feast.

The attendance at such feasts depends on the nature of the

occasion. At a marriage feast, for example, most of the guests will be of the same *jati*, while the celebration of some other life-cycle or exceptional event may involve friends from other *jati*s. Feasts normally take place in the *vadi* (*jati* hall) of the organizing group (*jati* or section of a *jati*) or individual, and all utensils are provided for the diners. The feasters sit in long rows on thin strips of cloth and eat with their fingers, in the normal Gujarati fashion, from *thali*s and *vadki*s (small metal bowls). Men and women sit separately and, if there are large numbers attending, in shifts. The food is generally cooked by hired cooks (no longer exclusively Brahmans), but distributed by friends and relatives of the donor. For reasons of practicality the servers are often young men (who can tread nimbly down the crowded rows of diners, carrying large trays of food), but it is considered an honour to serve food to others on such occasions and there is no lack of helpers. The giver of the feast distributes the sweetmeats, generally *gulab jambu*, and mock-aggressively force-feeds these to protesting guests.

For the most part communal feasts are of little importance as culinary events. The food served is a mixture of everyday items and delicacies, substantial food (*khorak*) and snacks (*nasto*), those items being chosen which are easy to prepare in bulk, simple to serve, and relatively cheap. While both the quantity and the quality of the food may tell the participant (and the observer) something about the status or wealth of the giver, these features in themselves are not *dharmik* (religious) matters. Nor do such feasts normally convey much information about the formal social order. If inter-*jati* non-commensality was ever common among the middle and upper trading *jati*s of market towns and trade centres such as Jamnagar (see Fox 1969*b*: 96 for historical data from Uttar Pradesh) it certainly is not today, and for the most part the feasts I attended laid no stress on *jati* exclusivity (although some, such as the post-*parana* feasts involved only Jains of a single *jati*) and people sat with their friends, or wherever there was space. Below, I describe two exceptions to this, the first where Jains met together to consume food within a religious framework during the festival of *ayambil oli*, the second contrasting two different criteria by which the basis for deciding who could and could not be invited to the feast was fixed.

Ayambil

Ayambil is the name given to a specifically Jain form of restricted diet, which can be practised at any time. However, twice a year (starting Chaitra *sud* 7 and Ashwin *sud* 7—around March/April and September/

October) a nine-day period of *ayambil* 'fasting', called *ayambil oli* is observed. This austerity is followed by both men and women although, as always, women predominate. It consists of taking one meal a day composed of specially selected items. As *ayambil* can be observed at any time of the year and as the preparation of the foodstuffs is quite complicated and would be laborious to produce at home (especially if other members of the household were following a normal diet), one *bhojansala* (eating-hall), attached to an *upasraya* in Jamnagar prepares the food daily. Anyone wishing to observe *ayambil* may eat for nothing here, although it is common to make a donation. During *ayambil oli*, however, the various Jain groups in the city make their own arrangements for the provision of food, and it is taken communally by members of each group.

> I have been invited to attend the Chaitra *ayambil oli* austerities of the Jamnagar Sthanakavasi Jain Sangh (JSJS). Once a day for the nine days about 100 women and fifteen to twenty men meet together at noon in a hired hall and courtyard to eat (the building they would normally use is undergoing repairs). There are no ceremonies or speeches; as each person arrives he or she joins the appropriate line of seated diners, and is given a *thali* and served with the various food items. Many of those attending continue with their domestic affairs or daily business as normal (apart, of course, from eating), simply coming to the *upasraya* for the midday meal from home or from their place of work. The women, however, will be continuing to prepare food for their families in the normal way.

Although it is reported that *ayambil* 'fasters' in Rajasthan may eat a different item of food on each of the nine days, following a colour symbolism derived from the *siddhacakra* (Josephine Reynell, personal communication), in Saurashtra the same selection of foods is served each day. The restrictions of *ayambil* demand that six items (known as *vigai*) must be avoided: ghee, milk, yoghurt (*dahin*), oil (*tel*), butter (*makhan*), and sugar (*gol*).[8] Butter as such is not commonly used in Gujarat and although I translate *gol* as 'sugar', strictly it refers only to unrefined cane-sugar molasses. However, Jains say that by extension

---

[8] Marie-Claude Mahias, working among Jains in Delhi, reports a similar restriction on six flavourings: butter, oil, milk, yoghurt, salt, and sugar. This restriction is observed by (Digambara) ascetics and for the laity during *ayambil* (Mahias 1985: 249). A section of Mahias's book is also devoted to fasting (ibid.: 111–25).

the prohibition refers to all sweeteners, such as refined sugar (*khand*) and honey (*madh*). In addition many people told me that salt and spices were also prohibited. In fact at each day's meal, salt, black pepper (*mari*) and powdered asafoetida (*hing*) are available to season the food.

I am initially surprised by both the variety of foodstuffs served and the large amounts that are consumed. Although only eating once a day the *tapasvi*s make sure they eat enough to sustain themselves for the next twenty-four hours. Even to Western palates the *ayambil* food is bland and unappetizing; the penance (*tapascarya*) of *ayambil* lies entirely in the restrictions of taste. The foodstuffs are mostly familiar items prepared without the *vigai*, some bearing special names to signify this. Every day, we are served a choice of three *dal*s (from chickpeas and mung beans); five kinds of bread (*rotli*, *rotlo*, *khakhara*—made from chickpea, wheat, and millet flours); *papad* (rice-flour popadum); *mamra* (puffed rice); *mag nu pani* and *kariatun nu pani* (thin soups of mung beans and bitter herbs); 2 chutneys (chickpea and *sunth*—dried ginger); and a variety of other small items. All this is followed by rice, rice mixed with *dal* (*khicadi*) and *kadhi* (a chickpea flour-based sauce).

On the tenth day a feast is given for the ninety or so *tapasi*s and *tapasvi*s who have completed the full nine days' austerity (a figure which, I must confess does not include myself, though I am generously invited to the feast anyway). The feast is being hosted by Shantaben, a Visa Srimali Sthanakavasi widow from Leicester who has come to Jamnagar in order to visit her brothers and to arrange her son's marriage. The food, prepared for 100, is said to have cost approximately Rs 600, in addition to which Shantaben gives each *tapasi* and *tapasvi* Rs 10 and a plastic plate in honour of their feat. The total cost is thus some Rs 1,750, or approximately £115. Various other people also give gifts of one or two rupees, bringing each *tapasi*'s and *tapasvi*'s total to some Rs 25. This money is placed in each person's *vadki* (a small bowl, usually used for serving food) at the side of their *thali*. The food at the feast is in complete contrast to that eaten on the previous days: rich and heavily spiced, employing each of the six *vigai* (with the exception of butter as far as I can tell) in abundance. Throughout the meal Shantaben bustles around, making sure that no one's plate is empty. Most people I spoke to later agreed that the food was of very high quality and delicious in its own right as well, of course, as being a pleasure after the dull *ayambil* fare.

Each day during *ayambil oli* the *tapasvi*s had attended the morning *vyakhyan* at the JSJS *pathsala*. At the end of any *vyakhyan* it is common for the senior ascetic to ask who is observing *ayambil* that day; those who intend to stand up and a short *mantra* is said over them by the ascetic. During *ayambil oli* the numbers standing were large, and others present at the *vyakhyan* drew my attention to them with pride. The sense of respect for, and solidarity with, the *tapasvi*s was strong, as demonstrated by the gifts made to them at the post-austerity feast.

Navnat and Naukasi Feasts

When I asked in Jamnagar about food and feasts and whether *jati* feasts were still held I was often given descriptions of Navnat and Naukasi feasts. Indeed, most people when questioned about caste and *jati* sooner or later raised the issue of either or both of these meals to give me a practical example of the information I was seeking. I discussed the Navnat ('nine *nat*s') in the previous chapter, and there tried to describe the confusions inherent in this category. Similar confusions entered the discussion of these feasts and served to make a simple situation complex. I have tried below to eliminate this complexity as much as possible.

A Navnat dinner is a feast given by an individual to which all members of the Navnat in that town or area (that is in Saurashtra or Kaccha, which is as far as my information extends) are invited. A Naukasi feast on the other hand is given by an individual to which all who know and abide by the Naukar *mantra* are invited. Thus the former may have a mixed Jain–Hindu attendance, while the latter is exclusively for Jains, the Naukar *mantra* being the closest there is to a creed to which all Jains subscribe.[9]

One informant in Jamnagar told me that Naukasi feasts are a fairly recent innovation, in Jamnagar at least, being only some forty or fifty years old. They were introduced after disputes between Jain and Hindu *vania*s at Navnat dinners over *ahimsa*. The Jains claimed that the food residue on the leaf plates (in common use at that time) was a breeding-ground for small life forms (*nigoda*s); Jains consider it just as harmful to cause 'unnecessary' life to come into being and then let it die through neglect as it is to destroy already existing life. At an

---

[9] While the Sthanakavasis are known to themselves and other Jains as *pancpadi*s (five-liners) because they hold only the first five lines of the *mantra* to be the authentic words of Mahavira, they do not deny the truth of the concluding four lines (*eso panca namokkaro* ... 'this fivefold salutation ...') but simply assert that it is a later gloss.

exclusively Jain gathering, however, the disposal of uneaten food could be controlled more carefully. Hence the Jains turned to Naukasi feasts as an alternative to Navnat feasts. Briggs, however, commenting on Hindu (Vaishnava) *vania* and Jain *vania* interaction (mentioned in Chapter 2), states that only up to 1830 had the two groups 'indiscriminately mixed in the social entertainments and part[aken] of meals at each others hands'. He goes on to say: 'Since then a sweeping religious revolution has taken place, which not only debars this incongruous admixture, but even marks among the Jainas a comingling of those alone who subscribe to the peculiar number of the Naukasari, or theological dicta' (Briggs 1849: 336).

Both feasts are rare. One informant told me that they only occur once every five years or so in Jamnagar and I managed to gather information on only four. I attended one Naukasi feast myself in the town of Dhrangadhra, some 200 km. east of Jamnagar; I was told that the most recent Naukasi feast held in Jamnagar was given by the Halari Visa Oswals in 1982, when construction of their *ayambilsala* (hall for performing *ayambil*) was completed; finally I was told on several occasions about Navnat and Naukasi feasts in the past. Two of these were specifically mentioned to me by several informants because they were considered to be focal points for the issues I was interested in.

To take the earliest of these first: in 1939 a leading Jamnagar Visa Oswal, Sheth Popat Dharshi, organized a Navnat feast on the occasion of his return from a pilgrimage to Shetrunjaya Hill—a famous pilgrimage site in Saurashtra. It is not entirely clear why he decided to hold a Navnat rather than a Naukasi feast to celebrate what was after all an exclusively Jain pilgrimage, although my informant was adamant on this point. Possible explanations are that, (i) Naukasi feasts may not yet have been introduced, at least in Jamnagar and thus there was no precedent; (ii) the question of whether Oswals (both Jamnagaris and Halaris) are or are not in the Navnat is a complex one given the fluid nature of the organization (similar ambiguity may well have been present in 1939, in which case Popat Dharshi was seeking to affirm his *jati*'s position within the body); and (iii) the story is a good story because of its 'punchline' ('We can't hold an eight-and-a-half-*nat* feast') and my informant may well have twisted the circumstances to make a better story.

At the time of the feast the Tapa Gaccha in Jamnagar was divided over the issue of *baldiksa*, that is, *diksa* taken by a minor. The practice was (and still is) supported by all the Tapa Gaccha ascetics and by the lay Tapa Gaccha Jamnagar Visa Oswals. It was condemned, however, by lay Tapa Gaccha Visa Srimalis who said that no child of eight or nine years was capable of making such a major decision and that the practice was open to abuse, for example by parents wishing to rid themselves of unwanted daughters.

On this matter of principle the Visa Srimali Tapa Gaccha refused to attend, although the Loka Gaccha accepted (that is, the Sthanakavasi section of the Visa Srimali *jati*: *baldiksa* was, and is, allowed by Sthanakavasis). Another Jamnagar Visa Oswal asked Popat Dharshi if he would hold the feast in such circumstances; his reply was, '*sada ath nat bhojan na cale*' (We can't hold an eight-and-a-half-*nat* feast). Instead he went to the Visa Srimali Tapa Gaccha *pathsala* in Chandi Bazaar where *vyakhyan* was being held, removed his turban (*paghadi*)—an act of deference—and pleaded with the Visa Srimalis to attend his feast. Eventually they acquiesced and the feast was held; the issue of *baldiksa* was not resolved, however, and continues to this day.

The other famous feast of which I heard was a Naukasi feast—that is, for Jains only. It was held some fifty years ago when a famous layman from Ahmedabad passed through Jamnagar with a group on pilgrimage. He organized a feast for all the Jamnagar Jains, to thank them for their hospitality during his stay in the city. The Halari Visa Oswals living in Jamnagar were also invited, but when they arrived they were forced to sit separately from the rest on account of their farmers' clothing and suspected coarse behaviour. This particular story was told to me (by Srimalis) to illustrate the final splitting off of the Halari Visa Oswals from the rest of the Jamnagar Jains. After this the Halari Visa Oswals began to buy up land outside Khambhalia Gate (that is, outside the old, walled city), and to create their own self-contained colony. (A. M. Shah's description of *corasi* and *bhandaro* feasts among Gujarati Brahmans indicates that they seem to fulfil the same function as the Naukasi feasts: that is, they serve to unite the constituent parts—what Shah calls 'second-order divisions' and others might call *jatis*—temporarily as a 'first-order' division. He also notes that 'very low' Brahmans were made to sit separately from the higher Brahmans (A. M. Shah 1982: 22)). In Chapter 6 I shall describe how a very similar event in Leicester produced a very similar outcome.

The practical aspects of Navnat or Naukasi feasts do not differ from those of other feasts in any significant way, except that a Naukasi feast commences with a recitation of the Naukar *mantra*. The feasts are held in the largest available *vadi*. This need not even necessarily be Jain: for example, the Naukasi feast I attended in Dhrangadhra was in fact held in the courtyard of the Dhrangadhra Brahman Boarding as this was larger than any Jain *vadi* in the town. The feast was given by the father of a *diksarthi* and was open to all Jains in the town as well as Jains who had travelled for the *diksa* ceremony from other parts of Saurashtra. A large Jamnagar contingent was present as a *sadhu*, originally from a Jamnagar Visa Oswal family, was to be elevated to the status (*pad*) of an *acarya* during the *diksa* ceremony. At the subsequent feast there were about 3,500 people, eating in shifts. It was a fairly simple meal consisting of green bananas (as a vegetable), butter beans, mango pickle, a sweetmeat (*mithai*), and *bhajiya* (deep-fried chick pea flour snacks), followed by rice and *dal*. Unusually, there was no bread (*rotli*, *rotlo*) of any kind. As at other feasts the donor was in constant attendance, ensuring that the diners were all satisfied.

Food has an overriding importance to the Jains, being a constant diacritical marker of their 'otherness' and the Jains have an elaborate schema of how, when, where, and what to eat. The likelihood is high that the Jains have also influenced the dietary patterns of other groups, at least in Gujarat. The *ayambil* example above shows how the type of food can unite the Jains, while the Navnat and Naukasi examples show how the occasions for food can unite them. Although in both cases the actual food consumed is given by others, the implications of this differ. At the *ayambil* austerity the *tapasi*s and *tapasvi*s were of higher status than the givers by virtue of their austerities. The givers, however, received status from their selfless act of devotion, and merit from honouring worthy persons. The giving of a Navnat or Naukasi feast on the other hand involves a far simpler status relationship between giver and receiver, the gift of the former asserts his status over the latter.

A New Form of Coming Together: The Jain Social Group

Several of the more affluent and educated Jains in Jamnagar belong to organizations such as the Rotary Club, the Lions' Club, or the local sports club (of which being a member is far more important than merely playing sports), as indeed do many educated and wealthy men elsewhere in India. An analogous organization exists, however, which is specifically for Jains: the Jain Social Group. For a variety of reasons the only Jain Social Group meeting I ever attended was a short business meeting of the committee (all men) and thus I can only give a very general account of its activities.

The first Jain Social Group was started in Bombay in the early 1970s, and there were almost one hundred in India ten years later, including a Group in London (the first outside India). Membership is for married couples only, although children may also attend certain functions. Each group is autonomous and largely responsible for its own affairs, although there is an annual, pan-Indian, meeting of representatives from all the groups at which ideas for successful functions are shared and guidelines established for the smooth running of the Groups. The emphasis is overwhelmingly social and cultural, although functions may have a specifically Jain bias, such as a visit (by luxury coach) to a nearby temple site.

The Jamnagar group was founded in 1978 with a membership of seventy-five couples—a number which had risen to almost ninety by the time of my fieldwork. The membership cut across both *jati* and sectarian divisions. The President was a local businessman, involved, with other members of his family, in a variety of commercial concerns. He and his five brothers, their wives, children, and grandchildren lived together in a large two-storey house built by the brothers' father. The oldest brother was in his early sixties when I arrived in Jamnagar. He had recently resigned (for reasons of ill health) as president of the Visa Srimali Tapa Gaccha—one of the most prestigious lay positions in the city for a Jain. The Social Group's president (the fifth brother), was eighteen years younger, and represented a different generation with a more 'modern' outlook. This, combined with his business acumen and connections made him the ideal leader for a Rotary-type organization and he was re-elected every year.

The Jamnagar Jain Social Group organized eighteen to twenty functions a year, which ranged from privately organized drama and film shows, to meals and outings. Membership in 1983 cost Rs 150 per couple per annum with a token charge of Rs 1 being made for each function attended. Membership, as with Rotary and Lions' Clubs, is by invitation only.

Early in 1983 the All-India Federation of Jain Social Groups praised the Jamnagar group for a successful trip they organized to visit the Jain temples at Bhadreswar in Kaccha. The trip, by luxury coach, lasted two and a half days, and cost only Rs 75 (about £5) per head, including food and accommodation. I was told that, in fact, most functions run at about Rs 5–10 loss per head, the difference being met from the membership fees.

The Jain Social Group is too exclusive a body ever to become a major force in Jamnagar. In the more sophisticated environments of Bombay and Ahmedabad the Social Group may be the only contact some Jains have with other members of their faith, and one day the Federation as a whole may achieve the status and power of, say, the Lions' Club. In Jamnagar, however, it remains a pastime for the élite.

Contrasts and Comparisons

The *samavsarana* discussed at the beginning of the chapter featured some elements which help us in drawing out important aspects from the other events described. First and foremost, the *samavsarana* represents unity: unity of all souls and therefore unity of all Jains. Secondly, the *samavsarana* is a religious symbol in the sense that the gathering is predicated on the message of salvation preached by an enlightened soul to unenlightened souls. Other biological or social factors which may unite those present—their species, race, *jati*, occupational group, and so forth—are subordinate to this soteriological unity.

The *samavsarana* is also, paradoxically, ahistorical. Although, in its contemporary physical representation, it commemorates a specific event at a specific time, there is no indication as to which *particular* event (out of twenty-four or more possible ones) is being commemorated. Indeed, by being in this sense timeless—iconic of all possible such events, past, present and future—the use of the metallic structure at any *diksa* ceremony allows the intersection of contingent, historical, and lived time with ahistorical time or eternity. Jainism is what we might term a non-processual religion: that is, it does not progress, nor is there a cosmological 'end-point'. Instead, the universe is eternal, time is cyclical, and adherence to religion remains entirely a man's or woman's responsibility—no god or higher being enforces it. No soul automatically reaches salvation, and the rise and fall in the quality of the universe over time ('light' and 'dark' halves) means that opportunities to do so are rare. Although none of these factors is a logical justification for the concept of eternity, merely that the universe (and hence humankind and society) will continue for a very long time, nevertheless Mahavira is said to have claimed that the universe is eternal and that there will never come a point when it is emptied of all souls capable of achieving salvation (P. S. Jaini 1977: 98–9).

Hence no Jain event or celebration today aims to change the universe (as the rituals of millenarian movements do, for example), nor is the community of believers transformed in any permanent or holistic way. Rather, the rituals and ceremonies described above constitute a set of 'eruptions' of the sacred and the timeless into the experiential world of mundane existence. While such 'eruptions' are particularly characteristic of religious traditions which posit a radical separation of the sacred and profane (the Catholic act of the Holy Sacrament and enmeshing doctrine of transubstantiation being a particularly good example), it is none the less possible to apply such an analysis to the radically material and non-transcendental doctrines of Jainism. The passage of events within the Jain universe is eternal, yet as human beings the Jains know themselves to be mortal. The *tirthankara* knows himself to reside unchanging in eternity and his trappings (the *samavsarana*, temple idols, etc.) attest to this. Thus interaction with the *tirthankara* through his iconic presence at a gathering or through mimesis of his actions (fasting, for example) allows for a temporary intersection of the two qualities of time. As we shall see in Chapter 7, certain strategies adopted by the Leicester Jains or forced upon them by necessity have had the effect of minimizing or even negating such 'eruptions'.

Diksa is the only event which constitutes a truly Jain rite of passage (all other life-cycle rituals that Jains observe being largely Hindu in form and content with a Jain gloss) and this is only for the individual concerned. Of course, many other rituals and ceremonies will form part of the continual influx and shedding of *karma*s for those present. Because of the many varieties of *karma* and the complexity of their operation it is not possible to calculate exactly how many 'wholesome' *karma*s are accumulated (or *karma*s of either kind shed) during any particular meritorious activity. Thus, although an absolute and exact accounting system operates, an individual cannot know (until he or she achieves enlightenment and omniscience) exactly how his or her 'account' stands. Thus the soteriological aspect of the *samavsarana* is not stressed or even acknowledged in the collective gatherings of the Jamnagar Jains.

However, the unity demonstrated in the *samavsarana* was in fact only a partial unity in the events I have described. At the ascetic level it was the unity of *gaccha*, at the lay level, unity of *jati* or *jati* section; only the Naukasi feast engendered the possibility of total lay unity, and even that was spoiled in the feast described from Jamnagar. All the events, bar the Navnat feasts, did, however, express Jainism as a religious identity—it was in following the symbol or the example of the *tirthankara* that the Jains gathered. However, the *mumuksa* (*moksa*-seeking), aspect of the *samavsarana*—that one who has achieved enlightenment instructs others in his path—was not the fundamental theme in the events I have described. To many Jains today, the here-and-now experience of life is more important than the distant goal of *moksa*; the maintenance of some level of group stability is more important than the solitary quest of the individual soul. The death of the woman who fasted, mentioned above, was thought to have breached these former considerations. That she may have speeded her soul's progress to *moksa* was considered secondary or irrelevant.

Solidarity among the Jamnagar Jains is of many different types; functions they hold and attend may be regular or sporadic, 'religious' or 'secular', exclusively Jain by decree, exclusively Jain by default (a domestic ritual, for example, to which only close kin and friends are invited—all of whom happen to be Jain), or open to all (the Navnat feast is a limited example of this, a political or business meeting would be another). There are also many informal occasions for coming together—senior men meeting to drink tea and gossip in a temple trust office for example, or women within a Jain neighbourhood getting together in small groups to sew or sort grain. Such events occur daily and form the domestic structure of many people's lives.

One of the most important aspects of coming together, however, is the relationship between the potential, or the stated, and the actual. Do the stated grounds for cohesion effect that cohesion? In the events described above, I have emphasized both cohesion and division, and I shall return to examine the link between the two in Chapter 9. In the next chapter I wish to examine the links between the stated and the actual with specific reference to Jain-held property in Jamnagar.

4

Who Owns What?
Jain Religious Property in Jamnagar

The previous two chapters presented the Jains of Jamnagar and discussed their communal activities. In this chapter I wish to examine in more detail the framework within which this commonality is expressed, both through a fuller analysis of the sects and the *gaccha*s (already begun in Chapter 2) and through an analysis of the various properties these groups control.

Throughout Jain history, corporately owned religious property, particularly temples (*derasar*s), has been especially important to the Jains. There are many types of such property. Famous temples and temple complexes (ancient and modern) attract thousands of pilgrims annually. Their fame may derive from architectural merit, from

association with particular *tirthankaras*, from a reputation for miraculous events, or from a combination of any of these. In each town (and even large villages) with any Jain population, there are one or more temples, *upasraya*s where ascetics stay and hold *vyakhyan* (religious discourses), and other buildings such as Jain libraries. In the larger towns of Gujarat and Rajasthan there are also hospitals, animal shelters, schools, and boarding-houses which Jains support or which individuals have endowed. Religious buildings, such as temples, are a permanent public expression of the religious tradition and differences between sects, particularly between Digambara and Svetambara, are readily identifiable through differences in temple design and furnishings. Unlike some Hindu temples, Jain temples are (nominally) open to everybody, although access to the idols is restricted. In practice non-Jains rarely enter Jain temples, except famous ones of particular architectural interest. However, some temples have become a focus of cults popular with non-Jains; the Digambara temple at Padampura, near Jaipur in Rajasthan, for example, is widely visited in cases of spirit possession.

An indicator of the importance of such physical manifestations of tradition are the disputes which sometimes occur, both between Jains and non-Jains, and between rival Jain groups, over the ownership and control of religious property, particularly temples. In Jamnagar I encountered no current disputes over such property, but several ambiguities, and it is with these ambiguities that this chapter is concerned. It should be noted, however, that property relations in Jamnagar are essentially static (unlike the situation I describe for Leicester in Chapters 6 and 8); two temples in the city have been recently constructed but most of the Jain groups and organizations I deal with corporately own and manage a given stock of properties.

'The greatest of tirthas'

By way of setting the scene, however, I wish to discuss briefly one of the most famous of all Jain temple sites, Shetrunjaya Hill near Palitana, some 220 km. south-east of Jamnagar. One author, in the mid-1800s, described the hilltop thus:

Street after street, and square after square, extend these shrines of the Jaina faith, with their stately enclosures, half palace, half fortress, raised in marble magnificence, upon the lonely and majestic mountain . . . far removed in upper air from the ordinary tread of mortals. In the dark recesses of each temple one image or more of Adeenath, of Ujeet, or of some other of the Teerthunkers is seated, whose alabaster features, wearing an expression of listless repose, are rendered dimly visible by the faint light shed from silver lamps; incense perfumes the air ... (Forbes 1924: 7)

Beautiful and edifying as the temples may be, the major problems for the Jains until Indian independence lay in the fact that they never controlled the kingdom (Palitana) in which the hill was situated. In AD 1589 Emperor Akbar made a grant of the hill to the Jains.[1] An inscription made by the Jains at the time reveals their appreciation in no uncertain terms:

Gratified by their eloquent discourse, rendering worthless, in comparison, streams of ambrosia itself—the prosperous Akbar, the Lord of the Earth, with a heart full of joy, not only remitted the large income derived as taxes from the mountain, but, to gain their hearts, he presented to the Jainas the mountain of Satrunjaya—the greatest of Tirthas. (cited in Burgess 1869: 13)

The Gohil Rajput chiefs of Palitana frequently tried to usurp the Jains' rights, questioning, for example, the authority of Shah Jehan (Akbar's grandson) in Saurashtra during the breakup of the Moghul empire, when Akbar's original grants were reinforced (M. J. Mehta 1927). In the eighteenth century, local unrest caused by roving bands of Kolis and Kathis led the Thakor (ruler) of Palitana to levy a tax on pilgrims to the hill, so that protection might be afforded to them (Burgess 1869: 14). The Jains objected, largely because they claimed the money raised was actually being used to pay mercenaries to defend the Thakor rather than themselves. In the meantime, certain local Jain merchants had been advancing money to the Thakor; in 1808 the British found him deeply in debt and decided that he was incapable of managing his own affairs. In 1821 what is today the largest Jain trust in India, Anandji Kalyanji, was set up to gather taxes from the pilgrims, some part of which revenue was paid to the Thakor (ibid.: 15). In 1821 the Thakor's revenue from this amounted to Rs 4,500 per annum, increasing by 1886 to Rs 15,000. The Jains' problems were far from over, however, and until independence successive rulers harassed the Jains. For example, in 1877 the Thakor allowed a fair (*mela*) of Dheds (an untouchable group) to take place on the hill, after which the Jains asserted that temple property and even idols had been damaged

---

[1] It is not clear to which particular Jains the grant was made; the likelihood is that it would have been to the largest Deravasi group—probably the Tapa Gaccha of the largest local *jati*—or to a federation of such groups.

(M. J. Mehta 1927). In part, the Jains at Shetrunjaya and elsewhere in India experienced administrative problems relating to religious property during the British period because of their insistence on the inviolability of temple funds. They refused, for example, to use a percentage of these funds to fund the work of the Charity Commissioners as the British desired.

It is common for Jains in India to think of financial gifts to Jain trusts either in terms of the *sat* (*punya*) *ksetra* (seven fields of merit), or in terms of *devadravya* (god's money) and *sadharana* (general funds). The seven 'fields' in which a donor can 'sow' his wealth are described most clearly by Hemachandra (AD 1089–1172), one of the most famous of the Svetambara scholar-ascetics, in his Yoga Shastra. He lists them as:

1. *jina bimba*: the setting-up and worshipping of Jain images (that is, images of the *tirthankaras*);
2. *jina bhavana*: building and restoring Jain temples;
3. *jina agama*: copying sacred texts and giving them to learned ascetics for commentary;
4. *sadhu*: giving alms to male ascetics;
5. *sadhvi*: giving alms to female ascetics;
6. *shravaka*: aiding Jain laymen with food and clothing etc., as well as inviting them to feasts and festivals and encouraging them in their religious duties;
7. *shravika*: as for (6) but with respect to Jain laywomen.

(after R. H. B. Williams 1963: 165)

The first three of these fields unquestionably count as *devadravya* (god's money), that is, money given for the service of the temple and its idols. This is the most common form of gift for Jains today; all gifts placed in temple collection boxes at the morning and evening *puja*s are *devadravya*, for example. This money can be spent for no other purpose. *Sadharana* (common) funds, which comprise the remaining four 'fields' and any other form of gift, are less restricted, and 'fields' (6) and (7) are open to wide interpretation. In an interview, the then president of Anandji Kalyanji explained the distinction between *sadharana* and *devadravya* to me and pointed out that the bulk of the Trust's funds today are in the form of *devadravya*, this being thought by the laity to confer many benefits, from rebirth in one of the heavens to *moksa* itself. In contrast, the Trust found it difficult to raise *sadharana* funds for the upkeep of the *bhojansala*s (eating-halls) and *dharmasala*s (pilgrims' rest-houses) which form part of the properties the Trust manages.

In the 1940s the Tendulkar Committee was set up in Bombay by the

British to investigate the management of temple finances (Hindu and Jain). In their report the committee recommended firstly that all trusts belonging to one 'community' should be thrown open to all. Secondly, that for the Jains 'surplus Devadravya can be used for purposes other than for which it is established and collected' (Jhaveri 1949: 4).[2] The president of Anandji Kalyanji at the time explained that *devadravya* was inviolable and that even expenses for the management of *devadravya* funds must themselves come from other sources. He claimed, moreover, that in certain instances monies donated to the latter four 'fields' of the *sat ksetra* might be considered as *devadravya* (ibid.: 3). During the British period, this point was frequently in debate and never adequately settled. Post-independence court judgments in Bombay ruled that *devadravya* funds could be diverted (see Baird 1976: 52–3) but these were later overruled by the Supreme Court (Derrett 1968: 467). Thus, as well as causing disputes amongst the Jains themselves (see *India Today* 1981; 1984), religious property and its attendant finances have been a point of contention between the Jains and those holding secular authority or power. There is, however, a further dimension to the importance of corporate property to the Jains, one which is concealed by simply referring to 'the Jains' as the above discussion (and the literature on which it is based) has done.

Lay and Ascetic

Implicit, for example, in all discussions of Jain corporate property and financial management is the assumption that these are lay affairs, of little or no importance to the ascetics. Already above I have pointed out that one of the documents I used (Jhaveri 1949) was written at the instigation of an ascetic. Before turning to the management of similar types of property among the Jamnagar Jains, it is necessary to discuss lay and ascetic relations in a more general sense. Unlike Buddhist forest monks, who retreat from the Buddhist laity to seek their own salvation, Svetambara Jain ascetics remain in close contact with the laity.[3] (This point is possibly less true of the highest grade of

---

[2] This particular document (*Jain Views Regarding Religious and Charitable Trusts*), which was a reply to the Tendulkar Committee's report, was written at the instigation of a Tapa Gaccha *acarya* (Sagaranandsuri) and should not therefore be taken as a guide to the feelings of all Jains at the time. Sthanakavasis, having no temples or idols, have no concept of *devadravya*, for example.

[3] Tambiah (1984: Chap. 5) discusses the relationships and occasional tensions between these renouncing monks, the village-dwelling monks, and the laity.

Digambara ascetics.) In the Jain case, the twin aims of community support and maintenance, and ascetic retreat and renunciation are held in balance, rather than there being a cycle or swing between the two poles over time, although empirically the need to maintain the cohesion of community overrides the desire to renounce totally. This 'need' has two aspects: the 'need' to unite when faced with persecution, and the 'need' to maintain the core of belief and practice, which the laity might be tempted to abandon if totally deserted by the ascetics. Consequently the ascetics and the laity are tied to each other on numerous levels and not just on the level of the ascetics receiving physical maintenance in return for spiritual guidance. Ascetics own no possessions and are prevented by the tenet of *ahimsa* from performing many tasks necessary to sustain life; they cannot cook, construct shelters, light lamps or use electricity, earn or carry money, or drink unboiled water to name but a few restrictions. Furthermore, as enlightenment is attained through austerities and meditation, ascetics have neither the time nor the inclination to pursue such mundane tasks.

Ascetics are thus provided with food by the laity which has been prepared with due regard to *ahimsa* (and which also conforms, when necessary, to the rules of abstinence which are part of *tithi* observance), and shelter, in the form of *upasraya*s. While food is necessary for the ascetics' immediate survival, the provision of *upasraya*s and *pathsala*s (teaching-halls), beyond providing shelter, creates an area of space in which lay and ascetic can interact and can influence each other. Temple worship, for the Jains, is either individualistic (for both lay and ascetic) or else consists of formal and elaborate *puja*s during which prescribed codes are adhered to. In contrast, interaction within the *upasraya* and, to a lesser extent, within the *pathsala*, is informal and largely unstructured. Laity bring specific problems and issues to discuss with ascetics known to them personally and ascetics themselves form certain bonds with individual laymen and -women, relying on them to perform certain mundane tasks (posting letters, for example) and as a source of news and information.

Certain collaborative projects may also be undertaken from within the *upasraya*. A rich business man, for example, will tell an important ascetic that he wishes to dispose of a large sum of money and asks how it should be done. The ascetic may suggest some building project (or have this suggested to him by the business man)—a new temple, for example, or an *upasraya*—as this is the most tangible form of donation.

The ascetic will then lend his presence at the various ceremonies of donation and commemoration, thereby legitimating and publicizing the merit (*punya*) which the layman earns through his action. The *upasraya* is also the location where a prospective candidate for initiation, a *diksarti*, may seek a *guru*—a *sadhu* or *sadhvi*—who will guide and instruct the candidate until he or she feels ready to undertake the more formal procedures that lead finally to initiation. Jainism in practice, therefore, is a collaborative project, undertaken by both lay and ascetic (rather than the graded project implied by P. S. Jaini's (1979) account of lay and ascetic paths, where the former is seen as wholly subordinate to the latter). It should come as no surprise, therefore, that in the discussion that follows the social and religious organization of both are equally interpenetrated.

Corporate Religious Property in Jamnagar

Although all property I describe below is owned or administered by the laity, the ascetics have an important interest in it. Both Sthanakavasi and Deravasi ascetics need somewhere to stay, as well as halls or other buildings in which to teach or instruct. There is no lack of such property in Jamnagar: almost every main street (and many of the minor residential streets and *gali*s) in the old city contains one or more specifically Jain building and there are a significant number of temples and *upasraya*s in the newer residential areas, beyond the old town walls. Almost without exception these are well maintained, prominent buildings, easily identified by large name plates or inscriptions. The properties I am going to consider in this chapter are all either owned or managed by the various Jain groups (*jati*s, sections of *jati*s, sects and *gaccha*s) that I discussed in Chapter 2 or else are privately owned properties to which the (Jain) public has general access.

Property-Owning Groups

The composition of these groups is almost exclusively ascriptive in Jamnagar. One or two individuals I encountered expressed dissatisfaction with the religious tradition into which they had been born and had consciously embraced another (I met more who claimed to be dissatisfied but did nothing about it), and in the early part of this century there was movement too as people joined the new Kanji Panth. However, most lay Jains are content to see their religious affiliation as an inheritance from their parents, or husband (in the case of women who are expected to adopt their spouse's religious affiliation on marriage) along with other formal status criteria such as surname and *jati*-affiliation, and informal criteria of taste and preference in matters of food, personal morality, and so forth.

Certain lay Jains, especially the more devout, may attempt to assert the superiority of their religious affiliation, and this is especially true of adherents to the Sthanakavasi and Kanji Swami traditions.[4] Their claims, however, are generally made on the basis of atemporal theological considerations—a stress on *ahimsa* in the case of the Sthanakavasis and on *moksa* in the case of the Kanji Panthis—and do not seek to draw legitimacy from a lineage charter (in the way, for example, that Digambara ascetics would denounce Svetambara ascetics on the basis of decisions reached at the third canonical council at Valabhi). That is, it is not which group (sect) is more 'original' in terms of a historical progression, such as that given in Figure 1.1, but which group asserts practices and beliefs that are thought to be closest to what Mahavira and the other *tirthankara*s espoused and propounded.

Jamnagar Jains usually refer to religious affiliation in terms of oppositions: Deravasi to Sthanakavasi, Digambara to Svetambara (as there are no authentic Digambaras in Saurashtra, followers of the Kanji Panth consider themselves—and are considered by others—to be Digambaras), Jain to Vaishnava or Hindu. Of these asserted categories only the Sthanakavasis in Jamnagar have a *de jure* existence that cross-cut *jati* divisions (discussed below); the rest are category labels only, there being no formally constituted groups bearing these names. The only difficulty lies with the Kanji Panth—the followers of Kanji Swami. There is a Kanji Panth organization in Jamnagar, linked to the parent body at Songadh (a small town near Palitana, south-east of Jamnagar) and concerned with the management of the Kanji Panth temple in the city. Some members of the parent body claimed to be Digambaras when I spoke to them but most acknowledged that Kanji Swami merely drew on Digambara tradition for inspiration, particularly the works of the second- or third-century scholar-ascetic Kunda-Kunda. As the vast majority of Jamnagar Kanji Panthis are Mahajan (Halari

---

[4] Interestingly both movements were instituted by laymen. Although Kanji Swami's status is ambiguous in some ways—he was a Sthanakavasi ascetic before founding his neo-Digambara movement—most followers stress that he renounced his ascetic status and then began his reforms.

Visa Oswal) and as the Songadh organization is backed and largely run by Mahajans, I treat the Jamnagar Kanji Panthis below as a part of the Halari Visa Oswal *jati* .

The Sthanakavasi organization is called the Jamnagar Sthanakavasi Jain Sangh (JSJS). It has a membership list (which I wasn't able to see) and members pay a nominal annual subscription. In practice it is dominated by the Visa Srimali Loka Gaccha but it also represents the Sthanakavasi members of the Dasa Srimali, Kandoi, Bhavsar, and Khatri *jati*s (the last two are non-*vania jati*s which have Jain members: both are 'traditionally' textile printers and dyers, although today Bhavsars are known as dealers in household utensils). The JSJS is largely concerned with financial organization. It provides support to low-income member families, as well as organizing the *samvatsari* (last day of Paryushan) donations for all the member *jati*s, except the Visa Srimali Loka Gaccha which is sufficiently large and important to organize its own.

There is, by contrast, no overall Deravasi organization and none of the Deravasi *gaccha* organizations cut across *jati* divisions—for example, the Jamnagar Visa Oswals and the Visa Srimalis both have their own Tapa Gaccha, which organizes lay and ascetic Tapa Gaccha affairs. On the ascetic level, however, there is another kind of division within the Tapa Gaccha that is reflected among the Jamnagar laity. Some fifty years ago there was a difference of opinion between two Tapa Gaccha *acarya*s, Ramchandrasuri and Sagaranandji (also known as Devasuri and Anandasuri). The two had been '*guru*-brothers', that is, disciples under the same teacher, but had differed over the method used to calculate the *tithi* (the auspicious days in the lunar month, which also affect the start of Paryushan). Later on, I was told, Sagaranandji wanted to publish the *agama*s—a part of the Svetambara canon—to make them more accessible to scholars (he did not wish them to be translated necessarily) and this was opposed by Ramchandrasuri. The ascetics who now follow Sagaranandji's path (he himself is now dead) are greatly outnumbered by the followers of Ramchandrasuri, but the Jamnagar Visa Srimali Tapa Gaccha supports the Sagaranandji followers and invites these ascetics to spend the monsoon period in its *upasraya*s. (Some individual members of the *gaccha* maintain a preference for Ramchandrasuri, however.) The Halari Visa Oswals on the other hand are unconditional followers of Ramchandrasuri, and it is his ascetics who are to be found in the *upasraya*s controlled by the Halari Oswals. The Jamnagar Visa Oswals

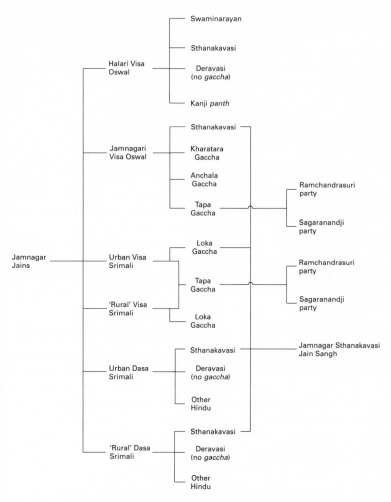

FIG. 4.1. Jamnagar Jains: Sect and *Gaccha* Divisions

are divided in their support, and maintain two sets of *upasraya*s, one for each section.

I have summarized these divisions in Figure 4.1. It will be noted that this diagram has the effect of subordinating religious affiliation ('sect') to *jati* ('caste'). It could be argued (and would be by ascetics and other keepers of the 'lineage perspective' tradition) that the relationship should be reversed—that is, that I should start with a list of the sects

(Deravasi, Sthanakavasi, etc.) and *gaccha*s (Tapa, Anchala, etc.), and then show which *jati*s or *jati*-sections have members who ascribe to the tenets of these religious groups. However, I justify my arrangement on the basis that all the groups named and isolated in this way (except the Ramchandrasuri and Sagaranandji 'parties') are corporate groups or organizations which can act or be mobilized for some purpose (marriage, *samvatsari* donations, appointing trustees, etc.). As further justification of this arrangement which subordinates 'sect' to *jati* I examine below the various types of corporately owned Jain religious property in Jamnagar (and some individually owned property which is used by a corporate group) and discuss whether the obvious religious ('sectarian') affiliation is the most important aspect to consider.

This property may be divided into three categories: temples, *upasraya*s and *vadi*s. There are also one or two other types of corporately owned property, such as libraries, but they are less frequently used and often located on the same site as an *upasraya* or temple. All the property described is formally and legally owned by certain groups (or in some cases, individuals) which appoints trustees to administer the property. At first sight these groups appear to be religious groups, the *gaccha*s, but as I shall demonstrate below, these *gaccha*s function for the most part as *jati* subdivisions. The ambiguity I encountered in Jamnagar lies not so much in which groups own and control particular pieces of property, as in the status of these groups. For the most part, each building stands as a separate unit, not attached to any other building (four of the temples were attached to a school boarding-house, an *upasraya*, and to two private houses respectively, but each had its own separate street access). All the buildings can be locked to prevent unauthorized access.

Temples

There were, in the early 1980s,[5] seventeen Jain temples in Jamnagar, ranging from tiny, dark *ghar derasar*s (house shrines with public access) to magnificent, many-chambered constructions beautifully painted and carved, situated within a courtyard or garden. All the temples contain at least one major *murti*, or idol (*mulnayak*) of one of the twenty-four

[5] In 1988 the Visa Srimalis opened a new temple in a recently established housing colony some 2–3 km. north-west of the city centre. I have only visited this temple once and know very little about its organization or the way in which the money for its construction was raised and so have excluded it from the following discussion.

tirthankaras, seated in a posture of meditation and carved from alabaster or marble. In the Svetambara temples (sixteen of the seventeen) the idol has bright, staring glass eyes, fixed into the carved eye-sockets: these symbolize his omniscience (*kevaljnana*). The eyes of the Digambara idols in the Kanji Panth temple are concealed behind half-closed lids, symbolizing inner, not outer, awareness. The temples are all open twice-daily—from early morning until noon, and again from early evening till 8 or 9 p.m. All but the two *ghar derasars* are staffed during these times by Bhojak Brahman *pujaris*, easily identified by their red *dhotis*. Their duty is to keep the temple clean, to remove old offerings (flowers, etc.) to make way for new ones, and to perform the daily *puja* of anointing those idols which have been omitted by the morning worshippers. In the larger temples in Chandi Bazaar this is a significant task—there are literally hundreds of idols, many tucked away in dark corners and, in one case, nestled in tiny shrines dotted about the roof; once an idol has been installed and consecrated *puja* must be performed before it every day.

During the morning period lay Jains come to anoint the idols with sandalwood paste, to meditate or recite prayers, or simply to take *darsana* ('beholding' the idol, viewing it with devotion). The period spent in the temple can range from a couple of minutes to almost an

(10)

hour, depending on the complexity of the devotions an individual chooses to perform. Worship is solitary and people in a temple do not generally communicate with each other. In the evening, the light-waving rituals of *arti* and *mangaldivo* are performed before the images, and people may bid—as in an auction—for the privilege of holding the lamp.[6] During the year, the birth and enlightenment of each of the *tirthankara*s is celebrated, and on these occasions the idols of the *tirthankara* concerned (and often all the other main idols) are decorated with *angi*—jewelled crowns, and breast-plates of silver overlaid with coloured fabrics. On these occasions there may be a *bhajan* (devotional song) session in the temple in the evening, and many Jains come simply to admire the splendidly adorned idols, sitting in their kingly majesty, surrounded by many flickering oil-lamps.

Jain temples are open to anyone who cares to go in, though one is not allowed to touch the idols unless one has bathed and donned clean clothing first. In practice, non-Jains would rarely have cause to enter a temple (although in other parts of India some Jain temples are visited by non-Jains because of their beautiful architecture, and a few—particularly in Rajasthan—have become the focus for regional non-Jain cults). The Deravasi Jains may freely worship at any of the fifteen Svetambara temples (Kanji Swami devotees follow the Digambara rite and can only worship at the Kanji Panth temple, though this does not preclude others from worshipping there if they so wish). In practice, most Deravasi Jains worship at the temple closest to their residence—my 'local' temple, for example, was a small shrine containing only a handful of idols which was attached to a (now empty) boys' hostel; some of the older men in my (exclusively Jain) boarding-house would visit it early each morning, performing the full *puja*; the younger men tended to take *darsana* at one of the central temples on their way to work (if they did anything at all). The temples in the centre of the city, in Chandi Bazaar, are foci for special occasions, such as the birthday of Mahavira, and are seen as a minor tourist attraction. I was told that Jamnagar is known as *ardho* (half) Shetrunjaya, because the splendour of its many Jain temples is thought to be at least half as impressive as that of Shetrunjaya Hill, near Palitana (although, in truth, I never heard anyone use the term spontaneously—in or out of Jamnagar).

---

[6] I discuss a similar form of bidding among the Leicester Jains in Banks 1991.

Upasrayas

There are seventeen *upasrayas* in Jamnagar, mostly located, like the temples, around the central Chandi Bazaar area. They are large airy buildings almost empty of furniture, cool and dark inside, with stone floors and shuttered windows. They are primarily used by ascetics who sleep there on low wooden benches, and perform their various rituals of meditation during the day. The *upasrayas* are also used for the morning *vyakhyan* or religious discourse; the ascetics will seat themselves on wooden benches along one wall of the main hall, and the laity sit facing them on the floor. The lay men and women always sit separately, sometimes with a low screen or curtain dividing them. The men generally sit directly in front of the ascetics and the women to one side. Occasionally, lay men and women retreat to an *upasraya*, especially during Paryushan, and will spend a day or more there, studying and meditating. Some of the *upasrayas* have facilities for cooking and serving food, perhaps a shaded courtyard, or a separate ground-floor hall, and it is common for lay Jains to perform certain dietary austerities communally in these places. Deravasi *upasrayas* generally have photographs or paintings of worthy ascetics adorning the walls, but the Sthanakavasi dislike of images extends to this also and the walls of their *upasrayas* are bare, save sometimes for edifying mottoes painted at eye-level.

Although the atmosphere inside the *upasrayas* is generally stark and austere, in the afternoons they come alive as the laity—mostly women —come to consult the currently resident ascetics on various spiritual and, indeed, domestic matters. Caroline Humphrey provides a particularly vivid description of a visit to an *upasraya* in Jaipur, Rajasthan, in a short article for the magazine of the Leicester Jain Samaj (Humphrey 1982). During these afternoon sessions families are able to obtain news of relatives who have become ascetics, children are given informal instruction in Jain practice, lay religious experts consult with the ascetics over the correct form of certain rituals, lay leaders discuss itineraries and try to 'book' prominent ascetics for certain key rituals and ceremonies (that is, try to entice the ascetic to arrange his or her peregrinations so as to be resident in Jamnagar on an agreed date), women seek an impartial and respected ear for their personal and domestic problems, and—crucially—those contemplating taking *diksa* can seek an ascetic who will become their guide and teacher. I was often taken to several of the *upasrayas* to meet and be displayed before new groups of ascetics (male and female—lay men, as far as I could tell, trust and respect female ascetics). Once seated, after the appropriate salutations had taken place, I would be urged by my lay friends to 'perform'—to sing or recite the various *mantras*, *stavans*, and *bhajans* that I had learned or could read. The ascetics invariably praised my performance and congratulated my companions on the skill with which they were training me. My day-to-day circumstances were also enquired after—where I lived, what I ate, who I spoke to—and again won approval which was again attributed to the close supervision of my companions. In this respect, I was treated as a child might be when presented by its parents.

Vadis

These have no religious connotations for Jains but I include them in my discussion for the purposes of comparison. Each *jati* in Jamnagar—Jain and non-Jain—has one or more *vadi*, or *jati* meeting hall. A *vadi* typically consists of an open courtyard, enclosed by a one-storeyed building with a wide, roofed veranda. To my knowledge, the Jain *jatis* in Jamnagar do not have a *pancayat* nor do the members meet on any regular basis to settle disputes or to act in any other self-regulatory way. The *vadi* is used nowadays for feasts, generally at marriages, although if a man is rich he may give a feast when his wife completes a major fast, or on some other occasion. Food is cooked over deep fire-pits in a covered part of the courtyard and served to the guests, who sit cross-legged and sexually segregated, along the veranda. The rooms opening off the veranda serve as offices and store-rooms. Some of the rooms may be set aside for accommodation if, say, a marriage party has come from another town. There are five *vadis* in the city which belong to various groups of Jains.

The *vadi* and its contents—stacking chairs, cooking utensils, and perhaps a *mandap* (open-sided tent-like structure) and other wedding paraphernalia, although this is usually hired from specialist firms—constitutes the corporate, secular, movable property of a *jati*. Funds raised by a *jati*—through annual 'membership' fees (that is, membership in the formally constituted *jati* organization or association) and the hire of the *vadi*, go towards renewing these fittings and maintaining the *vadi* itself. During the main marriage season in Gujarat—in the height of summer when agricultural work, and the trading activities related to agriculture, come to a standstill—marriages and engagement functions are held almost daily in the city's *vadi*s and competition for space becomes intense. Astrologers determine the most auspicious time for a marriage and, although this can be adjusted if necessary, it is incumbent upon the bride's family to find a suitable location, the *vadi* of their own *jati*, or section of a *jati* in the Oswal and Srimali cases, being the first and desired choice. For a period of three to four weeks I was visiting one or other of the Srimali- or Oswal-owned *vadi*s once or even twice daily, as an honorary if rather peripheral member of many friendship, kin, and *jati* networks. As the marriage ritual is long and of little interest in its details to anyone except the participants, these occasions were an excellent chance to consolidate contacts and to conduct fairly lengthy interviews.

Who Owns What?

Superficially these thirty-nine pieces of corporately owned property fall into two categories: those with a sectarian link (the temples and *upasraya*s), and those with a *jati* link (the *vadi*s). This was the way the situation was presented to me when I first arrived in Jamnagar. The sectarian affiliation of the temples is obvious. As I have said, attendance at the temples depends largely on residence, but inasmuch as residence locations show a *jati* or sectarian bias, so do the temples located in these areas. For those living away from the traditional residence location of their *jati* or *jati* section, daily *darsana* might be taken at the nearest convenient temple, but they might choose to hold a particular ritual—for example, a *siddhacakra puja* (worship of an auspicious diagram which represents cardinal Jain doctrines and persons) in another.[7] For example, the 'Digambara' temple of the Kanji Panthis is located on the edge of the Halari Visa Oswal residence area, and the majority of Kanji Panthi followers are of this *jati*. All temples have a more permanent affiliation to (as opposed to ownership by) *gaccha*, however, beyond the vagaries of lay attendance (excepting those controlled by the Halari Visa Oswals—see below). In each temple, besides the idols of the *tirthankara*s and other objects of devotion, one

---

[7] As I understand it, the new temple mentioned in n. 5 was built when a sufficiently large number of Srimalis had concentrated in the new colony and it was more convenient for them to hold larger rituals there than for them all to travel to the *jati*'s main temple in Chandi Bazaar. When I was living in Jamnagar many of these Srimalis tended to perform daily *puja* and *darsana* at my local temple—which was not far away—although it is owned and managed by the Jamnagar Visa Oswals.

finds shrines associated with *acarya*s or *guru*s of a particular *gaccha*, thus demonstrating a unique and permanent link between the temple and the *gaccha*. These shrines are generally of two kinds: either a set of footprints in bas relief (*paduka*) or an alabaster or marble statue of the person. The statue is not in the meditation posture (*padmasana*) of the *tirthankara*s but in the teaching posture of the living, a book in one hand, a *muh patti* (cloth held to the mouth) in the other. The statue may or may not have the staring glass eyes of enlightenment (strictly it should not as no one has achieved enlightenment since the time of Mahavira, this present age being a *dusama kala*, or unhappy time, when enlightenment is not possible). The idols and the footprints are often anointed by the laity in the same way that the idols of the *tirthankara*s are anointed.

Similarly, while one can judge the *gaccha* affiliation of an *upasraya* from those laymen who attend the morning *vyakhyan*, it is far more reliable to view the *gaccha* affiliation of the resident ascetics as indicative of the *gaccha* affiliation of the *upasraya*. Ascetics of a particular *gaccha* are always to be found in a particular *upasraya*, which usually has the name of the *gaccha* written over the doorway;[8] this strictness even reflects the division between the Sagaranandji and Ramchandrasuri parties in the tapa *gaccha*. Ascetics of the two parties are never to be found in the same *upasraya*.

Thus, if the seventeen temples and seventeen *upasraya*s are listed according to their religious or 'sectarian' affiliation we see that they are fairly evenly distributed between the *gaccha* and sectarian groups, although the Tapa Gaccha (the largest *gaccha* in India in numbers of ascetics) outweighs the rest. This listing is shown in Table 4.1.

There are some problems with this way of looking at things. For example, the two temples designated '*gaccha*—none given' were built and are run by the Halari Visa Oswals who tend to deny *gaccha* affiliations. Their *upasraya*s, however, are used by Tapa Gaccha ascetics of the Ramchandrasuri section of the Tapa Gaccha and so I have included their *upasraya*s in the Svetambara Deravasi Tapa Gaccha group.

The Kanji Panth has no *upasraya* as there are no travelling Kanji

---

[8] This is not always the case in Jamnagar as the Kharatara and Anchal Gacchas have only one *upasraya* apiece. If both male and female ascetics of either *gaccha* come to Jamnagar (a rare occurrence) the *sadhvi*s (female ascetics) will stay in one of the Tapa Gaccha *upasraya*s. Male and female ascetics cannot touch (nor can they touch a lay person of the opposite sex) and it would be unthinkable for them to sleep in the same building.

TABLE 4.1. *Corporately Owned Jain Religious Property in Jamnagar by Sectarian Affiliation*

'Sect'	*Gaccha*	Temples	*Upasrayas*
Deravasi	Tapa	11	8
	Anchala	2	1
	Kharatara	1	1
	none given	2	—
Sthanakavasi	Loka	—	7
'Digambara' (Kanji Panth)	—	1	—

Panthi ascetics (although there are two orders of male and female ascetics—*ksullak*s and *ailak*s—who visit and reside at the major Kanji Panth centres—Songhad in Gujarat and Jaipur in Rajasthan). 'Authentic' Digambara ascetics do not recognize the claims of the movement to Digambara status and rarely visit Saurashtra and its neo-Digambaras.

However, it is equally if not more illuminating to consider the actual ownership of the property discussed rather than its religious affiliation. With the exception of two, very recently built, temples, all the temples and *upasraya*s in Jamnagar have been built by individuals and handed over to a body of trustees at some later date. Two temples and one *upasraya* still remain in private hands, however. (The newly built temples were built by public subscription and have never been privately owned.) By listing the properties' actual ownership (as opposed to religious affiliation) I noticed that eighteen of the thirty-four temples and *upasraya*s are owned specifically by a *jati* or *jati*-section (by *jati*-section I mean the rural or urban section within a *jati*). Furthermore, an additional eight properties are, by default, wholly owned by a *jati* or *jati*-section. That is, they are owned by a *gaccha* which is wholly subsumed within a *jati*, such as the Anchala and Kharatara Gacchas which are represented only in the Jamnagar Visa Oswal *jati*. Retabulating, then, produces the arrangement found in Table 4.2.

The six temples and two *upasraya*s that are 'by default' managed by a *jati* or part-*jati*, belong to the Anchala and Kharatara Gacchas, or are managed by trustees of another institution (such as a school) which owns the temple. These trustees themselves are recruited from a single *jati*. It so happens that the Anchala and Kharatara *gaccha*s are only represented within the Jamnagar Visa Oswal *jati*. It is conceivable that

TABLE 4.2. *Corporately Owned Jain Religious Property in Jamnagar by Ownership/ Trusteeship*

Form of ownership	Temples	*Upasraya*s
trustees legally limited to a *jati* or *jati* section	8	10
trustees limited to a *jati* or *jati* section by default	6	2
trustees limited to an inter-*jati* sect group	—	4
property privately owned	3	1

non-Visa Oswal individuals moving to Jamnagar who claimed to follow Anchala and Kharatara Gaccha ascetics could be appointed trustees of these properties, but it is highly unlikely.

The individuals or families who privately own the three temples and one *upasraya* are of course members of a *jati*. One temple, very large and impressive, is owned by a family of Visa Oswals from Kaccha (Kacchi Oswals). Another is owned by a Jamnagar Visa Oswal family, while the third, a *ghar derasar*, is owned by a Visa Srimali family of Jamnagar origin. The *upasraya* is owned by a Jamnagar Visa Oswal family. But technically they are free to dispose of this property as they wish, unlike the *jati*-owned property managed by trustees, which could only be disposed of after a vote by all eligible members of the *jati*.

Thus only four of the thirty-four pieces of property considered above actively transcend *jati* divisions; these four are all *upasraya*s owned and maintained by the Jamnagar Sthanakavasi Jain Sangh. The other thirty buildings are divided along *jati* lines in the same way that specifically 'secular' corporately-owned property—such as the *vadi*—is. Table 4.3 summarizes the divisions and the property they control.

TABLE 4.3. *Summary of Jamnagar Jain Corporate Ownership*

Property-Owning Groups	Property			
	Temples	*Upasraya*s	*Vadi*s	Total
Jamnagar Visa Oswals (all *gaccha*s)	9	5	1	15
Halari Visa Oswals (all)	3	4	1	7
Visa Srimali Tapa Gaccha	2	2	1	5
Visa Srimali Loka Gaccha	—	1	1	2
Dasa Srimali (all)	—	—	1	1
Private ownership	3	1	—	4
Jamnagar Sthanakavasi Jain Sangh	—	4	—	4
Totals	17	17	5	39

Note: I have not divided the Jamnagar Visa Oswals by *jati* on this table because they have an overall *jati* organization which transcends *gaccha* divisions. The Visa Srimalis do not have an overall organization and president, and therefore I list the *gaccha*s separately.

This final breakdown of property ownership reveals again the tension between lay and ascetic, between 'secular' and 'religious' paths. The only sectarian body to maintain property which transcends *jati* divisions, the Sthanakavasi Sangh, maintains it purely for the ascetics.[9] Needing no temples, none is built and therefore none can be bequeathed by an individual to his prime focus of loyalty—his *jati*. For non-religious functions Sthanakavasi Srimalis have the Visa Srimali Loka Gaccha *vadi* or the Dasa Srimali *vadi*. (Khatris, Kandois, and Bhavsars also have their *vadi*s in the city, used by both Jain and Hindu members of each *jati*).

In a way this result is not so surprising. The principles of caste and division have been linked throughout Indian history just as caste and hierarchy have, and there is no reason why the Jains should have been untouched by these principles. When one considers that caste, not religious affiliation, is the key determinant in so many other areas of the Jains' lives—marriage, residence, occupation, etc.—it would be strange if the management of their corporately owned property were not similarly governed. Stevenson claimed that 'there are no people more caste-bound than the Jainas' (1915: 293) but I think that is an unfair accusation. They are no 'better' or 'worse' than their Hindu neighbours. Equally one-sided, however, is to take the view, as some Jains themselves do, that religious affiliation ('sect') is the be-all and end-all. As I mentioned earlier, the Jains sometimes think in terms of caste and sometimes in terms of sect. They act this way too; *samvatsari* donations, though for 'religious' purposes in part (upkeep of temples, medical care for ascetics) are for the most part collected and distributed by *jati*s or part-*jati*s.

My aim in presenting these data has been simple and straight-forward. I wanted to demonstrate that the principles of caste and sect—the 'secular' and the 'religious'—are intricately intertwined for the Jains. Such mixtures can be found in many aspects of Jainism in practice: the study of temple and other such property ownership above is just one example. Nor would such examples be confined to the Jains alone; all transcendent religions (by which I mean major, world religions, as opposed to small-scale tribal religions) are faced with the

---

[9] Even when no Sthanakavasi ascetics come to Jamnagar, the laity will construct a symbolic presence at religious functions in the *upasraya* by putting a book on a reading stand with a *mala* (rosary) and placing this where the ascetic would normally sit. All aspects of Sthanakavasi religious expression require an ascetic presence. Deravasi ascetics in contrast, while they may attended temple rituals, are not necessary for their performance.

problem of living out a religious code and philosophy which may—especially in the case of some of the more 'world-denying' traditions—conflict with the ideals and organization of the secular world encompassing the adherents. Several traditions—Christianity, Hinduism, Buddhism, Jainism—seek to solve the problem through renunciation. The contemplative orders of post-medieval Christianity, for example, are predicated on a belief that not only is withdrawal from the world a solution for those who do so, but also that their actions (prayers) once within the confines of the monastery, can be beneficial for those who remain without the walls.

The establishment of monastic orders, however, brings its own attendant problems. The 'secular' cannot wholly be abjured when the order owns (or makes use of) property, is dependent upon the laity for material support, and so on. More importantly, such religious orders often exist within the boundaries of a nation state and are subject to political whims and state policies (as seen in the discussion of Shetrunjaya Hill which opened this chapter). Nor does the existence of renunciatory movements and monastic orders wholly remove the problem from the laity. As we saw at the beginning of the chapter, in the discussion of *devadravya* and *sadharana* funds, the laity too seek to bound the domain of the sacred (the fact that such a distinction may be 'forced' upon them by ascetics—for example, by Jinasena, the author of the Adi-purana—is merely further testimony of the ascetic inability to dwell wholly within the sacred).

Thus there seem to be two conflicting principles at work—that of *gaccha* or religious division, which we can identify with the ascetics, and that of *jati* or caste division, which we can identify with the laity (without in either case attributing any kind of 'blame'). Both groups are (and have always been) tied to each other on several different levels, and each must accommodate to the other, while at the same time extracting maximum profit from the relationship—a symbiosis. The divisions important to each group have been 'imposed' upon the other presenting a pattern that is at once confused and unique. The ascetics have 'imposed' their *gaccha* divisions on the laity in, for example, the form of *tithi*: each *gaccha* maintains a separate calendar (*pancang*) on which auspicious and inauspicious days are marked (good deeds on the auspicious days will bring additional good *karma*, bad deeds on the inauspicious days will worsen the load of bad *karma*). These marked days are auspicious and inauspicious for both lay and ascetic. As the *tithi* are calculated differently by each *gaccha*, the laity, if they wish to be 'good Jains', must commit themselves to one *gaccha* and observe its *pancang*. (For the laity, differences between the *gaccha*s are otherwise minimal.) Conversely, the ascetics, though they have renounced all ties of *jati* and the structuring principles of caste on taking *diksa*, ally themselves with particular *jati*s or sections of *jati*s by their choice of *upasraya*. Lay Jains in Jamnagar will talk about 'our' ascetics, meaning the ascetics installed in their *jati*'s *upasraya*s. Ascetics must maintain a balance between lay contact (and hence, involvement) and renunciatory retreat, and I believe that it is this balance that is expressed through the two ways of viewing property ownership and management given above. On the one hand, by considering *upasraya*s and temples as the property of sects and *gaccha*s the transcendence of the religious path over worldly affairs is emphasized; on the other, by allowing these properties to be controlled by *jati*-based groups, the laity can be involved in the maintenance of their religion and at the same time subscribe to the ideology of caste which structures the Hindu universe around them.

The reader may, however, feel that the discussion of corporately owned religious property in Jamnagar has raised a far more immediate and pragmatic problem, which is, why do the Jamnagar Visa Oswals own or control so much of it? For this, I'm afraid, I have no simple answer and my own researches provided no conclusive evidence (though it might be the case that diligent historical and archival research could). The most I can offer is informed speculation along the following lines: of the three major groups owning property—the Jamnagar Visa Oswals, the Visa Srimalis (both Tapa and Loka Gacchas), and the Halari Visa Oswals—the Jamnagar Visa Oswals seem to be the most tightly bounded and historically deep-rooted in the city. Their commercial enterprises are all located within the city or in Bombay and—as far as I can tell—marriages are contracted exclusively within, or between, the two cities. The Visa Srimalis on the other hand have extensive kin and *jati* networks across the region which appear to 'shade off' in a more arbitrary fashion, so that, for example, a marriage may be contracted from Jamnagar with a family bearing the *jati* name 'Visa Srimali' in one town near by (Lalpur, for example, to the south) but not with a family bearing the same *jati* name elsewhere. Thus there are temples owned and managed by Visa Srimali groups elsewhere in the region which may have marriage links with the Jamnagar Visa Srimalis but whose members are not members of the Jamnagar Visa Srimali *sangha*.

It seems as though the split which occurred between the Jamnagar Visa Oswals and the Halari Visa Oswals (possibly rapidly, but more probably gradually, as mentioned in Chapter 2) left each group with a very clear sense of self-identity. The Halari Visa Oswals, of course, have only begun to reside in the city in large numbers since the turn of the century, or even later, and this is reflected in the small numbers of temples and *upasrayas* they own or manage there. Moreover, they are ready to admit that their interest in Jainism had been much lower prior to their moves to East Africa and into Jamnagar city. If I were to include in my tables all the temples and *upasrayas* owned or managed by Visa Srimalis and Halari Visa Oswals in Jamnagar region (and possibly those elsewhere, such as in East Africa, as well) then there would probably be a far greater parity between these groups and the Jamnagar Visa Oswals. However, it has not been my intention in this chapter to discuss how and why each of the groups controls the property it does (although that is undoubtedly of importance and interest) but rather to understand how they conceive of this property and what this reveals about Jainism as a practised religion.

5

In and Out of Africa

Hugh Tinker has pointed out that 'Indians overseas represent no more than one (or at the most two) per cent of total population. For the mother country they are only a tiny offspring' (1975: 25), and moreover that those in East Africa are neither the largest nor the densest part of that minority (ibid.: 15). Nevertheless, the influence of these expatriates was and is disproportionate to their group size, not only because of the economic significance for their relatives in India (through remittances) but also in terms of the attention they have attracted from Western academic observers. The literature on the East African Asians—resident now in both East Africa and England—is

(11)

large and comprehensive (if now somewhat dated), and many issues are covered in such detail (see especially Mangat 1969; D. P. Ghai 1965) that it would be pointless for me, with no direct experience, to cover them here.[1] Instead I concern myself in this chapter only with the experiences of the Jains, using data that I gathered from former East African residents that I met in Jamnagar and Leicester. The data are interesting for two reasons. First, while the activities of Hindu and Muslim Asians in East Africa are fairly well documented, the Jain experience has largely been passed over, despite their obvious economic importance to the former colonies.[2] Secondly, the details of Jain social and religious organization that I give below go some way towards bridging the gap between the relatively stable—if ambiguous —forms of organization that I discussed in Part I and the fluid and very different forms of organization discussed in Part II.

Migration

Contact between India and Africa is by no means a recent phenomenon. Most works on the Asians in East Africa point out that as early as the first century AD a Greek guidebook to the Indian Ocean describes ships from the Gulf of Cambay (modern Khambat) and Broach in Gujarat, bringing foodstuffs and cloth to East Africa, while in the thirteenth century Marco Polo noted that ships from Malabar visited Madagascar and Zanzibar (Hollingsworth 1960: 11, 12). However, it seems unlikely that the Indian traders established any kind of permanent settlement in the region before the sixteenth century, and that the modern phenomenon of the ubiquitous *duka* (Indian shop) owes much to the *pax britannica* in India and the recovery of Islamic influence in East Africa under Seyyid Said (Mangat 1969: 1–2). With reference to Tanzania, Iliffe (1979: 138) notes that the Asian control of retail trade in the interior of the country was not established until after the First World War. In the colonial period the fortunes of the Asians revived and many large investors and financiers were active on the

[1] The term 'Asian' was used in East Africa (and subsequently in the literature) to denote any person of Indian or Pakistani origin, regardless of their place of birth and ethnic or religious status. The issues discussed in the quite substantial literature include such things as the economic status of the Asians, their political influence, the effects of Africanization, patterns of settlement and occupation, and the question of nationality. Of course, facts relating to these and other issues will be used in this chapter where necessary.

[2] Zarwan (1975; 1975) and Murray (1978) give some very narrowly focused data on this economic importance.

coast in the mid-nineteenth century, and were in part responsible for the strength of the British influence (Mangat 1969: Chapter 1). The main growth of the retail trader (who was almost always Hindu in contrast to the earlier Muslim dominance) came at the end of the century.

Asians came from almost all parts of India and Pakistan to East Africa in the colonial period for many different reasons. However, we can class the bulk of these individuals into two general categories—the indentured labourers (that is, those brought over with a prepaid passage and a contractual obligation to perform a certain task within a certain period of time, during which they would—in theory—earn enough to repay the passage and accumulate a capital sum) and the entrepreneurs (using the term 'entrepreneur' not so much in the narrow sense of possessing business acumen, but in a more general sense to denote people controlling their own movements and seeking their own opportunities. Hence for the purposes of this discussion doctors, lawyers, civil servants, and shopkeepers are all 'entrepreneurs', although the prevailing stereotype is that of the shopkeeper/business man). Each of these two categories can furthermore be identified with a cluster of characteristics—the indentured labourers were generally from the far west of pre-partition India, represented a variety of different *jati*s and religious groups, were generally recruited for a fixed period, and then returned to India (unlike the indentured labourers in South Africa or Fiji who tended to stay) and had little impact on the emergent East African nationalism. By contrast the entrepreneurs generally came from Gujarat or Panjab, represented—in the Hindu/ Jain cases—only the trading *jati*s (or those *jati*s that had aspirations towards trade), established themselves permanently in East Africa (eventually moving on to Britain in many cases), and had a decisive impact (albeit passive) on native African society (Tinker 1975: *passim*; A. Gupta 1975).

The indentured labourers were needed in East Africa for the construction of the Uganda railway, and by the end of the nineteenth century some 32,000 men (many from around Karachi) were employed. The Gujarati entrepreneurs were always at pains to dissociate themselves from the 'coolies' and it is likely that few, if any, of the East African Asian migrants in Britain today are descendants of indentured labourers.[3] By contrast, the chain migration methods of the

[3] Because of the method of recruitment and employment the movements of the indentured labourers can be followed with some accuracy. Of the 32,000 brought over, only about 20% stayed on, the rest either returning to India or dying (Morris 1968: 8).

entrepreneurs make it difficult to judge the exact numbers of them in East Africa at any one time. By the late 1960s (that is, after the Kenyan panic, but before the Ugandan expulsion) there were some 367,000 Asians in East Africa—182,000 in Kenya, 105,000 in Tanzania, and 80,000 in Uganda; in all three countries about half the Asians were British passport holders (figures compiled by Mariyam Harris, cited in Ghai and Ghai 1971).

Although to the Asians themselves their purpose for being in East Africa was clear and obvious (that is, to make money, from which stems other benefits such as improved standards of living, higher educational levels, and possibly an improvement in the status of the *jati* as a whole in India) their position was ambiguous in the eyes of first the Colonial administration and later the African national governments, as well as in the eyes of the Government of India itself (an ambiguity well documented by A. Gupta (1975)).

The Gujarati Hindus, who made up about 45 per cent of the entrepreneurs, were and are renowned for their conservatism, and the influence of the East Africa political environment must be considered when discussing social and religious changes within the community. At the same time it is important to be aware of dynamics internal to the Asian 'community'—both between different Asian groups in East Africa, and between 'parent' and 'offspring' groups in India and East Africa. Michaelson (1983) has pointed out the importance of the East African experience for raising the status of the Halari Visa Oswals both in Africa and in India, and Pocock (1955) makes a similar observation for the Patidars and other groups.

Jains in Africa

Of all the *jati*s in India which are exclusively Jain or which have Jain members, only two—the Visa Srimalis and the Halari Visa Oswals— were represented in any number in East Africa. Members of the Navnat also emigrated and so those member *jati*s which had some Jain families also contributed to the Jain population, but, because of their common Navnat membership, these few families are counted in this chapter as Srimalis. Dasa Srimalis from Saurashtra and Gujarat also emigrated and again are counted as Visa Srimalis for the purposes of discussion.[4] Why members of only those two large Jain *jati*s should

---

[4] I justify this merging together on the grounds that the few Dasa Srimali families and the one Kandoi family I knew in Leicester initially claimed to be Visa Srimalis when I

have emigrated is not immediately clear. The most important factor is probably that they were the two largest Jain groups in the Saurashtra–Gujarat region from which much of the emigration came and processes of chain migration would certainly have been organized along *jati* lines. One of my Leicester informants, for example, told me that Visa Srimalis from Lalpur, a village some 35 km. south of Jamnagar (his own *jati* and village), had emigrated in chains to Uganda around the turn of the century. In the late 1960s some had migrated on to Manchester, and the rest had followed in the 1972 expulsion. (He and his brother, for a variety of reasons, had moved to Leicester instead.)

Generally the great famine and crop failure in Saurashtra between 1899 and 1901 is cited as the principle 'push' factor from the region (for example, Zarwan 1975: 221) although many of my older informants (all of whom were born at least twenty years later) who had travelled from India to East Africa had done so simply in a spirit of commercial enterprise. Zarwan notes that, for Oswals at least, early 'push' factors were later replaced by 'pull' factors: 'Word would get around that conditions in Africa were good: other people would emigrate' (ibid.: 222).

The Oswal migration was exclusively from the *bavangami*, the fifty-two villages of Oswal origin around Jamnagar, although some migrants may also have spent a period in either Bombay or Jamnagar also. In contrast, the Srimalis came from Jamnagar itself, the surrounding villages, other towns and villages in Saurashtra (generally to the east and south—Wankaner, Rajkot, Junaghad, Bhanvad) as well as towns and villages in Gujarat—Ahmedabad and Valsad, for example. More precisely, they did not come from Kaccha (Kutch), North or East Gujarat. While the Oswals constituted an endogamous group and freely married within it (apart from rules of surname exogamy), the Srimalis in East Africa were constituted from parts of endogamous *jati*s and even in 1982 Leicester Srimalis of Saurashtran origin (the majority) told me that they would not marry their children to Ahmedabadi Srimalis in Leicester for preference. Although for many migration to East Africa was permanent and preceded migration to Britain, there were many other options. Several Oswals and Srimalis

first met them and had difficulty in explaining why they were in any way different from 'true' Visa Srimalis. Although they claimed they could marry their children to Visa Srimali families I saw no evidence of this and in none of the cases that I know of was this a problem—all had so far found spouses within their own *jati* from India.

had always planned to return to India, their timing perhaps prompted, but not forced, by the East African political situation after independence: the father of one of my Oswal informants spent only two years in Kenya (1935–7) before returning to his village (Changa) on the death of his father to take over the family farm. The link with Halar (the area around Jamnagar) for the Oswals cannot be overstated for it defines their identity in many ways.

Indeed, many of the stories informants in both Leicester and Jamnagar told me, revealed quite complex migratory strategies. Several of these demonstrate an interplay of factors—personal, familial, and *jati*-based. As an example, let me describe the case of another of my Oswal informants, Jayantilal.

Jayantilal was born in Nairobi in 1947, the oldest of four children (three sons and a daughter), and was sent back to India at the age of 11 to complete his education. His father's father was managing the family farm in the village of Rasangpar (about 30 km. east of Jamnagar) but Jayantilal stayed in Jamnagar in the Halari Visa Oswal Boys' Boarding in Digvijay Plot, where he received his education.[5] In 1936 Oswals in Kenya had organized a relief fund to help famine victims in Saurashtra and when, at the completion of this project, some money remained, it was decided to establish a fund to help Oswals remaining in the *bavangami*, principally by giving children access to education.

Although his father owned a small retail business, Jayantilal returned to Kenya in 1963 to enter service, as a clerk in another Oswal wholesale business. Two years later he had saved enough money to buy a ticket to England where he hoped to start a small business, and for the next two years he worked in a food-processing factory in north London in order to build up more capital. Although he enjoyed the experience of living in Britain he had underestimated the difficulties of starting a business. He was also lonely—there were few other Indians in Britain at the time and the few Oswals were either business men or students, not factory workers. In 1967 the grandfather in Rasangpar died and Jayantilal and his father (from Kenya) returned to India. His father effectively retired and Jayantilal took control of the farm. Using his savings from England, supplemented by a loan, he bought a tractor —the first in the village. The farm flourished and more land was

---

[5] The 'Boarding' (i.e. residential accommodation for pupils attending nearby schools) was opened in 1942. Since then, a new Boys' Boarding has been opened at Sat Rasta (in 1963), at the northern end of the city and the old building has become a Girls' Boarding (girls previously stayed in a rented house).

bought, the tractor was replaced and a deeper well dug. The two younger brothers had also been sent to India for their education and were reunited with the rest of the family in 1967. (The sister had also been returned with her father and lived with the family until she married. Like the two younger brothers she did not return to Kenya.)

Sanat, the second brother, now lives in Surat where he is a textile dealer, buying from mills and selling to dyers. He had initially wished to study for his B.Comm., but Jayantilal dissuaded him, saying that while a certain amount of education was desirable, degrees were not necessary and that he had seen unemployed graduates during his stay in England, the land of plenty. (Of course, he exaggerated, but he wished his brother to earn money to support the development of the farm.) Instead, Sanat was sent to Bombay for a year's unpaid service in a textile mill, owned by distant relatives. He then established a textile workshop in Surat—on his own insistence, Jayantilal claimed—but failed, due largely to his own youth (he was only twenty-one) and inexperience. The present concern is thriving, however. In the meantime, the youngest brother, Dharmendra, had been educated and was trained by Jayantilal in farm management. Jayantilal gradually withdrew from the farm and then, using capital from the farm and the Surat business, bought a shop unit in the newly built 'Supermarket' in Jamnagar (a purpose-built bazaar on three levels, incorporating a hotel and offices as well as shop units: the owner is a Jamnagar Visa Srimali), where he sells school exercise books and other stationery. He travels in daily on his scooter, having his lunch with his sister and her family who live in Digvijay Plot. Jayantilal, his wife, son, and daughter, live with his parents and his youngest brother and his wife in a new and spacious house in Rasangpar. (Their old house is now a grain store.) Unlike bungalows built by East African returnees in other parts of Gujarat, Jayantilal's house and those of other village-dwelling returned Oswals is a traditional compound house with plain whitewashed walls, a cool veranda, and sparse, simple furniture. On his life-style now he told me: 'Mahajans [Halari Visa Oswals] are the most advanced people in the *bavangami* [Rasangpar has a population of around 2,000, some 25 per cent of whom according to Jayantilal are Mahajans], and it is we who are responsible for all changes, such as the introduction of tractors and electric water-pumps. We Mahajans have an organizational mind—not like the rest—and we can see the value of such things.' More to the point, he added that returnees from East Africa had become used to certain standards and amenities, and demanded these in their villages. The case of Jayantilal is obviously not typical of the experiences of all Jains in East Africa—indeed, the large numbers of East Africa-returned Oswals now resident in Jamnagar city itself indicates that not all find rural life as attractive as Jayantilal did. Nevertheless, for many like Jayantilal, the experience in East Africa was largely of economic significance which, without consolidation, left their life-chances largely unaffected.[6]

Sneh Shah (1979: 371) reports that as early as 1826 there is reference to two Jain (probably Oswal) customs officers in Mombasa, but the first major emigration from Halar came in the last two decades of the nineteenth century and reached a peak between the wars (Zarwan 1975: 222). Although Zarwan's and Shah's data relate to the Oswals, information from my informants in Leicester and Jamnagar confirms such a timetable for the Srimalis also. However, while the Srimalis settled in all three countries of East Africa, the Oswals confined themselves to Kenya for almost the entire period. Until 1940 there were only two or three Oswal households in Tanzania, a number which increased to about twenty in as many years, the settlers all coming from Kenya. Uganda by contrast never saw more than a handful of Oswals. (In addition, some Srimalis from Saurashtra migrated not to Kenya, Tanzania, or Uganda, but to other British protectorates such as Aden and Sudan.)

Using census and other official documentation Mangat has estimated the post-war Jain population of the East African countries as shown in Table 5.1.

TABLE 5.1. *Jain Population in East Africa*

Country	No.	% of all Asians
Kenya (1948)	6,000	6
Uganda (1948)	400	1
Tanzania (1957)	1,000	1

Source: After Mangat 1969: 142.

The figures, especially those for Kenya, are likely to be underestimates as Jains are known to have entered their religion on census forms as 'Hindu' in India (Sangave 1980: 291) and may well have done so in East Africa. If we assume that the majority of the 6,000 Kenyan Jains were Oswals (note that Zarwan (1975: 223) gives a figure of 7,000

---

[6] For others, of course, East Africa was a turning-point. Zarwan (1975) and Murray (1978) document the business success of important Kenyan Oswal families.

Oswals in Nairobi alone in 1948) and that the majority of Jains in Uganda and Tanzania were Srimalis, then we have some idea of the Oswal–Srimali balance.

While the Oswals were a 'crystallized community' (following Morris's (1968: 34) use of the term) in East Africa, due partly to their numerical strength and partly to their strong links with Saurashtra, the Srimalis were in a more ambiguous position. Not only were they from different regions of India and did not constitute an endogamous group, they were a comparatively weak group numerically. They were therefore instrumental in recreating the Navnat, using as member *jati*s (i.e. '*nat*s') whichever Gujarati *vania* groups were in East Africa. The number of constituent *jati*s varied from region to region as well as over time.[7] Grouping themselves together in this way allowed these *jati*s to 'compete' with larger *jati*s such as the Lohanna and Patidar. As in India, the Navnat had dual functions as a trading guild and marriage pool (intra-*jati* endogamy being preferential, of course).

However, relations between Oswals and Srimalis, as in India, were not entirely smooth, and the Navnat's existence should also be viewed in this light. In the early part of this century, the Oswal's educational background was low (see Zarwan 1975: 224 n. 7) and on arriving in Kenya they moved immediately into retailing and other forms of commodity exchange (ibid.: 224). Moreover, internal solidarity meant that entrepreneurial activities could be exploited to the full. In East Africa Oswals 'sent' for relatives and other *jati*-mates from the *bavangami*, trained them in their shops and businesses, gave them stock on credit and encouraged them to start their own concerns. The Srimalis, by contrast, had greater literacy and managerial skills (primarily through urban residence and involvement with bookkeeping in India: the surname of many Srimalis, Mehta, indicates a clerk or accountant), and although many became shopkeepers and traders, many more entered Government service. Although secure and moderately well paid, service obviously did not provide the opportunities for great economic advancement and capital reinvestment: several of my Leicester Srimali informants expressed resentment that the less-well-educated Oswals had, through individual success and corporate

---

[7] Michaelson (1983: 101) lists 13 member *jati*s that were considered to be part of the East African Navnat: Visa Srimali, Dasa Srimali, Modh, Gurjar Oswal (that is, non-Halari Oswals from Gujarat), Sorathia Srimali, Kandoi, Lad, Vanik Soni, Porwad, Mewar, Deshawar, Khedayta, and Kapol. Mostly small *jati*s in Gujarat, the numbers of these *jati*s' members in East Africa must have been very low.

solidarity, raised their status, power, and prestige in East Africa (both as individuals and as a group) while the Srimalis with their better education and 'commitment' to East Africa had not. Moreover, this difference in occupational strategy is probably the reason the Oswals settled only in Kenya, where they were able to develop a network of business contacts and information, while the Srimalis were free to seek government service in any of the three countries.

Not all Srimalis entered government service, however, and some followed quite typical patterns of entrepreneurial activity supplying goods wholesale or retail that were needed either by the Asian population (such as saris and spices) or by the British, black Africans, and Asians alike (grain, china, etc.). One of the senior Leicester Srimalis, Charandas Sanghvi, had built up an extremely successful enterprise, due partly to the unexpected success of a commodity— pickles—that he had begun to retail in an entirely casual way.

I first met Charandas in Leicester, technically 'retired', but still active—both socially and economically. He was born in Kenya at the end of the First World War and was sent back to India (to Jamnagar) for his education, before returning in the late 1920s. Although his father was a shopkeeper (selling groceries) Charandas went to work for a distant relative, managing the stock of a pharmaceutical warehouse. During the Second World War, one of the partners was killed and the other (Charandas's relative) ran into financial difficulties over another venture and was forced to sell up. Charandas bought the Mombasa office and began to run it himself.

In the mean time, his wife, Nanchaben, was achieving local renown with her home-made pickles. Her father had had a small pickle-making business back in India and she had brought some of the recipes with her and begun distributing the products to family and friends. One of these owned a grocery shop in Mombasa and eventually asked if she could produce enough jars to sell in his shop. Nanchaben, pressed by Charandas, did so, but had no desire to make anything further of the business. Therefore Charandas, whose own business was beginning to stagnate, took over the concern. By the late forties they were employing one worker and had set aside a room in their house for pickle production. By the mid–fifties Charandas had bought premises back in Khambhalia (his 'home' town, some 50 km. south-west of Jamnagar) and was employing two workers there (Nanchaben's father had died in the meantime and his business closed). Screen-printed labels for the jars were made in India, together with the pickles (a range of four or five varieties), and the produce was packed and distributed from Mombasa (smaller quantities were also sold locally in India). Salesmen and a small fleet of vehicles carried the products throughout Kenya and into Uganda and Tanzania. The salesmen and shop-keepers who bought the pickles were other Gujaratis, but the salesmen had native Kenyan assistants, partly because Charandas believed in employing Kenyans, and partly because there was an increasing demand for the pickles from the black population and the assistants were believed to be important in attracting custom. So great, however, was the demand for the pickles among the Asian population, that after the exodus in the sixties and seventies, Charandas began exporting from Khambhalia to Canada, New Jersey, and Britain (the Mombasa operation ceased at about this time).

Charandas and Nanchaben had six children, four of them girls (three of whom were still living in Kenya in 1982). Neither of the sons, however, took any interest in the business and the elder—an accountant—came to England with his wife in 1968. Charandas, Nanchaben, and the younger son, Bharat (now also married, to a British passport-holder), remained in Kenya until problems with Bharat's health brought them to Britain in search of treatment. Bharat, trained as a pathologist, quickly found part-time employment in Leicester (where the elder brother had settled) and the family was given priority housing by the council because of Bharat's chronic health problem. Charandas and Nanchaben, both Indian passport-holders, were allowed to stay in Britain on compassionate grounds and have lived there on and off since the late seventies. Charandas's heart lay in Kenya, however, and they visited the country once a year or so when I knew them, travelling on to India to keep an eye on the pickle factory (now being managed by Charandas's brother's son). Although I have no figures, Charandas left me in no doubt that the business was highly profitable, a success he attributed to his ability to attract a large Kenyan and Ugandan clientele through his extensive knowledge of East Africa and his sympathetic handling of local labour. He told me once that the condiments used in the pickles were mentioned in ancient Jain texts and had beneficial properties. Certainly the converse applied and Jainism in East Africa benefited from Charandas. He was instrumental in organizing the first Mombasa Jain temple and gave large sums of money towards Jain activities.

Jainism in Africa

With regard to the practice and organization of Jainism, some Oswals, as mentioned in Chapter 4, readily admit that a corporate (i.e. *jati*-wide) interest in Jainism coincided with and, in part, was undoubtedly precipitated by, the migration of part of the *jati* to East Africa. The construction by them of impressive temples in Jamnagar (1948, 1961, 1983)[8] and Mombasa (1963) can be seen as marking the development of this interest, with the construction of one in Nairobi in 1984 probably marking the summit.

The first temple in East Africa that I have knowledge of was founded in a private house in 1916 by the Srimali owner and visited by both Oswals and Srimalis. In 1921 or 1922 a separate house was purchased specifically for this purpose and the Mombasa Jain Svetambara Derasar Sangh (basically, the temple's management committee) established. In 1926 the Oswals founded a small temple in Nairobi and began to institute local *jati* associations in the major Kenyan cities and towns; they also began to buy land and build *vadis* (Zarwan 1975: 229). Charandas Sanghvi (discussed above and mentioned again in Part II), had been general secretary of the Mombasa Sangh in the early 1930s; he outlined to me the pattern of worship in the temple—a short, twice-daily *arti* (offering of flame) and recitation of short *mantras* and *stavans* before an unconsecrated idol— a pattern that is very similar to that which I observed in Leicester fifty years later (where Charandas was—perhaps by default—the main ritual specialist). All of these temples, once constructed, became a focal point for the local Jains—women would visit them early in the morning before beginning the household chores and thus meet one another, men would gather in the evenings to chat and play cards (there were, of course, no *sadhus* or *sadhvis* to visit).

For some individuals, changes in the affective aspects of their religion took place in East Africa. In Leicester I noticed that my presence, as—ostensibly—a student of Jainism, caused some Srimalis I knew to bemoan their lack of 'deep knowledge' of their own religion. These people usually went on to express the opinion that the damage thus caused to Jainism (in a general, rather than a personal sense) could be traced to the East African experience, where as children or young men and women they had lacked regular religious education,

---

[8] The 1961 temple is the only Kanji Swami temple, situated in the Digvijay Plot; the remainder are all Svetambara temples.

consecrated idols (at least initially) which demanded the full range of ritual observance, and, most especially, the guidance and stimulation of the ascetics. In short, the absence of many of the infrastructural aspects of the religion rendered the superstructural and affective aspects unintelligible.

There are, of course, exceptions. One of my older Leicester informants, Manilal, a man born and educated in India, but working for most of his life in East Africa, expressed a contrary opinion. Equating religious commitment with (intra-personal) morality—an idea common throughout India (see Bharati 1965: 43) as well as elsewhere—he maintained that the 'decline' in Jainism (which he certainly perceived) had occurred when the Srimalis came to England. East Africa had provided a good environment for religious belief and practice, partly because there had been few distractions of the type experienced in Britain (television, for example), but mainly because the Asians had been segregated not only racially but also sexually. Women were far less likely to work than they were in England and thus 'interfere' with men's affairs; girls and boys, moreover, were educated separately in the Asian schools. However, as a rider it should be noted that Manilal, while pious in his own way, had—in my opinion—a fairly idiosyncratic interpretation of Jainism and rarely if ever manifested overt displays of religiosity. More to the point, he had clearly enjoyed his life in East Africa—where he had been a moderately successful trader—and was less happy in England. In Leicester he was jobless and living with his daughter and son-in-law, both of whom went out to work and whose three young children were extrovert anglophones.

Another contrasting example is provided by the Shah family whom I met in Leicester. Also Srimalis, the family again consisted of the father, Rajabhai (also in his late seventies), living with his son, the son's wife, and their two children (a teenage boy and girl). Rajabhai's son, Ramesh, was anxious that I should meet his father who, although frail, unfailingly worshipped each morning at the domestic shrine that he had erected in his bedroom and spent much of the rest of the day in prayer, meditation, and reading improving tracts. Ramesh claimed that his own knowledge of and fervour for Jainism was a direct result of his father's insistence that, as a young boy in Kenya, he spend an hour or so each day in prayer and study. Ramesh in turn had instilled a similar rigour in his two children (both born in Kenya) and, indeed, the family's ritual and orthopraxic knowledge did seem much deeper than that of others I encountered. Ramesh was one of the key organizers of communal activity in the Leicester Jain Samaj, although he had never held any of the committee posts.

As I say, these examples seem to be exceptions. However, the lack of ascetics in East Africa, while detrimental to traditional or 'orthodox' Jainism, provided a foothold for new religious forms. In particular, the Kanji Swami movement (*panth*) with its anti-ascetic stance and emphasis on education (religious knowledge disseminated through publications of sacred texts and edifying books for children, rather than through the traditional *guru–chela* or teacher–disciple relationship), proved popular with the Oswals, who perhaps felt intimidated by the traditional forms they had apparently ignored previously. Jayantilal, whose experiences in and out of East Africa are recounted above, became a follower of Kanji Swami in East Africa and now worships at the Kanji Panth temple in Jamnagar. The manager of the Digambara Jain Swadhyay Mandir Trust in Songhad (the centre of the Kanji Swami movement in India, from where all literature is disseminated) was, in the early 1980s, a Kenyan-returned Oswal, who claimed, when I spoke to him, to have invested one lakh rupees (about £6,700 at the time) from his East African earnings in the work of the movement.

Of the traditional sects, the various *gaccha*s described in Chapters 2 and 4 devolved into two groups in East Africa—Deravasi (idol-worshipping) and Sthanakavasi (non-idolatrous). This was a development of more importance to the Srimalis than to the Oswals (cf. Chapter 2) and reflected, to some extent, the distribution of the two *jati*s in East Africa (as well, of course, as reflecting the absence of ascetics, to whom *gaccha* is far more pertinent). In Tanzania, for example, some 80 per cent of the Jain population (informants' estimates) were Sthanakavasi, which effectively means all Srimalis, as the Oswals have very few Sthanakavasi adherents, leaving a 20 per cent Oswal Deravasi population. However, the Oswals demanded religious facilities and could afford to pay for them, so a building was erected, paid for by both Oswals and Srimalis, for the joint use of Sthanakavasis and Deravasis. In Uganda, by contrast, where the Oswals were very few, the largely Sthanakavasi Srimalis (many of them the chain-migrated Srimalis from Lalpur, mentioned earlier) erected a large Sthanakavasi *upasraya*. This building also contained a meeting-hall (with a capacity of 500 or so) which was hired out to Hindus and Muslims for marriage and other functions, when not being used by the Jains. An arcade of shops lined the outer walls and these were rented to any trader who applied. Table 5.2 briefly summarizes the position of

TABLE 5.2. *Jain Organization in East Africa*

Country	*Jati*s present	Sects present	Type of organization
Kenya	mostly Oswal some Srimalis	mostly Deravasi some Sthanakavasi some Kanji Panth	Deravasi (separately founded Oswal and Srimali temples)
Uganda	mostly Srimali a very few Oswals	mostly Sthanakavasi	Sthanakavasi (large *upasraya*)
Tanzania	mostly Srimali some Oswals	mostly Sthanakavasi	joint Oswal and Srimali multi-funct-ional building

Jain organizations in East Africa.

It is difficult to assess the importance Jainism had for the Srimalis; they were interested enough to build temples and *upasraya*s in East Africa, but they compromised on many issues also. Many Sthanakavasis adopted practices of idol-worship by creating domestic shrines as their Hindu neighbours did—shrines that devoted as much space to oleographs and small statues of Ambamataji, Jalaram Bapa, and Krishna, as they did to representations of Mahavira or Parsvanath. To the Oswals, however, Jainism offered a legitimation and a sanctification of their status aggrandizement. Not only did they build handsome temples in Mombasa, but they could patronize Jain movements in India such as the Kanji Panth.

Out of Africa

In 1962 Uganda attained independence, followed in 1963 by Kenya and Tanzania (as newly independent Zanzibar joined with independent Tanganyika). Four years later came the first panic exodus to Britain as the rights for non-citizens resident in Kenya were withdrawn, to be followed by the mass expulsion of Ugandan Asians in 1972. The *laissez-faire* immigration policies of successive British governments over the period—allowing each crisis to develop and then reacting belatedly and blindly—caused additional confusion and upset to the immigrants, especially the later ones who had to combat the quota scheme (see, for example, Rees 1982), and the fears expressed by the white population of being 'swamped' only created further tension. Once in Britain, the Asians dispersed to urban areas—primarily Greater London and the Midlands. Some went initially to India on leaving East Africa and then came on to Britain after one or two years to settle with already established relatives. Others, particularly the young, rich, and successful, made attempts to move on to the United States and Canada as quickly as possible. As far as I am able to establish, the Jains' experience of this migration had no outstanding or unique features. The rich and prudent had foreseen a possible transfer to Britain and had planned accordingly; others have used intelligence and luck to regain their previous prosperity and position, while still others remain unemployed and without prospects today, nearly two decades after coming to this country.

Of course, many Asians—and thus Jains—remain in East Africa (mostly in Kenya), though they were badly shocked by the 1982 attempted coup in which many of them found themselves targets. I was working with the Leicester Jains as news of the coup came through and their reactions to it perhaps served to increase their nostalgia (and consequently my perceptions) of a peaceful East Africa of the past, and to highlight the distaste some of them felt (metaphorically and literally) of life in Britain.

PART II
ENGLAND

(12)

6

The City of Leicester:
Its Jain Inhabitants

Leicester is a compact city in the Midlands, with a population of 276,000 (1981 Census). There has been a slight decline in the city's population over the last ten years due to a migration, felt in all British cities, away from the inner city to the suburbs. According to a pamphlet issued by the city council (LCC 1981) the site of the city had been continuously occupied since the first century AD when the Romans established a garrison town on the Fosse Way. From as early as 1700 the city has had a predominance of small-scale industries, mostly in the textile, hosiery, and footwear sectors; Leicester's development as a manufacturing centre during the Industrial Revolution was unusual in that it occurred without the use of conventional power-

driven machinery. Instead the 'stocking frame' device was used which mechanically multiplied a worker's labour power. Because there was no need for clustering around an energy source, small-scale family businesses developed, rather than large factories, and set the pattern for power industrialization in later centuries. The small industries are surviving fairly well in the current economic climate, and indeed new businesses are opening as individuals acquire sufficient capital to buy their first knitting machine and bale of yarn. As elsewhere in the country, however, larger industries are passing through a difficult time, and closures and redundancies are frequent.

Spatially the city is compact, with large areas of parkland and easy access to the surrounding countryside. To the east of the city centre is an area of high-density Victorian and Edwardian housing stock known as Highfields. Prosperous one hundred years ago, it is now a classic zone of transition, populated by students, prostitutes, and ethnic minorities, with a sprinkling of long-term resident white working-class families. Highfields was designated a 'priority zone' by the City Council in the late 1970s and numerous improvements have been made to the housing and the environment. In the late 1960s and early 1970s, however, the area was probably at the low point of its decline and it was here that many of the early Asian migrants initially settled.[1]

Today, however, it has become known as the centre of West Indian culture and it is also the area where most of the Pakistani and Gujarati Muslim mosques are situated. To the east of Highfields, around Spinney Hill Park, lies the area of highest Panjabi concentration and one of the main *gurduara*s. Although many Gujarati Hindus live in these areas, the most popular area among them is Belgrave, north of the city centre. Here, the Belgrave Rd./Melton Rd. shopping area, in decline in the mid-1960s, has been revitalized and now almost every shop is owned and run by Asians. Many of the shops are strictly 'internal', that is they stock goods such as saris or shrine paraphernalia that are of interest only to Asians. Other shops sell items such as fruit and vegetables that are not so exclusive, although because the area is largely Asian residentially (between 20 per cent and 35 per cent of the population) and is used by Asians from other parts of the city, the

[1] There is an added difficulty of terminology in the British context as, of course, many of the 'Asians' I refer to are technically British. To avoid awkward circumlocutions I will continue to refer to 'Asians' and to 'Gujaratis', asking the reader to bear in mind that not only do most people so designated hold British passports but that most children under 20 have been born in this country and may have never seen India. (Nor for that matter may their parents if they themselves were born in East Africa.)

clientele is almost exclusively Asian.[2] In recent years more affluent
Asians have moved to the Rushey Mead housing estate, north of
Belgrave, where the housing stock is newer (ten to fifteen years old)
and the housing density lower. Map 6.1 shows the main areas of high
Gujarati concentration in the city.

Leicester is regarded by Gujaratis in Britain as a resource centre:
many East African Asians who initially settled elsewhere in Britain
later moved to Leicester to join kin and friends (Phillips 1983: 95), and
several Gujaratis I know in other parts of Britain travel to Leicester to
meet kin and friends, and to shop. (Tambs-Lyche (1975: 355)
provides an interesting if, by now, dated perspective on the way various
British towns and cities are 'ranked' by British Gujaratis.) Although in
some streets in Highfields and Belgrave the Asian occupation is as
high as 80 per cent of the residents (Phillips 1983: 90), in 1951 only
638 Asians lived in the city (ibid.: 92). In this decade, large numbers of
West Indians and Panjabis arrived in Leicester, followed a decade later
by some 5,000 of the Kenyan Asian immigrants to Britain. Another
5,000–6,000 Ugandan Asians arrived in 1972, mostly to join kin, and
by the end of the decade a further 5,000 or so Ugandan Asians had
made their way to Leicester from other parts of the country where they
had initially been placed by the Uganda Resettlement Board (ibid.: 96).
The Ugandan expulsion was particularly embarrassing for the
Leicester authorities. Information sent from Kampala in 1972 alerted
the Uganda Resettlement Board to the fact that the majority of those
Ugandan Asians who were asked intended to settle in areas of Britain
where the Board felt 'housing, educational, and social services were
already under severe pressure' (Uganda Resettlement Board 1973: 7).
As a result notices were inserted in the Uganda *Argus* by Leicester City
Council, warning the Asians not to come to Leicester.

A survey by the Leicester Council for Community Relations
(LCCR), using data from the 1981 Census and the 1982 Electoral
Register, estimated the 'ethnic minority' (i.e. non-white) population of
the city to be approximately 20 per cent of the total (some 50,000 to

---

[2] There has been a tendency in the media to popularize the idea of an Asian 'success
story', particularly with regard to small businesses (see, for example, Forester 1978).
Many academics have since disputed this. Cater and Jones for example, in a study of
Asian business men in Bradford, claimed that many of the businesses were 'under-
capitalized and frequently unprofitable, classic cases of the marginal firm' (1978: 81).
They also pointed out that such businesses were usually located in areas of high Asian
population where the ratio of shops to Asian customers was 1:68, as opposed to the
national average of 1:95 (ibid.: 82). See, however, the essays collected in Ward and
Jenkins 1984 and Westwood and Bhachu 1988 for alternative and less-simplistic
assessments of ethnic minority business enterprise.

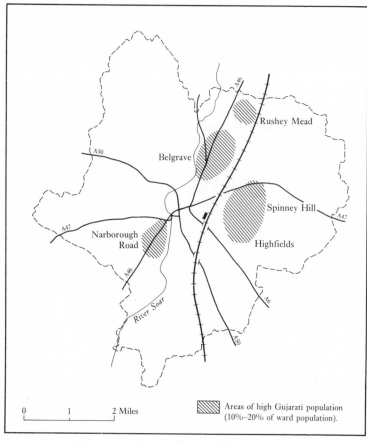

MAP 6.1. Leicester: Gujarati Residence Areas
Source: LCC 1981 and LCCR 1982*a*.

58,000 inhabitants out of a total of 276,245). Gujaratis were thought to make up approximately half of this 'ethnic minority'. Further details are given in Table 6.1.

Although the total number of Leicester residents originating from the New Commonwealth and Pakistan (NCWP) may be as high as 58,000, the 1981 Census gives a figure of 41,459 for those now resident in Leicester who were born in the NCWP (the Census did not ask about ethnic identity, only birthplace, so this figure also includes any white Britons born abroad). The LCCR estimated that 45,000–49,000 of the NCWP population was of Asian origin, while the 1981 Census records only 38,000 (approximately) residents of Leicester

TABLE 6.1. *Leicester: 'Ethnic minority' Population Figures*

	Approximate numbers (000s)	%
Gujaratis	31	57
Panjabis	8	15
Muslims	8	15
Afro-Caribbeans	7	13
(Estimated) Total	±54	100

Note: The 'Muslim' category is the nearest one can get to describing Pakistanis and Bangalis in numerical terms, though the category also includes a few Gujarati Muslims. Otherwise the categories should be taken as a very rough context, to provide a feeling for the balance of the Leicester Asian community.

Source: LCCR 1982a

born in India, East Africa, Pakistan, and Bangladesh. The difference —anything from 7,000 to 11,000—therefore gives some idea of the numbers born in Britain to Asian parents. (Phillips claims that in 1978 births to parents of NCWP origin in Leicester formed 33 per cent of the city's total (1983: 94), while the NWCP population forms only 19.5 per cent of the city's total.)

As mentioned in Chapter 5, it is potentially misleading but occasionally useful to refer to the 'Asian community'. In Leicester, this 'community' is divided in many ways—there are, for example, some eighty Asian organizations in the city, only one or two of which are umbrella bodies, claiming to represent or serve all Asians. In addition there were in 1982 four Asians on the City Council (three Labour and one SDP), although those I spoke to said they specifically avoided being 'Asian representatives'.

A useful analysis of the Asian population is by religion, as religious differences usually correspond to cultural and/or linguistic differences. Thus, akin to the discussion in Chapter 4, I discuss corporately owned Asian religious property in the city as it was in 1982. There are five mosques in the city, catering for Pakistani, Bangali, and Gujarati Muslims, as well as a centre for the Ismailis and a research centre, the Islamic Foundation. With the exception of these last two, all the mosques are situated in the Highfields area of the city and gradually the indigenous population and initial non-Muslim Asian migrants are being replaced by the city's Muslims.[3]

[3] Detailed population density maps for many of the ethnic and religious minorities in the city were published by the LCCR (1982b) but are doubtless now out of date. They are reproduced, with additions, in Phillips's thesis (1983: Figs. 3.2–3.8, pp. 110–22).

Three *gurduara*s cater for the Sikhs, the major one (a converted factory) being situated in the Spinney Hills area. The city's Hindus have now largely settled in Belgrave and it is here that the largest Hindu temple, Sanatan Mandir (opened in 1971), and one of the smaller ones, are situated. The first temple in the city—Hindu Mandir, in Cromford St—was opened in 1969.

There were in 1982 four Hindu temples, the largest being the Sanatan ('eternal' or 'universal tradition') temple which has Radha and Krishna as its main images. There are also two additional shrines, both fairly large, one for Shiva and one for Jagadamba-mata, a form of the mother goddess. Smaller images (Hanuman, Ganesh) are placed at the foot of the main images. The other three temples are dedicated to Radha and Krishna (Hindu Mandir), the mother goddess (Shakti Mandir), and Jalaram Bapa—a nineteenth-century Saurashtran saint associated with Rama.[4]

All the temples have an 'open' policy of admitting anyone, regardless of ethnic or *jati* origin. The four temples have a 'core' of regular attenders, although there are always casual visitors dropping in for the evening *puja* or to attend the major festivals. I never saw another white English person in any of the temples although I heard several stories— all second- or third-hand—of white Leicester residents who had 'converted' to Hinduism, or who had been 'adopted' by Gujarati neighbours. Affiliation to any one particular temple seems to rest as much on personal preference and residence as on any theological criteria. Map 6.2 shows the location of all the mosques, temples, and *gurduara*s. In addition, the Jain Centre and the Swaminarayan Centre (both discussed below) are marked.

The Swaminarayan Centre and temple are situated in the centre of town, in the old Trade Hall. As elsewhere, the Swaminarayans are highly organized in Leicester, although there are casual visitors to the temple (R. B. Williams gives further details of the Swaminarayans in Britain (1984: 186–93); the Leicester temple is associated with the Ahmedabad 'diocese'). There are also numerous Hindu worship circles, which meet in private homes. Many of these are popular with women and provide a reason and a legitimation for older women to gather together.

Literature on the Asians in East Africa (for example, Bharati 1965),

---

[4] Although important in Saurashtra, especially to Lohanas, Jalaram Bapa is little known outside the area. The only documentation of the sect that I know of is based on a study of the Leicester temple (Sapsford 1980).

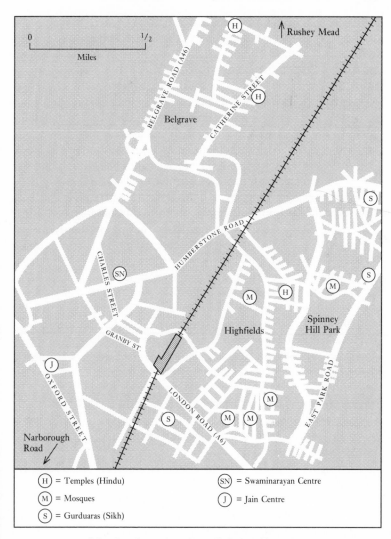

MAP 6.2. Leicester: Asian Religious Property

has shown that there was a break with traditional and textual Indian Hinduism. Hindu religious ideology in East Africa, lacking its infrastructure, brought to the fore the unassailable doctrine of *bhakti*— the right of every individual to meet with and satisfy his or her god. In Leicester, twice removed from context, this has led to a casual approach to religious practice, and rituals are generally simple and arranged around the commitments of the British working week. Some Hindus feel shamed by the religious organization of the Muslims, especially in their provision of religious teaching for the young, and are aware that their own young people show little interest in the beliefs of their parents. However, despite the current anomie of Hindu religious practice, social customs and morality have retained their traditional intensity and pervasiveness. In part this is again attributable to the experience in East Africa where the strict racial segregation was found —in their own eyes at least—to be beneficial to both Europeans and Asians. For all groups, the mosque, temple or *gurduara* serves a social as well as a religious function, and thus great care is taken in choosing a location. The majority of temples and mosques have opened in the last fifteen years or so, the 'congregation' having previously met in people's homes. The City Council has tried to be fair in granting permission to convert buildings to places of worship (of all the Asian religious buildings in 1982 only one, a mosque, was purpose-built), but there have been complaints in the past from local (white) residents angered at the alleged noise, crowds, and traffic congestion (see for example the *Leicester Mercury* 5 November 74; 12 January 78; 24 June 81). Ideally the Council would like the groups to use disused churches, but as there are few available (and in one case permission was refused by the Bishop), the Council is forced to compromise. Leicester City Council laid down numerous guide-lines and regulations in the 1970s (see LCC n.d.*a* and n.d.*b*) which were later revised (LCC 1981: 54). The guide-lines are, of course, for all places of worship, but as most Christian congregations are established, they really only affect the Asian groups.

Three of the Hindu temples are converted churches which are fairly well suited to the new use although, being located in areas of dense population, parking still remains a problem at major festivals. All the temples remain, apart from a small sign (in English and sometimes also in Gujarati or Hindi), entirely unaltered on the outside, making it possible to miss them altogether. The Muslims, on the other hand, have tended to refurbish the façades of their mosques (generally converted houses) and to erect large signs. The Sikh *gurduaras* (two houses and a disused factory) fall between the two in terms of public visibility: generally unostentatious exteriors, surmounted by their sacred flag. The Jain Centre, which will be discussed in greater detail later in this chapter, is a converted church, unadorned at the time of my fieldwork. There were plans, however, to erect an elaborate marble façade and make it, among other things, a tourist attraction for Leicester (*Leicester Mercury* 24 November 83).[5] As will be discussed in this chapter and in Chapters 7 and 8, the 'public face' that the Jains present is an important issue.

'Indian' or 'African'?

Before leaving the general issue of Asians in Leicester to focus on the Jains, I should perhaps make a brief comment on the 'Indian'–'African' divide. Several authors have pointed out that it is not simply enough to distinguish between the various groups that constitute the Asian 'community' (in Leicester and elsewhere) on the basis of religion, language, or *jati*, but to examine whether the subjects in question have migrated directly to Britain from India, or whether they have come from East Africa (see, for example, Tambs-Lyche 1975). Of course there are further refinements: Phillips, for example, found a difference between the housing constraints on Kenyan Asians and Ugandan Asians, the Ugandans being more likely to rent property (1981: 108). Work on the 'Indian'–'African' issue has so far concentrated on the idea of 'assimilation' (for example, Robinson 1982; Patel 1971), although the liberal melting-pot theories have little currency in the field of British race relations today. More recent work, however, is exploring the political implications of the issue, particularly the differential strategies of 'Indian' and 'African' halves of the same *jati* (see, for example, Eriksson 1984). In fact the vast majority of the Visa Srimalis and Halari Visa Oswals (referred to from now on simply as Srimalis and Oswals) I worked with in Leicester had come from East Africa, and other differences I shall discuss in this chapter and in Chapter 8 for the most part overrode the 'continental divide'. Indeed, the matter is by no means so clear-cut—while individuals may have a clearly identifiable 'Indian' or 'African' strand to their identity, they may be members of larger kin groups which combine both. Indeed, significant experiences in both countries may be equally strong, as with the example of Jayantilal given in the last chapter. However, while Jayantilal ultimately returned to India, others stayed on in England. Although much of the remainder of this chapter is concerned with the Srimali Jains of Leicester, I will conclude this section with the example

[5] This façade has since been constructed together with an elaborate reconstruction of the interior.

of another Oswal individual, Mansukh Shah, the elder brother of Rajesh Shah who was discussed in Chapter 2.

As mentioned in Chapter 2, Mansukh and Rajesh are the youngest of five brothers, one already dead when I met the family. The middle three brothers had made a career of Kenya, while the eldest and youngest (Rajesh) had stayed for only a few years and then returned to India. Mansukh had been in partnership with his brothers in a wholesale clothing enterprise, but they had bought him out shortly before he left Kenya, after a dispute. Mansukh was the only one of the brothers to contemplate moving to England, although the eldest, Ramniklal, paid a visit after I left Leicester.

Unsure of what to do with himself, a wife, and three children (all of school age), Mansukh used his small amount of capital to buy a house on the new Rushey Mead estate and embarked on ten years of part-time and short-term jobs in factories and warehouses. His wife, Nita, also worked occasionally during this period and together they brought in enough money to pay the small mortgage and to run a car. Mansukh spent a lot of time on Jain activities and was one of the initial founders of the Jain Samaj (discussed below) and, after the Leicester Oswals withdrew from the Samaj (also discussed below), he was one of the very few who maintained contact, attending most of the major functions. He was also involved in the local branch of the Oswal Association (see below).

By 1980 Mansukh was working in a textile warehouse and Nita had a machinist's job with a local knitwear firm. Both were earning fairly good wages and, during my fieldwork, they decided to give up work and start a shop. Both their sons had left school by this time, one having married and moved away, the other working for British Telecom, on a wage that would support a wife when he married. Nita and Mansukh had saved not only the start-up capital for the shop (to be supplemented by a bank loan) but also enough money (about £2,000) for their daughter's eventual wedding. Their aim was a Post Office, a popular choice with many Gujaratis, for it combines a guaranteed income with scope for entrepreneurial activity. Eventually they found one for sale in a small side street at the very end of Melton Road, the continuation of Belgrave Road. It had been owned by an elderly English woman and was small and fairly run down. It was, however, all that Nita and Mansukh could afford.

They kept the Post Office for two years and lost most of their savings. This was not due to any failure of entrepreneurship—except possibly in the choice of location—for they had diversified the non-Post Office sales into a typical array of essential and quotidian provisions: newspapers, cigarettes, sweets, basic canned food, shoe-laces, and such like. What broke the business were two break-ins, after the first of which they could no longer afford full insurance cover with the increase in premiums demanded. After the second break-in, they sold up and went back to factory work.

Of course, Mansukh's story is not typical—there are many Gujaratis of his age who have established thriving concerns and many more who manage to keep their commercial enterprises afloat, if only just. But neither is it unique; I met several men, Srimali and Oswal, who had set up and then abandoned small businesses (shops and Post Offices, knitting workshops, catering businesses) and several more who had considered the idea but lacked the necessary capital. From what I heard from my friends and informants and read in the newspaper archives, Melton Road and Belgrave Road had been abandoned as centres of trade by the local white population in the sixties, yet today they thrive under the Gujarati influence. The problem is that there are more Gujaratis than shops.

The Srimali Jains of Leicester

Probably the first Jains in Britain were the (Halari Visa) Oswals, who began to take up residence in the early 1960s, coming in the most part directly from India (although some were sent from East Africa), for the purposes of business or study. It soon became apparent in the wake of successive crises in the East African countries that the Oswals in East Africa would have to regard England as their new home and, after large numbers came from Kenya, an Oswal Association was established in 1968 which by the early 1980s had approximately 4,050 member families representing some 15,000 Oswals. For reasons which will become apparent below I had far less contact with the Leicester Oswals than with the Srimalis. Consequently, the rest of this chapter (and indeed those that follow it) are largely concerned with the Srimalis; where possible I will make comparisons with the Oswals.

Srimalis began to arrive in large numbers after the East African crises, together with other members of the Navnat. In the early 1980s there were some three or four Navnat-type associations in Britain which were affiliated to a national organization (The National Council of Vanik [i.e. *vania*] Associations) and which represented perhaps some

1,200 individuals. Almost all the Srimalis and Oswals in Britain are Jain. The Oswals are exclusively Deravasi, as are about half the Srimalis, the other half being Sthanakavasi. As I shall discuss below these sectarian differences have little importance in the British context. In addition, there are several families of Jains in Leicester and elsewhere in Britain who are neither Srimali nor Oswal (nor are they necessarily Gujarati). I discount them from all the discussion and analysis below. At the time there were, however, only three pieces of property held by Jain groups in the country. The first is a large country house north of London which was purchased by the Oswals in the late seventies but which had not been developed due to planning difficulties. The second is a house north of Birmingham city centre purchased a little earlier by a group of local Jains (Navnatis, and some non-Gujarati Jains) in collaboration with an American Jain organization (consisting of a few Indian Jains and many white converts) but which now appears to be moribund. That leaves the Leicester Jain Centre, which was the focus of my research and which will be discussed in detail in a later section. In addition there was an (unconsecrated) idol of Mahavira in a Hindu temple in Wellingborough, while various Hindu temples in Leicester (and, I assume, elsewhere) had oleographs of Mahavira or other *tirthankara*s on their walls. The local paper, the *Leicester Mercury*, occasionally carries articles on the activities of the Jain Centre, but otherwise the presence of the Jains has been ignored by the media and, as mentioned earlier, by most academics working with Asians in Britain.

In 1982 there were some one hundred households of Srimalis in Leicester, or about five hundred individuals. In comparison there were only about eighty Oswal households in Leicester—although the larger group nationwide, they claimed to be marginally outnumbered in Leicester by the Srimalis. The Srimalis are not clustered in any one area of Leicester and the distribution patterns given by Phillips (1981: 107) for Gujarati Hindu households in the city (modified from a Leicester Council of Community Relations publication) largely reflect the distribution of the Srimali Jains, although the move away from the Highfields area that she discusses is now almost complete and parallels a similar shift to the Rushey Mead estate. One or two of the Leicester Srimalis are disproportionately wealthy and several are in status occupations (by both British and Asian ranking criteria) such as medicine and law.

Many times during the period of my fieldwork my informants

pointed out that Leicester had become the home of the poorer Asians (that is, those who had not been investing African earnings in Britain and who could not bring any wealth with them when they left Africa). The Srimalis and others in East Africa with capital to invest had gone either to London or Manchester, while the younger professionals had tried to go to the United States or Canada if at all possible. In contrast, Leicester had offered the attraction of easy employment. While some had been able to start their own business (a small shop or light industrial concern) many more of the Srimalis were employed in 'service' occupations. The employment situation in Leicester at this time was particularly suited to the needs of the East African immigrants, offering as it did a large number of low-paid, non-skilled jobs, for which a good command of English was not necessary. Not all the Jains had been self-employed businessmen in East Africa, and on arrival in England many more were obliged to take up 'service' occupations, either clerical or manual. The Leicester Jains generally considered themselves to be the poor relations of Jains in London and Manchester. None the less, over the ten- to fifteen-year period spent in England, some of my informants had accumulated enough capital to open a small shop or other retail business. Table 6.2 gives details of the occupations of 105 Srimali household heads.

Apart from their religion, however, there is little to mark the

TABLE 6.2. *Srimali Jain Household Heads: Occupational Data*

Job Type	Number
Factory Worker	17
Business (shop, etc.)	16
Doctor	3
Other medical	1
Accountant	2
Service and Clerical	
skilled	6
unskilled[1]	10
Unemployed[2]	6
Retired[3]	15
No information	29

[1] The unskilled 'Service' category includes three salesmen (two selling insurance and one selling clothing).

[2] The distinction between 'Unemployed' and 'Retired' is purely on the basis of age, except in two cases where the retired household head is below 65 but is unable to work through ill health.

[3] The 'Retired' category includes two female heads of household who are supported by their children.

Srimalis off from other Gujarati Hindu groups in the city. In terms of diet, clothing, language, aspirations for their children, etc. they are as alike, and yet as internally varied, as the Lohanas or the Patidars: intra-*jati* differences are probably as great as inter-*jati* ones. Some are conservative, some are liberal; some enjoy Western food (usually, but not always, within the bounds of vegetarianism), while others spend a large proportion of the household budget on buying imported vegetables from Africa.

Men, as noted above, follow a wide variety of career patterns and exercise different styles of patriarchal authority within the household. For example, some I knew were insistent that their wives and sons' wives should not work outside the home. Others allowed it for purely economic reasons, while still others seemed to encourage it or jointly ran an enterprise with their wives (such as Mansukh and Nita, described above). Women themselves varied in their attitudes towards life in Britain. Some women stuck resolutely to saris after marriage, whilst others wore Western blouses and skirts (some factories forbid their female workers to wear saris for safety reasons), and so forth. Most spoke English and all the women I knew were anxious that their children should not be disadvantaged by being 'too' Gujarati.

(14)

None the less, they were also concerned that their children should not become entirely divorced from Gujarat and Gujarati life.

The younger generation in Leicester (that is, those who came from East Africa as children) have, where possible, been encouraged to gain further education by their parents: a fact which seems as true for girls as it is for boys. Like their counterparts in Jamnagar the trend is to study a subject with opportunities for entrepreneurial activity. However, while I knew many men in the twenty-five to thirty age-bracket in Jamnagar who held B.Comm. degrees, I only met one or two such graduates in Leicester. Instead, the favoured degrees were those which gave or were equivalent to a professional qualification: accountancy, pharmacy, dentistry, medicine, pathology, etc. The feature all these qualifications have in common is that, while they allow one to find employment fairly easily, this period of employment may be regarded as a stepping-stone to full self-employment in the profession. In East Africa a common trend had been to send one's son or sons to work in the retail or wholesale business of a relative, where they received a minimal wage (or no wage at all, merely board and lodging) but learned enough business practice to set up on their own (note the cases of Charandas and Jayantilal's brother Sanat in the previous chapter). In Britain, the absence of an extensive network of such established relatives, together with free further education and paid, on-the-job, informal business training in one's first place of employment, meant that the professional route to entrepreneurial success became quickly established.

Mahesh Vora (a Srimali) came to England from Uganda in 1972, with his father, mother, and younger brother. His father, Ramjibhai, had been manager of a dry-goods shop in Uganda and had some capital tied up in various ventures and in their home. They lost everything in the exodus, however, and Ramjibhai considered himself lucky to find part-time unskilled work in a factory. Determined that his sons would succeed in England, even if he were too old to do so, he encouraged Mahesh to study as an optician in London, where he lodged with relatives. Once his training was complete, Mahesh returned to Leicester and married Lila, a medical technician and daughter of a friend of Ramjibhai's in Kenya. Mahesh found work with an optician in a nearby town.

While Lila was pregnant with their first child Mahesh would occasionally accompany her to the local health centre for ante-natal check-ups and advice. On one of these visits he noticed that a large room near the entrance was used only for occasional storage purposes and he set about devising a plan to turn it into an optician's shop. The internal door with the rest of the health centre could be blocked off and the window could be enlarged into a door and shop window. The room was large enough to be partitioned to provide a customer area and a consulting cubicle. He wrote first of all to the local Family Practitioners' Association, which advised him to consult with all the opticians in the neighbourhood as they would only consider an application from a consortium. This Mahesh was unwilling to do as it would, to some extent, defeat the purpose of setting up his own business. This was the point at which I got to know him and he asked for my help. I suggested at first that he should simply lease or buy a vacant shop in Leicester or elsewhere, but he—and his family—lacked the capital to do this, estimating that the lease of the health centre room and the necessary alterations would be cheaper. Furthermore, he felt that he had spotted an ideal 'niche', a location removed from most other commercial premises (and thus competition) and yet one in which people were already predisposed to think about their health. As the health centre ran regular check-up clinics he foresaw the possibility of the GPs eventually passing patients on to him to complete their check-ups.

There then followed several months of letter-writing which revealed an interesting difference in our outlooks. Mahesh had thoroughly researched the (complex) bureaucracy of the local area health authority and drew up for me a flow chart showing the various administrative levels, the interconnections between them and the names of the relevant officials. My advice was to start at the bottom (with the individual GPs at the health centre) and to work his way up. Mahesh, however, was in favour of starting at the very top, with the senior administrator in the area health authority. I felt that he would be too important a man to take any trouble over such a matter and would simply send the letter down to a junior. This, said Mahesh, was precisely the point: a letter travelling down from the top official would carry the weight of his authority with it, in the way that a letter percolating up from the bottom would not.

In the end, the proposal failed; not, I think, because of any problem with Mahesh and his suitability, but simply because, before the Thatcherite restructuring of the NHS got under way, it was administratively and bureaucratically too outlandish for those involved to consider such an unprecedented commercial use of such property.

However, although ultimately a failure, Mahesh's case does indicate a sophisticated assimilation of local circumstances and imported initiative.

To turn away now from a discussion of the Leicester Srimalis in terms of their housing, occupations, household structure and composition, educational level, and so on, I wish to focus on the notion of a more general—and shared—Srimali identity. This is done by examining the institution to which they all belong.

The Jain Samaj (Europe), Leicester

The full title as given above is somewhat cumbersome (an explanation of it is given below) and I shall refer to it as the Jain Samaj, as did all my informants. The Samaj was founded in 1973 with the dual purpose of being a social and religious organization. It was founded jointly by the Oswals and the Srimalis, although much of the initial impetus came from the Srimalis as the Oswals already had their national organization (mentioned above), which served their social purposes if not their religious ones.[6]

The initial membership was low—some 200 individuals—but grew gradually as all the Jains in Leicester were contacted, especially those recently arrived from Uganda. As the scale of the projects envisaged by the Samaj grew, members were attracted from all over the country, as well as abroad (principally Srimalis and others in the Benelux countries, involved in—amongst other things—the international gem trade). In 1982 the membership totalled some 200 families in the UK and a further fifty abroad. Prior to the formation of the Samaj, the Leicester Srimalis had maintained informal contacts with each other, based on their contacts in East Africa. Young couples with children had gone out together in small groups for picnics at local beauty spots, older retired or unemployed men had met together in the afternoons to play cards. Some of my informants spoke nostalgically of those days—hardly so very long ago—as their English counterparts might fondly remember the days of home entertainment before the advent of television. Now, they said, things were structured and organized in the Jain Samaj, with big functions for many people. Of course, informal activities still continued, but with only a limited amount of free time in

---

[6] The national Oswal Association had an informal start in 1967, and became fully bureaucratized as a registered charity in 1974, when regional committees were established.

the week it was deemed easier to attend those functions that were already pre-arranged.

The founding of the Samaj was the first time that the Srimalis and the Oswals—the two largest Jain *jati*s in both East Africa and in the Jamnagar region—had ever formally co-operated in such a venture and, given the degree of latent animosity between the two groups in East Africa and India (or rather, that between Halari Oswals and other Jain *jati*s in the region, not specifically the Srimalis), it is not really surprising that the alliance between Leicester Oswals and Leicester Srimalis disintegrated some four years later.

As it was related to me by Srimali informants, the scene of the argument that led to disintegration was, ironically, the Swami Vatsalyan Bhojan, or feast of affection, which is held each year after Paryushan, the principal Jain festival. The cause of the argument were some *ladu*s (sweet balls) provided by the Oswals which some prominent Srimalis criticized as substandard. (Compare the stories of Srimali–Oswal tension at feasts related in Chapter 4.) However, it would be wrong to make too much of this antagonism. By the time I was working in Jamnagar, relations between the two *jati*s were cool but not hostile: members of each *jati* had their own clearly separate occupational and residential domains and organized their religious functions entirely separately. Neither *jati* made any demands on the other. At an individual level I encountered several friendships and occasional instances of business partnership. In Leicester—where the city was, in a sense, pre-structured—Oswals and Srimalis, together with all the other Gujarati, Panjabi, etc. migrants, had to fit in as best they could. Business opportunities had to be seized as they arose, as did housing choices. Although I tried, I could see no way in which the Oswals or the Srimalis had made any kind of corporate impact upon the city or displayed any kind of epiphenomenal corporate structures except, of course, in their capacity as Jains.

Thus, a joint Jain venture was embarked upon, but quickly foundered. However, due mainly to dedicated public-relations work by certain leading Srimalis, the Jain Samaj in Leicester kept the support of Oswals in London and abroad. After the Leicester split, the Srimalis kept the name of the Samaj and began to consolidate their position as the true representatives of Jainism in this country. This support was necessary for attracting finance from other sources. (The first major step towards this goal was the purchase of a building for the use of the Samaj, discussed later.) During the period of the alliance, however, there was a common religious identity shared and perceived by both groups. Religious functions were held in hired halls—the high point of each year being Paryushan—and a school was established for the young people by one of the Srimali founders of the Samaj and a prominent Oswal. The school was held for a couple of hours on a Sunday morning in the home of one of the organizers. There the children were taught to memorize the basic Jain *mantra*s and recitations, and given simple explanations as to their meaning. (Schools like this—*pathsala*s—are held daily in Jamnagar.)

Even during this period of alliance, the constitution of the Samaj was challenged by other members of the Navnat, the group of trading *jati*s to which the Srimalis belonged, the challenge being one more reason for the alliance to dissolve. One or two of the Navnat *jati*s have Jain members (one or two of whom had become members of the Samaj) and the Navnatis felt that it was socially divisive to have a religiously exclusive body such as the Jain Samaj. Resentment was probably also felt at the alliance of the Srimalis ('true' *vania*s and the most affluent member of the Navnat through sheer force of numbers), with the equally, or more, affluent but ambiguously *vania* Halari Oswals.

Eventually a Navnat-type organization was formed (the Midland Vanik [i.e. *vania*] Association) which the Srimalis later joined as 'The Jain Samaj' after this body had ceased to include Oswals. Religious organizations are not unknown in the Leicester Asian 'community'— they are characteristic of Muslim and Sikh groups for example—and several Hindu temples and religious groups are caste-cutting in their attendance. The problems of the Jain Samaj—the tensions between Srimalis, Oswals, and Navnatis—stemmed, however, from the following factors: first, the Samaj was formed from the alliance of only two *jati*s and this alliance moreover had no meaning or significance outside the shared religious identity;[7] and secondly, despite what the Jains might say, their religion functions as an exclusive ascriptive tradition. Although they can freely enter Hindu temples in Leicester (and do), their ceremonies and communal events during the period of alliance (and in their Centre later on) were sufficiently esoteric (the *pratikramana* 'confession', for example) to discourage casual visitors.

[7] Muslim and Sikh groups, beyond a religious identity common to the member individuals, also capitalize on a common linguistic, regional, and cultural identity. Jains, as mentioned above, have little to mark them off, beyond their religious beliefs (which may be vague and unfocused—see Chapter 8), from other Gujarati Hindus.

The last point is equally well true for the Muslim and, to a lesser extent, Sikh groups. The issue is, however, that neither of these groups is thought to be Hindu, nor are they necessarily Gujaratis. The Jains on the other hand are thought to be Hindus (of a type) by other Hindus (and to some extent by themselves) and, perhaps more importantly, they behaved as Hindu *jati*s in East Africa: the Srimalis were involved with the East African Navnat association, while the Oswals had their own Oswal Association.

Contrary to the popular view that while West Indians are assessed as adapting negatively to their environment—evidenced in their (perceived) antisocial behaviour—Asians are seen as indifferent to adaptation, simply seeking like the Chinese to ignore the 'host' population (Watson 1977: 193), I found the ideas of adaptation and assimilation to be of great concern to the Asians I knew. (There may of course be a process of media reinforcement which presents the 'problem' to the Asians in the first place.) I was often asked by Jains and Hindus in Leicester for my opinion on their status within British society: did I think they were 'modern' enough? Did I think there was any chance of their being expelled from Britain as from Uganda? In addition I was asked for my opinion on their effect on British society: did I think more people would become vegetarian in Britain? Did English people enjoy the Hindi movies shown on the television? Admittedly, I was often told by members of the older generation that the 'community' was losing its 'culture' and that too much adaptation was taking place, and that this was undesirable. But despite these fears it would not be true to say that adaptation and assimilation were undiscussed issues in the Srimali (or any other) 'community'. However, before discussing the Srimalis' perceptions further I should briefly comment on the 'cultural' strategies of other Asian groups in the city in the early 1980s.[8]

Immigrants' own perceptions of their adaptation to the British environment is an issue generally not discussed in the literature, most authors preferring to rely on their own 'objective' analyses of marriage patterns, residence changes, and so forth (see, for example, Levine and Nayar 1975; Robinson 1982). It is evident, however, from my own

---

[8] Since I did my fieldwork in Leicester the topography of white–Asian relations in Britain has changed in many complex ways. Obvious new landmarks include the 'race' riots of the early 1980s, the Dewsbury (and other) parents who refused to send their children to Asian majority schools, and the 'Rushdie Affair'. The mapping out of this topography is a complex and subtle affair, however simplified it has become in media presentation, and I feel it is wiser to leave it out of my discussion altogether.

work and that of others who have looked at the religious life of
immigrant Asian communities (Michaelson 1983: 131 and *passim*;
Barot 1973; Jackson 1976) that Asians tend to look to the retention
and transmission of what they term 'culture' as indicative of their
stability in the new environment. Setting aside the easily assessable
components of this 'culture'—principally language, dietary customs,
and marriage arrangements—the Asians are left with the twin
complexes of caste and religion. For some of the Asian groups in
Leicester—the Sikhs, and more especially the Muslims—for whom
caste is of minimal importance, religion becomes the very essence of
their culture, and this is evidenced in the proliferation and sophistication
of their religious activities. While all Asian groups in Britain are aware
of second-generation 'problems'[9] (such as the breakdown in respect of
children for their elders, threatened sexual promiscuity, and the loss of
the mother-tongue), in Leicester it was the Muslims who were in the
forefront of organizing classes and activities for their children; the
second generation was at once contained and protected from the
perceived moral anarchy of British society, while being inculcated in
the religious values that would ensure the continuity of culture. The
Muslims were also the most militant minority in Leicester, threatening
to boycott, for example, two single-sex schools that were planning to
unite (*Leicester Mercury*, 3 February 80). Sikh and Muslim provision
was frequently cited to me as exemplary of the path that all immigrants
in Britain should be taking. Hindus in Leicester, lacking a paramount
textual basis to their religion, and not being divided radically by sect
(unlike the Muslims) tended to identify their 'culture' with the
ideology of caste and the practices of their own *jati*; thus, religious
festivals were often orchestrated within the framework of *jati*.

In 1978 Leicester City Council compiled a list of all the Asian
organizations the Council was aware of in the city.[10] While undoubtedly
incomplete, and certainly inaccurate on some points, it does reveal
some interesting trends and help us 'place' the Jains by revealing the

[9] While 'second generation' is usually meant to denote those children born to
immigrant parents in the 'host' country, I use it here more generally to include children
socialized in Britain, many of whom are now of a marriageable age. As with white–Asian
relations, one should be wary of any single assessment of first generation–second
generation 'problems'. Certainly to see the second generation as 'trapped' between 'two
cultures' is reductive and unhelpful.

[10] This list was unpublished and the copy I saw much amended. For this reason I
have not referenced it (as I have not referenced numerous other memos, letters, lists,
small circulation newsletters and the like that I had access to in both Jamnagar and
Leicester).

range of cultural and organizational choices that had been taken by sections of the Asian population. Out of the seventy-nine organizations listed, more than half (fifty-six) are Gujarati Hindu organizations including the Jain Samaj and the local branch of the Oswal Association. The remainder comprises eleven Muslim organizations, nine Sikh organizations, and three Bangladeshi organizations. Of the fifty-six Hindu groups at least thirty-one are *jati* organizations. More than one of these may represent the same *jati* (for example, the Limbachias and the Lohanas both have 'welfare' organizations as well as the regular *jati* body), and similarly one organization may represent several *jati*s. Apart from the specifically *jati* organizations there are ten Hindu groups which I classify as religious (mostly temple committees and worship circles), and fifteen cultural organizations (such as the Indian Art Circle and the Old Asian People's Association). The management of and recruitment to these non-*jati* groups may or may not be along *jati* lines—it is very difficult to tell—but it is certainly clear that groups which do recruit along *jati* lines (and which may indeed have religious and cultural functions) are predominant among Leicester Gujarati Hindus. By contrast, the eleven Muslim groups are, as far as I can tell, exclusively religious, as are six of the nine Sikh organizations (by this I mean that their primary aim seems to be to organize religious functions, administer religious property, or to disseminate knowledge about the religion; they are not concerned with burial, 'welfare', rotating credit, or youth clubs). There may of course be other lines of division within these communities in lieu of *jati* divisions—linguistic–regional divisions amongst Muslims, for example —but such divisions are not perceived by the Gujarati Hindus. Many times during my fieldwork Hindus and Jains referred to the Muslims and Sikhs as monolithic entities, their members united by their religion. The Leicester Jains, both Oswal and Srimali, therefore fall between these two poles, having both a distinct (if weak) religious identity, and separate *jati*-based identities.

Thus while the Sikhs and Muslims had tight, culturally educative organizations (all the mosques held classes for children, and some held them for adults also), the Hindus had formed *jati* bodies which organized 'passive' cultural events (music and dance evenings being the most popular) and acted as marriage-forums.

The temples provided inter-*jati* religious functions but little or no education. Nor was attendance particularly high, except at major festivals. There seemed to be few formal attempts by the Leicester

(15)

Hindus to reify a Hindu culture in the way that Sikhs and Muslims were seen (by the Hindus and Jains at least) to be doing, although of course parents might informally socialize their children in Hindu orthopraxy and in the particular manners and customs that were felt to be distinctive of their own *jati* (these often involve food preparation; on several occasions I was told that inter-*jati* marriages were not really feasible because the incoming bride would not prepare food to the taste of the groom and his family).[11] Thus the Jain Samaj was seen by

[11] I met similar arguments in India but simply did not eat in enough different homes to judge the validity of this claim—certainly there was variation (though not very much) but this was as much intra-*jati* as inter-*jati*. It might be interesting to speculate whether

both Jains and Hindus as being a religious body analogous to Sikh and Muslim groups, and, because of its exclusive nature and close organization, not comparable to Hindu religious groups. The Leicester branch of the Oswal Association, set up after the Oswal–Srimali split, conformed to the 'weak' cultural pattern of the Hindu *jati* associations in Leicester: no formal education for the second generation, religious functions organized on an individualistic basis and poorly attended, the *jati* association acting as a marriage forum and organizing musical and dance evenings sporadically. Yet the majority of my informants (Srimalis as well as Oswals) agreed that the Samaj had been better before the split, that their culture, the loss of which they now feared, had had a better environment in which to survive.

After the withdrawal of the Oswals from the Jain Samaj the Srimalis were left in the curious position of being able to 'choose' a corporate identity: they had been left with the name of the Samaj and had already begun a fund-raising drive (which soon involved the Leicester City Council, the Manpower Services Commission, and the Inner Area Programme) to purchase a property for a religious centre; on the other hand they could not honestly claim to represent all the Jains in Leicester, and they were themselves all of the same *jati*.[12]

Because of this, certain elements within the Srimali *jati*—particularly those in positions of authority—decided to press on with pursuing a religious course, feeling that their commitment to Jainism transcended their *jati*-identity. There are several factors to account for the direction the Samaj took at this point. First, the religious belief and dedication of the leaders, combined with the general apathy of the rest of the Srimalis, became a driving-force for the whole community (cf. Morris 1968: 40). Secondly, although the religious identity had not been strong enough to keep the Srimalis and Oswals together it was sufficient to unite the Srimalis who were otherwise rather disparate in terms of occupation, education, and origins (the elected President in the early eighties was neither Saurashtran nor had he been in East Africa, and hence was in a minority). Thirdly, a religious group was

this argument is the modern, urban vestige of 'traditional' rules of inter-*jati* commensality, or whether this merely seemed the most appropriate way of translating such rules to a foreigner.

[12] In fact some Oswals remain members of the Samaj and occasionally attend religious functions. One of these Oswals told me, however, that he always feels uneasy at such functions, and he and the other Oswal members are all also active members of the Leicester Oswal Association.

more likely to attract funding (especially from outside the Asian 'community') than a 'caste' group. Despite what I have said about Jainism being effectively an exclusive religion, and the prevalence of this belief among non-Jain Gujaratis, the ideology among some Jains is, and was, otherwise. A report in the *Leicester Mercury* (12 November 73) at the time of the Jain Samaj's formation referred to the group as a 'sect' and quoted a spokesman as saying its aims were to 'promote good relations between its members and other communities'. Four years later, after the split with the Oswals and when plans were being made to raise money for a building, another spokesman reported to the *Mercury* (17 September 77): 'Jainism is not a sect or just one more conflicting ideology. It is a way of thinking and living.' The 1973 statement reflected the view of the Srimali–Oswal alliance as a 'community', albeit a religious one, and therefore bounded. The 1977 statement in contrast indicated a much more 'open' position, pushing the fact of the almost exclusively Srimali membership into the background.

In 1978 a disused Congregational chapel in the centre of Leicester was purchased by the Samaj, at a cost of £41,000, to become the Jain Centre. Initially this was used simply in lieu of hired halls, for religious and social functions (dance competitions, marriage functions) and available for hire to non-members as well as members (although non-members paid considerably more). Money for the project was raised by a system of membership and patronage which drew donations from Leicester, other parts of England, and India, and successful applications were made to various local and central government bodies. The Jain Samaj had been formally constituted from before this time—that is, there was an elected committee consisting of President, Vice-President, Treasurer, etc.—and members had 'joined' the Samaj by paying a small annual fee (much in the same way that members of a *jati* in India 'join' the *jati* as a formal body by paying a small fee—cf. Chapter 2). However, once the fund-raising drive was under way and after the building was purchased, what had previously been formal roles of authority, now became infused with some degree of tangible power. Others (for example, the contributors to Werbner and Anwar 1991) have noted the prevalence with which elaborate committee structures and other bureaucratic trappings are established amongst minority migrant groups; however, as the Jain/Srimali case shows, to see these in a narrowly synchronic perspective as purely 'empty' structures or as solely 'symbolic' is to miss the point that they may be imbued at some future time with very real political force.

The ex-church which became the Jain Centre is a large building, although closed in on all sides by warehouses and offices. At the time of purchase there were two main auditoria and a number of smaller rooms, as well as facilities such as store rooms and a kitchen. Over the years that followed a balcony around the main chapel was roofed over providing two large spaces one above the other, the upper half becoming the temple (discussed further below). At the time of my fieldwork, however, the temple was located in a small room on the existing first floor; the large areas (including the old chapel) were used for meetings and the other, smaller rooms served as offices and store rooms. The use of the internal space did not present many problems to the Samaj—it functioned well as it was, although it is now more convenient since it has been refurbished. The external space provided problems, however, and these are more or less insurmountable. There is no room for car parking at the Centre itself and located as it is, in the heart of the city's business district, there is little parking space nearby.

Between July 1978 and June 1982 over £12,000 was raised in membership fees (including patronage). Over the same period, some £86,000 was raised by appeal for the building fund (intended to cover the costs of purchasing and refurbishing the Centre).[13]

Although most of the Samaj's members made gifts to the Centre over and above the price of the membership fee, gifts were also made by interested groups and individuals who approved of the Samaj's stated aims (these include the propagation of Jainism in Britain and research into the religion, together with more social aims, such as the development of recreation and child-care facilities), but were not directly involved. One typical example is the gift of the Centre's temple

---

[13] At the formation of the Samaj in 1973 ordinary membership cost £0.50 a year, life-membership £25, while to become a Patron cost £50 or over. (Patronage automatically confers life-membership. In addition the names of Patrons will in due course be prominently displayed in some part of the Jain Centre.) After the purchase of the building (and the consequent high costs envisaged for the future), ordinary membership increased to £1, life-membership rose to £100, while the cost of becoming a Patron stood at anything over £1,000. In fact, most of the ordinary members of the Samaj contributed more than the minimum £1, either by making gifts during the year on auspicious occasions (personal or public), or by responding to particular appeals. In 1979, a year after the project had started, Leicester Jains had contributed a little less than one-third of the total sum in the building fund (£12,600 of £43,600). A slightly smaller sum had been contributed by Jains in London—mostly Oswals—(£11,700) and a slightly larger amount by a small but wealthy group of Srimali diamond merchants in the Netherlands (£15,200).

by Jains in India, mentioned below. Various Asian-owned shops in Leicester also made gifts. After the acquisition of the Centre, the leadership made repeated attempts to obtain grants for refurbishment from local and central government. By the end of my fieldwork period, at least three of these applications had been successful: a grant each from the Manpower Services Commission, the Inner Area Programme (designed to help the regeneration of inner-city areas), and the Leicester City Council. In total these grants were worth some £75,000. Unlike the gifts mentioned above, these solicited grants had to be used for the specific projects outlined in the application—an application to provide new kitchens, for example, was granted because at the time of application there was a scheme (since abandoned, though it is not clear how serious it was in the first place) to turn part of the Centre into a drop-in centre for the unemployed. That the Samaj received these grants is a measure of its success *vis-à-vis* other Asian groups in the city.

The Leicester Jain Centre differs from most other Asian communal and religious property used or owned by Asians in Leicester in being situated in the city centre, away from residential areas. Thus possible objections from local white residents (excessive noise, for example) were not encountered, though car parking facilities (the other problem area defined by the City Council) were scarce, as mentioned above. As a consequence of its situation, however, few Jains in Leicester were able to reach the Centre easily; programmes had to be carefully structured and some degree of co-operation between the members was necessary to provide transport. Owning property at once focused the attentions of the Samaj and placed it in a position of potential power within the Leicester Asian 'community'. Not only did the Jain Samaj no longer have to compete with other groups for hired property and facilities at key times of the year (Divali for example), it was (in 1982) able to hire out its own property, when not needed for Samaj functions. At the same time, the way the property was managed, and the uses to which it was put, became of great importance to the Samaj members and provided a framework for some degree of internal factionalism.

The importance of corporate property ownership for Asian, and particularly Hindu groups in Britain cannot be overstressed. (The *Leicester Mercury* regularly carried stories of lock-outs at Hindu temples and other properties by rival factions, together with reports of claims that elections to boards of trustees were invalid or illegal. See, for example, 4 and 6 October 73). Unable to enter and dominate the economic sector of the country as they did in East Africa, and hindered in many ways from pursuing their own political and social organization, still less imposing it on the majority population,[14] absence or presence of property, and the functions held there, provide an alternative arena for corporate action and competition by the Asian 'community'. In this respect, however, the internal bureaucracy of the Jain Samaj proved remarkably trouble-free (see Banks 1991 for a much more detailed discussion of this bureaucracy).

Between 1978 and 1983 minor alterations were made inside the Jain Centre to render it more suitable for the Jains' use. In particular a room was sound-proofed and carpeted, to act as a temple, prior to the completion of the main temple. In addition, the kitchen was modernized and enlarged, and a platform-cum-stage erected in place of the organ in the main body of the chapel. In 1982 smaller gatherings and rituals took place in the temple room, larger ones in the upstairs hall (which was carpeted and without chairs), and large or formal functions in the main meeting-hall.

In 1980 a more ambitious project was embarked upon which involved a partial reconciliation of the Oswals and Srimalis. Various Oswal and Srimali leaders and representatives from London and Leicester met in London and decided, after some argument, that the Leicester Jain Centre should be a place of meeting for all Jains, irrespective of *jati*, origin, or residence, and that the name of the Samaj should be changed to 'Jain Samaj (Europe), Leicester'. In short this 'success' for the Srimalis (or at least their leaders) rested on the fact that the Srimalis were the only Jain group in the country with any viable property,[15] and, moreover, that the Srimalis had proved remarkably successful at attracting finance. This success it should be

---

[14] As a somewhat peripheral example I cite the case, reported in the *Leicester Mercury*, of a Hindu priest in a nearby town who was gaoled for trying to coerce a Hindu girl who had been raped and who had reported the incident into writing a letter to the police, retracting her previous statement and explaining that the incident took place of her own free will. The priest's argument (implied in the *Mercury* and expanded for me by Asian friends) was that the Asian 'community' should manage its own affairs and not involve the 'host' society's legal system. The incident, if it came to trial, would cause shame not only to the girl and her family, but to the whole 'community'. As a priest he felt himself to be a guardian of morality and wished to suppress this breach of it (*Leicester Mercury* 1 Mar. 80 and 5 Aug. 81).

[15] The Birmingham group, it will be remembered, had only a small house, while the London Oswals had up until then been refused permission to develop their North London estate.

said was largely due to the tireless efforts of the Leicester Samaj's president. In turn, the Srimali leadership had to promise to effect a reconciliation with the Leicester Oswals—a process which, to my knowledge, is still not complete.

The new image and direction of the Samaj expressed itself in part through a new journal, *The Jain*, which replaced *Jain News*, the Samaj's journal from 1977. In contrast to *Jain News* which was cyclostyled, largely in Gujarati, and a vehicle for local news and devotional articles, *The Jain* was professionally printed, had an English section equal to or greater than the Gujarati section, and contained book reviews, glossaries of Jain technical words in Prakrit and Sanskrit, and generally a more academic and educational content. The increased cost of such a publication was met through advertising. At about the same time plans for the use of the Centre were formulated which would involve gutting the building almost completely and reconstructing the interior around an elaborate sandstone and marble temple in a traditional Gujarati style. The total costs involved were estimated at half a million pounds. A large proportion of this (for the temple itself) was to be met by Jains in India. Various plans were also circulating during the period of my fieldwork (and on subsequent visits) for future developments, including building up a library, making the place a centre for international study, and employing a full-time worker to give short courses in Jainism and meditation. All such plans assume a clientele beyond the Leicester Srimali 'community'.

In 1982 the Srimalis were using the Jain Centre regularly (shortly after I finished my fieldwork the refurbishment programme rendered large parts of it unusable). The most frequent activities attracted the smallest numbers, so that the daily worship session was usually limited to three or four elderly men, and the evening worship session sometimes attracted no one at all. By contrast, *samvatsari*, the final night of the Paryushan festival, drew crowds of between two and three hundred.

Every morning, except Sundays, a handful of retired men met at the Centre for an hour or two, to read the Gujarati papers, gossip, and perform a small *puja*. Two or three of the men attended regularly, while others came as circumstances permitted. Three of the men were fathers of committee members; they were relatively wealthy, had been successful business men in East Africa, and made yearly visits to India. In some respects they behaved as community elders, giving advice, informally directing proceedings at the Centre, and occupying the most prominent place at any ceremony or gathering. The morning *puja* was short, and followed the form of the Indian Jain *puja*, adapted to suit the circumstances of the Leicester Jains. The light-waving ceremonies of *arti* and *mangaldivo* (which in India would have been preceded or replaced by anointing the idol; *arti*—with bidding—is generally performed in the evening) were performed, followed by a series of *mantra*s and verses praising the qualities of the *tirthankara*s and confessing sins committed. This was followed by the singing of *stavan*s (devotional songs) taken from various books the Centre had accumulated, and culminating in two Vaishnavite *bhajan*s (devotional songs), one acknowledging the lordship of Krishna, the other praising Vishnu as Lord of the Universe (*'om jaya jagadisha hare'*). The men saw no contradiction in this, though sometimes when women or strangers were present (other members of the Samaj came to the morning worship occasionally if they had a day off work, or had relatives or other visitors staying) the songs were not sung. The Leicester morning *puja* was an abbreviated and somewhat impoverished version of the Jain *puja* in India, or, more specifically, in Jamnagar. There are two reasons for this. First, many Jains at the Centre had little or no experience of *puja* in India and were simply unable to reproduce it in full (this was less true of the women, however). Secondly, the idol in the Leicester temple (of Mahavira) had not at the time been consecrated, and therefore the standard *puja* of anointing (*anga puja*) could not be performed.

Each Sunday afternoon there was a *satsang* ('association of the good'). Once a month this was sponsored by an individual or family who would perform the *arti* and *mangaldivo* ceremony at the end and who provided a snack (*nasto*) for the participants afterwards, typically consisting of small fried items (*cevdo, mamra, ganthiya*) with chutney, a drink—Coca-Cola or orange juice—and possibly some kind of sweet (*penda, jalebi*). The sponsors often took it upon themselves to telephone all their Jain friends and acquaintances and ensure their presence. Afterwards the sponsors would make a contribution (£15 on average in the early eighties) to the Samaj and the work of the Centre. The monthly *satsang* attracted anything from fifty to one hundred people, depending on the status and importance of the sponsors, the type of food they were likely to provide, as well as the weather. The non-sponsored *satsang*s attracted far fewer people, no more than fifteen, and it was typically the same people who came week after week: a group of three interrelated households (the household heads all being in their forties and including Ramesh, who is mentioned in Chapter 5) and some of their closer Jain friends. At all *satsang*s the procedure was the same: after singing or reciting the Naukar *mantra*, *stavan*s were sung for about an hour, individuals choosing their personal favourites by turns. The session concluded with *arti* and *mangaldivo*. The Bagini Kendra ('ladies' circle') was supposed to meet prior to the weekly *satsang*, but as often as not nobody came. The smaller *satsang*s were held in the temple room where the idol was the principle focus. The monthly *satsang* took place in the upstairs meeting-hall where a large painting, depicting Mahavira in meditation, and executed by one of the Samaj's younger members, served as a focus.

Throughout the year there were several annual events—Paryushan, Mahavira Jayanti, Divali—and these generally attracted large numbers. The Paryushan events in particular are described in greater detail in Chapter 7 and their form is similar to that of other annual events.

7

Coming Together in Leicester

In Chapter 3 I gave several examples of the ways in which Jains in Jamnagar 'came together' for festivals, fasts, and feasts. In this chapter I wish to do the same for the Jains of Leicester and it would be satisfying to construct this chapter as an exact parallel to Chapter 3, using the same types of events to draw a series of neat conclusions.

For various reasons this is not possible. First there is the factor of scale: there are far fewer Jains in Leicester than in Jamnagar and hence the range of their activities is far more limited. Moreover, there are only two groups of Jains in Leicester, only one of which I studied in depth, while in Jamnagar there is the whole variety of *jati*, *jati*-sections, and *gaccha* groups discussed in Chapters 2 and 4, each of which organizes its own functions. Secondly, few events in Leicester actually paralleled events in India. Those that did were Paryushan, Mahavira

Jayanti, the evening *arti* ritual, and one or two of the minor *puja*s, such as *snatra puja* (the bathing of a small idol of a *tirthankara*). Other events, such as the *ayambil* fasting, which were celebrated communally in Jamnagar, were observed only by a few individuals in Leicester. Such people (usually women) would gather informally in their homes during the daytime to fast or meditate, in groups of three or four. In Leicester there were no processions, no lavish feasts and few public displays of wealth. Although there was bidding at Paryushan for *arti* and *mangaldivo* (see Banks 1991 for an analysis of this), in general, 'functions' and events had an equalitarian bias to them. Roles and parts were distributed by consensus, and women were more to the fore than in Jamnagar. However, while the relative status positions of ascetic and lay in India are fixed and largely unassailable, tensions did arise between the leaders and the led in the Leicester Samaj. These tensions will be touched on in this chapter, and then explored more fully in the next.

I witnessed several events in Leicester that, in their organization at least, have no parallel in Jamnagar, the sponsored *satsang* being the most obvious example. In some ways the *satsang* does resemble a *bhavana* (or *bhajan*) session in India (a gathering, usually in the evening, to sing devotional songs). But the obvious social aspect of the *satsang* (the food and drink served afterwards, for example) give it a new meaning in Leicester, and some informants told me that the present form of the *satsang* developed in East Africa. Some of the events in Leicester paralleled Jamnagar events in form, however, if not in organization. For example, the series of lectures given by Sri Ananda that are discussed below, are analogous to *vyakhyan* for Jains in India. The contrast is that one was an exceptional event while the other is a daily occurrence.

The discussions in this chapter also differ from those of Chapter 4, in that the events in Leicester are, on the whole, described completely rather than as isolated incidents within a total programme. This is partly because the 'functions' (as they are known) that I witnessed in Leicester were shorter and took place at one location, and partly because the greater range of functions in Jamnagar meant that there was a 'menu' (as I called it) of part-events from which items could be drawn to 'construct' a function, following what I termed the rules of 'social collocation' (a procession, a ritual, and a feast, for example). Such a process enabled both actors and observer to view (and participate in) the function as a set of parts, which was not necessarily the case in Leicester.

Paryushan

Paryushan is the major religious festival of the year for all Jains, both in India and in Leicester. Although it is really a time for extra emphasis on those duties such as fasting, austerities, and 'confession', that should be observed throughout the year, most Jains in India and England seem to view it as a special period during which observance of these duties is necessary rather than merely desirable. That is, they see it as an event which is qualitatively rather than quantitatively different from those private and public observances which occur during the rest of the year.

The eight- to ten-day period of Paryushan (the duration and dates of which vary with sect and *gaccha*) culminates in the ritual of *samvatsari*, the 'annual ceremony of public confession' as P. S. Jaini (1979: 63) translates it, at which an extra long *pratikramana* 'confession' is said. This confession is for the sins of the past year, hence its length (the session itself is called *samvatsari*, but popularly the term refers as well to the day on which it takes place). The Paryushan period is technically constituted by an eight-day period of fasting and austerity (*atthai*) to bring the devotee to a suitable state in which to perform the great confession of *samvatsari*. In practice, however, through a series of feasts in Jamnagar and the exceptional daily communal *pratikramana* in Leicester, the eight-day period is experienced as an event in itself, rather than as the preparation for an event.

In India, the period occurs during *comasun*, the rainy season, when ascetics are resident in a town or village and can guide the laity in their spiritual development. Paryushan is seen as a period of catharsis during which vows of abstinence can be taken, such as abstinence (for the eight days, or for a longer period) from certain foodstuffs, and during which confession can be made for all sins committed during the year. The confession is technically to oneself, through an ascetic as mediator, by which one realizes one's failings, repents of them, and thus frees the soul from the bad *karma*s that have accumulated through evil thoughts, words, and deeds. Confession is made during the said-meditation of *pratikramana* during which various types of sin are enumerated (in a general, not a particular sense) and repented of.[1] The actual text of *pratikramana* is in Prakrit. While the gist of it may be

---

[1] Stevenson (1915: 165–6) makes reference to the ascetics' performance of *pratikramana* although, given her missionary bias, she makes it sound more like a Catholic confession than my experience of it in either India or Leicester.

known to individual Jains in Leicester, I met few who were clear about the meaning of all the verses. Towards the end of the popular editions of the text, however, is a section in the vernacular (the *aticar*, or 'transgressions'), which summarizes the basic theme of repentance (see ibid.: 173). Ideally, *pratikramana* should be said twice daily; failing that it is said once a day (in the evening), on all or some of the auspicious days in the lunar fortnight (the 2nd, 5th, 8th, 11th, and 14th), or at the very least, on *samvatsari*. Some women in Leicester meet together in each other's homes at the end of each lunar fortnight to say *pratikramana* and they may also fast on these days, but the only large-scale communal gathering of the Leicester Srimalis is during Paryushan.

Paryushan in Leicester

The Leicester Srimalis refer to Paryushan as '*pajusan*', which is the original Prakrit term ('Paryushan' being the Sanskrit form; I use this term as it is that which is commonly used in the literature) and began looking forward to it from July or so onwards.

Paryushan in 1982 began on Sunday, 15 August (Shravan *vad* 11 by the Vikram calendar). In India, the Loka Gaccha and the Tapa Gaccha begin the festival one day apart, owing to different calendrical calculations which affect the *pancang* (calendar). This is known to the Leicester Srimalis, several of whom receive *pancang*s from friends or relatives in India. However, the Leicester Srimalis are too few in number to follow this practice and it would be difficult to organize. Nor are there any ascetics to force such adherence. Instead they follow the different starting dates in alternate years, and 1982 was the year for the Tapa Gaccha (Deravasi) dates.

Each day for the eight days two sessions took place in the Jain Centre: a reading from the Kalpa Sutra in the morning, and a session of *pratikramana* followed by communal singing and *arti* in the evening. There were, in addition, one or two afternoon functions. Several Jains I knew took part of their annual leave (if they were employed), during the week in order to be free for the sessions. Many of the older women did not work, and were also able to attend, provided they had access to transport. Schools and colleges were also on vacation at this time, but on the whole there were few young people in attendance. The readings from the Kalpa Sutra followed directly on from the usual morning worship. This posed several problems. In India, an ascetic would read, so the first problem was to choose someone to read from among the Leicester laity.[2]

Charandas, who attends the Centre regularly in the morning, and who is also one of the most senior and respected Srimalis, has agreed to do the readings, and after the first morning (when he was first asked), brings a *dhoti* and *khes* to the Centre every day into which to change for the reading. Unfortunately the structure of the book causes him difficulties from the outset. The edition of the Kalpa Sutra at the Centre is a standard loose-leafed one—the modern equivalent of the ancient palm-leaf manuscripts. Each page measures about 250 cm by 200 cm and is folded in half lengthways, creating four surfaces, each of which is printed with text. It is not readily apparent in which sequence the four surfaces should be read and there is much fumbling and several false starts. Added to this is the difficulty that although the Prakrit text had been translated into Gujarati, the language employed is literary and obscure (or so I was told). A further difficulty is that Charandas and the other men are not very familiar with the Sutra itself and therefore have difficulty not only in following the sequence of events but also in dividing the readings up so that the passage describing Mahavira's birth will fall on the Thursday, which is fixed by the *pancang* (calendar) as *mahavira janma vancan*.[3]

Each morning during Paryushan some eight or nine men and some fifteen or sixteen women assemble in the temple room for the readings. For the first couple of days Charandas tries to encourage some of the other men to share the task, but they find it even more difficult than he. On the first day some discussion takes place as to

---

[2] If I give the impression in this passage that this was the first time the Srimalis had celebrated Paryushan communally, it is because in past years the form had been different, depending on who was available and what the general consensus had been. For example, in 1981 only the passage relating to Mahavira's birth had been read out from the Kalpa Sutra on the appropriate day (*mahavira janma vancan*—lit. 'reading of Mahavira's birth'). See also n. 3, below.

[3] The anniversary of Mahavira's birth, Mahavira Jayanti, is really celebrated in the month of Chaitra which falls around March–April time (see Chap. 3). However, as the birth is narrated in the Kalpa Sutra, which is prescribed reading during Paryushan, the event is celebrated again and known as *mahavira janma vancan*. During the morning *vyakhyan* on this day in India, silver plaques depicting the fourteen auspicious dreams of Trisala, Mahavira's mother, are lowered from the ceiling of the *pathsala* where the reading takes place. The laity bid large sums of money for the honour of garlanding these plaques as they descend.

(17)

whether women should be allowed to read; certainly they seem to have a clearer idea than the men of the sequence of events narrated and they join in loudly during the discussions of this. Eventually it is decided (by the men) that a senior lay man will be the best alternative to an ascetic. For the first couple of readings the women enter the speculation as to which sequence the passages on the loose-leaf pages should follow (these debates occur at the end of almost every quarter page), but as Charandas settles into a rhythm most of the women seem to lose interest in the readings and instead become absorbed in meditation with their beads (*malajapa*). They also read and worship books such as the *Jinendra Darshan Covisi* (which depicts each of the twenty-four *tirthankaras* together with an appropriate *mantra*) or simply gaze around. The men on the whole try to sustain their interest throughout the week, though one or two confided to me afterwards that it had not been easy.

In Leicester, attitudes towards the readings varied considerably. Some people felt that simply listening was virtuous and the correct thing to do during Paryushan, perhaps in the vein of a nominal Christian hearing a Christmas bible reading. Others felt that it was an inspirational exercise, that the issues presented, such as Mahavira's renunciation, or his adoration by the gods, were issues to inspire a greater religiosity in oneself. Charandas gave me his own idiosyncratic version, which was that the readings patterned ideal behaviour for mundane life, such as the proper care of a pregnant woman, or the importance of regular baths and exercise, which was the topic of one morning's reading (Kalpa Sutra: 60–1, 92; Vinayasagar and Lath 1977: 101–5, 139–41).[4] If this was the case, I asked him, why go through all the ceremony of gathering people together to listen, wearing special clothes, not allowing women to recite, instead of just letting people read it for themselves at home; he replied that all the preparations beforehand, the solemnity and formality, served to fix the lesson in one's mind. The readings were generally brief, thirty to forty minutes, and were followed by coffee and social chit-chat.

The evening sessions begin at about 6.30 p.m. and are devoted to the 'confession' of *pratikramana*. Although Sthanakavasis and Deravasis have agreed to begin Paryushan on the same date, their *pratikramana* sessions are held separately, partly because the text and mode of recitation varies to some extent between the two *gaccha*s, and partly because no room in the Centre is large enough to accommodate all the people who wish to perform *pratikramana*. Consequently, Deravasis meet upstairs in the large room next to the temple, while Sthanakavasis meet downstairs in the dining-hall. I sense some resentment among the Sthanakavasis about these arrangements because the dining-hall is the colder and bleaker of the two rooms. Moreover, food should not be consumed in an *upasraya*, which is what the dining-hall effectively becomes for the duration of the meditation.

The *pratikramana* generally lasts about one and a half hours. In both rooms some twelve or thirteen men and thirty to forty women gather each night. Men and women sit separately and each person sits on a small mat, known as a *pathranun*. Some of the men change into *dhoti* and *khes*, and one or two people bring along soft brushes (*rajoharana*—lit. 'dust remover'), looking rather like large dish-mops, with which one is meant to brush the ground before sitting down, although few actually do so. In addition most people bring

---

[4] It will be seen in the next chapter that this kind of interpretation is fully consonant with what I call neo-orthodox belief.

with them a *mala*, a folding reading stand and a handkerchief (Deravasis) or a *muh patti* (Sthanakavasis). Copies of the *pratikramana-sutra* are held by the Centre and are distributed to those without, although several people have their own copy. But for the absence of an ascetic, these preparations are identical to those I will later witness in Jamnagar for the ordinary, daily *pratikramana*.

At one end of each hall, a copy of the *sutra* is placed on a reading-stand and topped with a coiled *mala*. This is to represent the guru or ascetic who would lead the ritual in India (cf. R. H. B. Williams 1963: 102). The meditation is a dialogue between ascetic and laity, interspersed with periods of silent meditation. In Leicester the ascetic's part is shared out amongst the various speakers by Chimanbhai, who assumes the role of organizer. At the beginning of each Deravasi session, for example, a list of the various sections is drawn up and these are then assigned to different people, who read them when their turn comes.

There is not enough space here to present the entire meditation, nor do I have a full translation. The text is in Prakrit and clearly very old, dating at least from the time of the medieval *sravakacara*s. It begins with the words:

WORSHIPPER. Instruct me at my own desire to make *pratikramana* for all that I have done amiss this day in thought, in speech and in act.
GURU. Do so.
WORSHIPPER. May that evil have been done in vain (*micchami dukkadam*).

(R. H. B. Williams 1963: 205)

Several people in Leicester knew the entire meditation by heart and could rattle it off at enormous speed. As it is almost entirely in Prakrit, however, nobody I spoke to knew the entire meaning. With two exceptions the leaders and committee members of the Samaj did not attend *pratikramana* (the two that did were the token 'lady', and the assistant treasurer who was the only Sthanakavasi on the committee). Kesu Jain, the Samaj's president, told me that he did not understand the Prakrit and that he found the formalized gestures that accompany the ritual old-fashioned and pointless.[5] Instead, he preferred to meditate alone on his sins and failings.

[5] These gestures are of two kinds. The first are gestures of obeisance to the *guru* at the points at which he or she gives permission for confession to be made. The second are

The small number of people, and the close participation (in terms of chanting, gestures, and periods of communal silence) made the Leicester *pratikramana* an intense and intimate time for all who participated. One person told me that it was the only thing that Leicester Jains had 'feelings' for. Dark fell as we performed the ritual each evening (the meditation is timed to bridge day and night), and although one or two people used torches to read the text, the atmosphere was one of calm and quietness. However, while the form of the ritual in Leicester is close or identical to its performance in India, the context is not. In India, at the conclusion of the confession the participants walk quietly home (generally no more than a few hundred metres away), and read or talk quietly until they sleep, taking nothing to eat or drink (eating or drinking after dark is considered to be *himsa*—violence). In Leicester, the *pratikramana* was followed by *arti* and singing, after which people drove home by car, turned on electric lights, and perhaps had a late snack.

On the final day, many more people of both sects attend *pratikramana*—well over double the numbers for the Deravasi ritual alone. The parts that have been shared out on previous evenings are now bidded for, most going for £10 or so, the money going into the *arti* fund (see below). At the end of this session the participants greet each other with the phrase '*micchami dukkadam*'—an apology for any evil thought, word, or deed directed at the person over the past year. Men shake each other's hands as they say this, or make *namaskar* (the traditional Indian greeting with hands held together), as do the women. In India, it is traditional on *samvatsari* to send printed 'apology letters' (*samvatsarik ksamapana*), to friends and relatives who live at a distance and many of my informants did this; indeed the following Paryushan I will receive two or three such letters from friends in Leicester while I am working in Jamnagar.

At the conclusion of each day's *pratikramana* session the participants make their way into the main auditorium of the Centre (the old chapel). Several other people, who have not performed *pratikramana*, now join us and most nights the hall is quite full. From 9.00 p.m. *stavan*s are sung, either communally as at the *satsang*s, or by individuals coming to the front and singing into a microphone.

ritualized gestures to free the limbs of any insects that may have alighted on the penitent and may subsequently be crushed by inadvertent movement. Again, Kesu Jain's attitude is indicative of neo-orthodoxy.

The proceedings culminate after an hour or so with the auctioning of *arti* and *mangaldivo*, each of which goes for between £10 and £50 (similar auctioning happens in India; see Chapter 3). These sessions are a curious mixture of business and worship. The committee sit at a table to one side of the stage and process the accounts, update the membership lists, and do other administrative work. Between the *stavan*s, appeals are made by the President for donations, patronage, and applications for life membership. All the paperwork at the table —as indeed all the financial business of the Samaj and the Centre— is conducted in English, as is much of the conversation at the table. In contrast, the 'religious business' that is conducted at the start of each *pratikramana* session (drawing up lists of people to speak the parts, organizing seating arrangements, and so forth) is entirely in Gujarati.

Although more people attend the post-*pratikramana* sessions, the sense of a Turneresque *communitas* seems to be less. In part this is due to the nature of the auditorium—dark, gloomy, and chilly, even in August. The space, designed for Christian ritual, with hard, tiered pews facing a central point, cannot duplicate the intimate grandeur of an Indian Jain temple, or the cool spaciousness of an *upasraya*. One evening the President also complains to me of this lack of enthusiasm, particularly the lack of interest in the bidding for *arti* and *mangaldivo* (which is discussed fully in Banks 1991). His explanation is that he and the committee have worked so hard for the Samaj that the rest of the Srimalis have become complacent.

There is some tension, however, beyond sheer complacency. One evening, for example, the committee arranges for a videotape of Chitrabhanu's speeches to be shown. Chitrabhanu is an ex-ascetic who has married, left India, and now runs an 'International Jain Meditation Centre' in New York. He visited Leicester the previous year at Paryushan and gave a series of talks on his own eclectic brand of Jainism, which had been videotaped by the President on his own equipment. This year *arti* is the final event of each evening and so the videotapes have been scheduled for screening after the *arti* bidding but before the ritual. On the first night this proves unpopular, however, as few people are interested in the taped talk but simply wish to perform the ritual and go home. Eventually the tape is stopped half way through to allow *arti* to take place and then restarted afterwards. A few people stay on, but at the end of the tape there is only myself and a couple of others remaining. In other years the young people have held a session of Gujarati dancing after *arti* and *mangaldivo*, but Chitrabhanu's visit the previous year had prevented this. Although they wish to organize dancing again this year, the committee is reluctant to allow it, feeling that arrangements for musicians would be costly and involve too much organization. They also express an opinion that a solemn period of fasting and austerity is not really an occasion for dancing (although there were apparently no such objections in the years before Chitrabhanu's visit). In consequence the young people mill around aimlessly at the back of the auditorium, unable, some later tell me, to derive much pleasure from the *stavan* singing and speeches.

Paryushan, then, is the main occasion for Jains in Leicester to come together and almost all Srimalis in the city and from surrounding areas try to attend on *samvatsari*, if not on the preceding days. (The Oswals held their own parallel functions in 1982 in one of the city's Hindu temples which they had hired for the occasion.) It is also the main occasion to express solidarity. The Kalpa Sutra readings and the *pratikramana* observances were clearly perceived this way. People arranged to give each other lifts to the Centre (which, as mentioned, was far from most people's homes), and discussed the changes in their domestic arrangements that had to be made in order to attend the sessions. Even despite the slight apathy and tensions I have described, the post-*pratikramana* sessions were more successful in raising funds and encouraging commitment to the Centre than any other meetings in the year. Each evening there was a small but continuous stream of people to the business table, where subscriptions were renewed and donations made. Sometimes the subscriptions were upgraded (say, from ordinary to life-membership) or all the members of a family took out subscriptions in addition to that previously held by the household head.

Education: Learning the Path

During my Leicester fieldwork, while I was most often enquiring about people's occupations or quizzing them on family history, I occasionally asked people to explain an issue within Jainism itself, such as the difference between a *siddha* and a *jina*, or the meaning of the *siddhacakra*. More often than not my informant would give me an apologetic smile and tell me that they did not know, they had never had a chance to study Jainism as I was doing. Moreover, for many, religious commitment rested on knowledge: to be a good Jain one must have read and studied. Although *bhakti* and more extreme forms of ecstatic religion, such as possession, are evidenced within the Leicester Hindu community, and are to some extent practised by the Srimalis, the stress that ascetics in India place on books and learning carried over to Leicester, and caused in some a feeling of inadequacy.

As discussed in the previous chapter, religious education is a field in which Muslim and Sikh groups are thought to take the lead, by providing after-school and weekend classes for their children, on their own religious and other property, devoted to learning prayers and scripture.

During my period of fieldwork in Leicester there was no formal education provided in Jainism for either adults or children. As I discussed in the last chapter, a school had operated for children in the initial Oswal–Srimali Samaj but had become moribund after the split. Chimanbhai, the organizer of the Paryushan *pratikramana* sessions had been one of the school organizers, and told me that he had expected the President and the committee to help organize something in the Centre after its purchase, but they had as yet shown no interest. (Some years later, however, a lay teacher was brought over from India for a year.)

Chimanbhai's 'school' had provided basic instruction in written Gujarati and the elementary tenets of Jainism to some twenty to thirty children between the ages of ten and sixteen on Sunday mornings. The religious content of the Jain school's instruction was taught, in part, through a set of three booklets written by a Gujarati Tapa Gaccha monk (Bhadraguptavijayji) entitled, *Life of Children*, *Fragrance of Children*, and *Thinking of Children* (the booklets were used both in the Gujarati original and in English translation). Each booklet contains a series of short lessons combining practical instruction (the types of offering to be made to the *tirthankara*, for example), prohibitions (on food), and moral instruction, followed by a series of questions on each lesson. The introduction to the English editions states:

Children who have become some sensible, must be alert and Vigilant to keep their morality, religion and spirituality alive . . . You do make these three booklets your bosom friends and these booklets will be better and nobler guide. (Bhadraguptavijayji 1976: 3)

One of the chapters of *Life of Children* (Lesson 5—'Religious School'), makes it clear that such 'schools' are thought to be as important for the inculcation of moral values ('courtesy', 'duties', 'modesty', 'discipline') as they are for religious instruction—that is, specific information about the nature of the *tirthankara*, the meaning of offerings, etc. The teachers at Chimanbhai's school taught the Naukar *mantra* and its meaning, the use of the *mala*, and the various postures for *pratikramana* (small booklets are published in India on such topics and from these various *mantra*s were also taught), but it was less easy for me to discover whether issues of morality—by their nature, more intangible than practical instruction in the use of the *mala*, say—had been discussed. The amount of anxiety I encountered among parents about their children (see below and also compare the contrasting cases of Manilal's and Ramesh's families in Chapter 5) indicated that this was none the less an area of concern.

Apart from the school, the other means of informal religious transmission at the Jain Centre was through visiting speakers. As mentioned earlier, the ex-ascetic Chitrabhanu came to speak at the Centre during Paryushan 1980. This, I was told, had been very popular (even if the talks shown subsequently on videotape were not), partly because he is well known among the Jains, and partly because several Leicester Oswals came and swelled the numbers. (Chitrabhanu had in fact been invited to England from America by the national Oswal Association.)

Just prior to Paryushan 1982, three lectures were given at the Jain Centre by a member of the (Indian) Theosophical Society, Sri Ananda. A man in his sixties, Ananda had been a touring lecturer for the Society and now lectures by invitation all over the world. Although a Theosophist he comes from a Jain background and was a friend of the Samaj's President. The lectures he gave were entitled 'The Search for Health' and were concerned with the importance of attaining one's own spiritual balance within modern industrial society. He indicated that the anomie of Western consumerism and materialism could be redressed by rediscovering spiritual values and absolute standards of morality, in one's attitude to oneself and one's relationships with others. The talks placed no special emphasis on Jainism, though Mahavira's teachings and aspects of Jain philosophy—especially *anekantavada*: the doctrine of multiple viewpoints—were introduced as appropriate. The content, however, was sufficiently general and platitudinous as to be palatable to all but the most sectarian listener.

The talks, which were given in Gujarati, were held on consecutive evenings and lasted thirty minutes or so. The last talk was followed by a short time of questions. Several of these were asked in English, although I was the only non-Asian present, perhaps because it was felt to be more scholarly.[6]

Each evening finds Sri Ananda and his wife, Swartiben, seated on the stage at the dot of 8.00 p.m. People drift in for the next half hour or so, while officials of the Samaj check the tape-recording equipment, adjust microphones, and generally busy themselves. On the first evening I am deputed to take photographs. By 8.45—when the programme finally gets under way—there are about 100 men and women seated expectantly. The events start with Swartiben singing a short devotional song and accompanying herself on a *tambora* (a 'drone' instrument, like a sitar). Ananda then gives his talk which is followed by questions. Swartiben and Ananda remain alone on the stage for the entire evening.

All the questions tend to be fairly general in nature and do not seem to bear specifically on any issue discussed by Ananda. However, several of the questioners phrase their queries within the context of Jainism even though Ananda has not made this a particular focus; for example, one night a friend of mine asks: 'Sometimes you kill an animal unintentionally; what is it that makes one kill? What should one do after the animal is killed? Has Jainism an answer?' In his reply to this question, as in his replies to others, Ananda does not invoke any specifically Jain principles at all. In this instance he declares that the issue of intentionality is irrelevant, all killing is wrong. Moreover, we should not confine the debate to killing but extend it to all forms of harm caused to other beings, be they animals or people. He goes on to quote a verse of Shankaracharya: 'Shankaracharya says happy and unhappy situations will arise . . . accept life as it comes . . . without any regret, without any resistance . . . If you act in the present . . . you can be completely free from what *karma* has generated provided one knows how to respond

---

[6] On a visit to Jamnagar in 1984 I attended some sessions of a (Jain) *sibir*, a week-long religious 'camp' which was organized by a prominent visiting ascetic for adults and children. On one of the days I had not attended some friends, returning from the *sibir* in the evening, told me that another man known to us had stood up and asked the ascetic a question in English. A few other people, after checking that I was not present, called out for the ascetic not to answer him, saying that there was no justification for this, that only one or two people knew English and that he was just showing off.

to situations that come. If you receive gratefully and give to life generously . . . then you will find that *karma* is no bondage whatsoever. You will find yourself completely free from all that you call *karma*.' I quote at length from Ananda's answer to demonstrate how far from 'orthodox' Jain teaching he in fact seems to be. In short, Ananda is advocating involvement in the world to rid oneself of *karma*, while Jainism is predicated on detachment from the world to achieve this. Later I question some teenaged friends as to what they thought the content of the lectures had been, but they are only able to answer in the most general terms: although Sri Ananda is well liked, his message seems hard to contextualize and thus hard to retain.

In India, education in Jainism is achieved through daily instruction at *pathsala*s, parental guidance, and most importantly, guidance by the ascetics, either formally through *vyakhyan* and *sibir*, or informally through discussion in the *upasraya*. This ascetic guidance applies as much to adults (if not more so) as it does to children. The *pathsala* had been tried in Leicester but became a casualty of the Oswal–Srimali split, and ill-feeling between the Srimali teachers and the Srimali leadership seemed to prevent its resurrection. Parental guidance in Leicester was negligible from what I could ascertain. Many of the parental generation who had been socialized in East Africa had received little in the way of formal religious education themselves— perhaps an evening session once a week for a year or so to learn the recitation of basic *mantra*s and to acquire familiarity with some of the story literature. In England these parents were teaching their children what they could remember of this, and familiarizing them with some of the *stavan*s popular in Leicester, and the technicalities of performing *arti* and *mangaldivo*. Others simply relied on the presence of their children at *satsang*s and other gatherings to instil in them the basics of Jainism. The absence of the ascetics was bemoaned widely, particularly because of their knowledge, but also because of the spur to learning they were thought to provide. Some, however, like Jayantilal, the Assistant Secretary of the Samaj, felt that the absence of the ascetics freed the Srimalis from the more old-fashioned and ritualistic side of their religion, leaving them to develop their own path suited to the constraints and demands of the British environment.

Coming together to learn was, therefore, not an established practice in the Leicester Jain community in the early 1980s. In part this seems due to the lack of facilities—no trained and dedicated teachers, and no easily replicable organizational structure. Furthermore, while several adults I knew extended their knowledge through reading when they had time (several people brought books of collected *vyakhyan* discourses and other devotional literature back from visits to India), many of the teenagers were interested (but only loosely) in the more modern ideas of teachers like Chitrabhanu—for example, that vegetarianism promoted a more healthy body and contented mind— ideas that did not necessarily need to be learned or practised communally. Such an individualistic stress, echoing Kesu Jain's comments on *pratikramana* mentioned above, will be explored more fully in the following chapter.

Honour and Respect

Of all the Asian religious groups in Leicester the Jains are perhaps the most lacking in religious specialists to approve and sanction their behaviour. It is possibly for this reason that much was made of people's achievements. The quarterly publication of the Samaj, *The Jain*, often congratulates those who have achieved examination success or who find a new job. A special issue of the predecessor of *The Jain*, *Jain News*, in 1977 carried an article entitled 'Our Youths—Our Pride', which gave a short educational career history of thirty young people, all sons and daughters of Samaj members. Many of them were studying at universities and colleges in Britain.

There is also another side to honour and respect, and that is money-raising. For example, the leadership of the Samaj encourages young people, on completing a degree or beginning work, to take out life-membership of the Samaj (in 1982, £100 or £25 covenanted for four years). Other members make donations to the Samaj or the work of the Centre on happy occasions such as birth or marriage, for which they are thanked in the magazine. Most prominently, most of those who perform *upvas* (a twenty-four-hour period of total fast) during Paryushan, as well as being honoured and given gifts by the Samaj, contribute money and useful items such as pots and pans to the Centre.

In India there is a similar reciprocity in honour; many of the *ayambil* fasters discussed in Chapter 3 made gifts to a *bhojansala*, or to the Jamnagar Sthanakavasi Jain Sangh, but these gifts are not publicly acknowledged as they are in Leicester.[7] In some cases there is

---

[7] All funds and trusts in Jamnagar issue an annual report of their finances but individual contributions are not recorded. One could try to consult the account books (where such information is recorded) but permission would not necessarily be granted.

reciprocal honour between lay and ascetic (for example, the *varsitap
tapasvi*s giving sugar-cane juice to the ascetics, mentioned in Chapter
3). In Leicester, the smaller numbers of Jains—the moral community
within which such exchanges of honour would normally take place—
makes the reciprocity at once more overt and more introverted. The
Leicester Srimalis, through the Leicester Jain Samaj, have corporate
goals and objectives in a way that the Jamnagar Jains do not: they have
acquired property but must now develop it, they must discover and
reify their position *vis-à-vis* the other Asian minorities in Leicester, as
well as *vis-à-vis* the majority population. Some wish to entrench, and
retain unaltered what remains from the past. Some wish to seek or
develop a new form of Jainism that is both relevant to life in late
twentieth century Britain, and attractive to non-Jains in the same
environment. (These aims and objectives are explored in detail in the
next chapter.) Thus the income derived from gifts is important to the
Samaj and may decide its future form, depending on the size of the gift
and any 'strings' that may be attached to it. Gifts in Jamnagar need not
materially benefit those who give them. For example, gifts made to
jivdaya (lit.: 'life compassion'; that is, charitable donations for animal
and human welfare), or for the welfare of ascetics are effectively 'lost'
to the lay community—they are Maussian gifts to god. Even those that
remain within the community of givers only add to or improve existing
organizations or structures, for example, repairing an *upasraya*, or
installing new idols in a temple. (Though this last may bring honour to
the temple, or even to the town, as well as to the individual who makes
the gift.)

The major portion of the Leicester Srimalis' gifts to the Jain Centre
were self-beneficial in that they were directed for the most part
towards the work and development of the Samaj and the Centre. For
example, during the four-year period for which I have records (1978–
82) only £56 was given to *jivdaya* (for famine relief in Gujarat) through
the Samaj, while all other gifts went largely to the building fund, to be
spent on the purchase and refurbishment of the Centre.[8] The reward
for gift-giving is honour. On a small scale this means simply having
one's name appear in *The Jain* and the honour that comes from pulling
one's weight in the community. On the large scale, giving the cost of
some major project in the Centre (refurbishing the kitchen or library,

---

[8] I have no indication how much individuals *qua* individuals gave to charities in
Britain or abroad, although I know that some did so quite extensively.

for example) would result in an engraved plaque being fixed in the appropriate place to commemorate the donor and the donation.

Below I give two ethnographic examples. They describe the two occasions I witnessed when the Leicester Srimali community honoured people: on both occasions those honoured made, or were expected to make, financial contributions to the Samaj, but in one case this was the reason for giving them honour, whilst in the other it was secondary.

Honouring the *Tapasis* and *Tapasvis*

Fasting is neither as elaborate nor as common among the Leicester Srimalis as it is in India. Various reasons and excuses are given for this by the members, such as the fact that one needs to eat more in Britain to keep warm, or that it is too difficult to fast and to do a full day's work. The fact that fasting is always approved and occasionally initiated by ascetics in India may be another reason for its lack of popularity in Britain. Nevertheless, fasting is a duty during Paryushan and each year some thirty people undertake *upvas* for anything from one to ten days, culminating on *samvatsari*.

By the end of the 1982 Paryushan, twenty-four people have made three or more *upvas* (that is, they have undertaken three consecutive twenty-four-hour periods of total abstinence from food), and twenty-three of these have come to the Centre to be honoured. Of these, two (both men) have fasted for the entire ten days. One is a man in his early twenties who has a slight mental disability and therefore does not work. He has spent a large part of the Paryushan period at the Jain Centre, using it effectively as an *upasraya*, and has been treated with great respect by the rest of those attending. People greet him with *namaskar* and enquire solicitously about his health, as well as providing him with boiled water from the Centre's kitchen, and making sure he is comfortable with pillows and backrests. The other ten-*upvas tapasi* is an old Oswal in his late seventies. The son with whom he lives no longer attends the Centre, but the old man has insisted on being brought, at least for some of the week's events, and he is duly honoured by the Samaj (he had known several of the Srimali members in Kenya). He commands even more respect than the young man, partly because of his age (austerities are thought to be more debilitating as one gets older), but mainly because he has chosen to abstain from water as well as food for the whole ten days, to the extent that he is said not even to clean his teeth, lest some of the water be accidentally swallowed.

At the Saturday post-*pratikramana* session rows of chairs are arranged on the stage of the main auditorium. As the *tapasi*s and *tapasvi*s enter from *pratikramana* or from outside (they have not necessarily performed *pratikramana* nightly) they sit on the front central pew, facing the stage. After a communal chanting of the Naukar mantra and '*cattari mangalam*' (a version of the 'four refuges' —see P. S. Jaini 1979: 164; J. Jain 1975: 177–8), there follows a devotional song by the Centre's resident musician and the bidding for the evening's *arti* and *mangaldivo*. The honour ceremony is then opened by speeches from the Samaj's President and the President of the All India Svetambara Conference, an architect who, although resident in Bombay, spends two or three months a year with his son in London (the family is Visa Srimali but not of Saurashtran origin). After the speeches the *tapasi*s and *tapasvi*s are called up on to the stage one by one, the old Oswal going first and the three one-day fasters bringing up the rear. As he or she comes up, each one is presented by the AISC President with a large stainless steel *thali*, a *vadki*, a coconut, and a small packet of *sakar* (large crystals of sugar) before taking his or her place on the stage. Some of the smaller gifts —the *sakar* and the *vadki*—have been given by individuals, while the Samaj as a body has purchased the rest out of general funds. Stainless steel ware is a standard gift between all middle-class Indians, while coconuts and *sakar* are commonly offered in both Hindu and Jain temples and are considered to be auspicious. Afterwards *arti* and *mangaldivo* are performed on stage, with the *tapasvi*s looking on but not participating. (In Jamnagar the *tapasi*s and *tapasvi*s are honoured after the breaking of their fast, at the *parana* ceremony. Although a *parana* will be held in Leicester on the following Monday morning, few people are able to attend because of work commitments.)

Honouring the Philanthropists

If the previous event demonstrates a net flow of honour from the Jain Samaj to some of its members in response to an action completed (several of whom made small financial contributions to the Centre's funds and all of whom confirmed the worthiness of the Jain path and hence the legitimation of the moral community's foundation by their actions), the event described below suggests the converse—the proactive bestowal of honour by which it is hoped an appropriate financial response will be stimulated.

One Sunday afternoon towards the end of September 1982, the Lord Mayor of Leicester, the Chairman of Leicester Inter-Faith,[9] the secretary of the Leicester Vegetarian Society, and representatives from the local paper arrive at the Jain Centre by invitation, along with members of the Samaj, to attend a reception in honour of two Bombay 'philanthropists' (as they are described on the invitation card). The two guests are a wealthy industrialist who had been, at one time, President of the Bombay Jain Social Group, and the President of the All India Svetambara Conference, mentioned above. Although nothing is overtly stated during the proceedings it is hoped that each will make a substantial contribution to the Centre's funds. About 200 people attend—mostly local members of the Samaj—taking tea in the dining hall before moving into the auditorium. After the Naukar *mantra* and *cattari mangalam* have been chanted by the wife of one of the committee members (renowned for her fine voice), there is a short display of Kathakali dancing by a local (Hindu) dance teacher. Then the visitors take their places at tables arranged on the stage and are garlanded with sandalwood garlands by young girls—daughters of committee members and others.

There then follows a series of speeches by visitors and committee members. The Lord Mayor welcomes the potential benefactors to Leicester and goes on to link the work of the Centre to the general good of Leicester, expressing the hope that the Centre will become a place of pilgrimage and bring many visitors to the City. He is the only one to speak in English, although outlines of some of the other speeches are provided for non-Gujarati speakers. The other speeches stress the previous philanthropic deeds of the two main visitors (in India), the potential the Centre has for aiding all future visitors—Jain and non-Jain—in the way of academic resources, as well as devotional inspiration, and the need for money to realize this potential.

Afterwards the two guests reply, indicating their general support for the Centre and its work, their approval of its non-sectarian stance, and its apparent openness to all comers. After their speeches

---

[9] An organization representing several religious groups in Leicester, Asian and non-Asian.

they are each presented with an embroidered Kashmiri shawl and a coconut by the Samaj's President. The ceremony is followed by a meal to which all present are invited, after which there is a brief *arti* and *mangaldivo* in the temple room.

The results of the reception were never clearly made public and my own enquiries received only the vaguest answers, indicating that the unconditional lump-sum gift that had been hoped for had not materialized. In fact both men, before and after the reception, had worked hard in India to raise funds (amounting to some £400,000) from various Jain trusts and temples, as well as from individuals, to pay for the carving and shipping of the temple that was later to be installed in the refurbished Jain Centre. Both also became Patrons of the Samaj (at a minimum cost of £1,000 each). The event was deemed to be a success, however. Not only did the two philanthropists attend— important men in their own right—but also several other leading Jains, including the President of the British Navnat Vanik Association (a Srimali from London), the General Secretary of the National Council of Vanik Associations (to which the Jain Samaj and the Navnat Vanik Association are affiliated), and the Secretary of the Mombasa Jain Temple (an Halari Oswal), demonstrating to the assembled Srimalis the importance, as well as the potential power, of the Jain Samaj. Moreover, the presence of the editor-in-chief of the local paper, together with reporters, resulted in a photograph and story in the next day's edition (*Leicester Mercury*, 20 September 82). As mentioned in previous chapters the Jain Centre has a far more distinct (and benevolent) profile in the Leicester media than any other single Asian group in the city. In this instance the coming together was publicly sanctioned and recorded.

Contrasts and Comparisons

Chapter 3, which parallels this chapter, opened with a discussion of the *samavsarana* as an archetype, a pattern against which communal occasions in Jamnagar could be compared for the purposes of analysis. I should perhaps stress again that this comparison was purely of my own devising to give a thematic neatness to the ethnographic examples that followed. There are many ways of presenting ethnography, and for a book which is as much concerned with the form and organization of a religion as with any possible 'meaning' this seems appropriate. In this chapter the *samavsarana* has not been mentioned, although the idea of 'coming together' that I drew from it in Chapter 3 has been retained.

On the whole, the form of Jainism in Leicester as I observed it was far less centred on the person of the *tirthankara* and the ideals he embodies, than on the lay community itself, the Srimalis. (The argument of Chapter 4 tried to demonstrate that this was in fact also true of the Jamnagar lay community.) The 'eruptions' of *tirthankara*-centred eternity that characterized communal events in Jamnagar had little or no place in Leicester. The Leicester Srimalis had no pre-existing physical structures around which to organize themselves, and the period without ascetics in East Africa that the majority of Srimalis experienced, combined with what Morris calls 'communal crystallization', had a levelling effect on the hierarchy of religious structures such as sect and *gaccha* (Morris 1968: 34 ff.).[10] In consequence, the Srimalis in Leicester, a minority religious group within a minority ethnic group, were doubly removed from their Indian religious context, quite apart from the social and structural changes that had taken place both for individuals and for the *jati* as a whole. Moreover, the Jains' experience of urban space differed greatly from that which pertains in Jamnagar: all the events described above took place within the confines of the Jain Centre and were thus invisible to the wider population of the city—no processions, no red and white bunting adorning the building, no gleaming chariots or carts. Rather there was an inwardness that was tempered only by controlled and highly mediated 'eruptions' (to use the same metaphor within a different context) into the the public world through newspaper interviews and radio broadcasts.

Far from the weight of tradition implied by the archetypal *samavsarana* and the yearly round of festivals and fasts, a main theme of this chapter has been the extent to which specific factors—the location of the Centre, the personality of various individuals, the need for money—have directed the form and outcome of the various events described. In truth, this last point is as much a feature of the size of the Leicester Jain Samaj as it is of its newness. Nevertheless, the new environment allowed several experiments with form to take place—for example, the Oswal–Srimali alliance and the formation of 'Jain Samaj (Europe), Leicester'. A further aspect of this development is discussed in the next chapter.

[10] To which one might add the point that only three sects—the Kanji Panth, Sthanakavasis, and Deravasis—were represented in East Africa, and only two *gaccha*s—Tapa and Loka—both of which are coterminous with two of the sects.

8

Which Way Forward?
Ways of Believing in Leicester

In Chapter 4 I presented a puzzle that had struck me while I was working in Jamnagar—who owned the various pieces of Jain property that were scattered throughout the city? To a large extent my interest in this issue had been brought from my earlier fieldwork in Leicester where a similar problem—though at a more abstract level—hovered over the Jain Centre, at least in my eyes. That is, in what sense was the Leicester Jain Centre 'owned' by the Leicester Jains? I have touched on this issue in Chapter 6 and discussed it in much greater detail elsewhere (Banks 1991). In this chapter I wish to consider a different, although related, puzzle concerning the types or varieties of belief people hold. Again, recognition of the problem was prompted by the

fact that I sensed ambiguity in what people said and what I observed, particularly in statements that claimed unity for the Leicester Jain 'community', while I thought I could see divisions. It is in this sense that the puzzles I examine in both Leicester and Jamnagar are related.

In Chapter 6 I outlined the division that had occurred between the Leicester Srimalis and Oswals and the consequences this had had for the subsequent development of the Jain Samaj. I also mentioned in passing that the Srimali 'community' itself was not free from internal tensions. As in any community or organization, no matter how small, there are perceivable and quantifiable differences between individuals, in terms of occupation, education, income, and so forth. There are also divisions engendered by the particular structure of the community, most noticeably between the leaders and the led. For example, one night during Paryushan when the bidding for *arti* and *mangaldivo* was slow, the *arti* was finally awarded to 'The Jain Samaj'. It was performed, however, by members of the committee. This later led to an disagreement, with some of the Srimalis present feeling that the (elected) committee was not necessarily synonymous with the Samaj, and that 'ordinary' (i.e. non-committee members) of the Samaj should have performed the ceremony. In part, the argument was simply the outcome of a personality clash (between Kesu Jain, the Samaj's President, and Chimanbhai Mehta who had organized the *pratikramana* sessions), but it was also an expression of more deep-seated resentment on the part of those who felt they were losing control of 'their' Samaj and Centre. Although I accept Morris's proposition that the progress and organization of *jati* (and other) associations rest largely on the aspirations of self-motivated leader figures (Morris 1968: 40), I do not believe that the other members are necessarily indifferent or apathetic. The disputes over temple boards and trusteeship of other Asian organizations in Leicester that I referred to in Chapter 6 belie this, or at least demonstrate that there is competition between self-interested leader figures. In this chapter I wish to explore the notion of a 'counter culture', the ideology of those not in power.

In Chapter 1 I stressed the distinction one should draw between the laity and patrons in the political organization of early Jainism. I argued that the attention of the ascetics only turned to the increasingly wealthy laity in the medieval period when the support of their earlier royal patrons began to wane and shift to Hinduism and Islam. In Chapter 4, I explored the nature of the relationship between lay and ascetic, and concluded that there was a symbiosis—each was dependent upon the other. With the infrastructural aspects of the religion intact (temples and other property, a regularized system of *gaccha*s and sects, and a strong ritual and ceremonial structure), and in a stable political situation, the need for patronage on the part of the Jamnagar ascetics was not great and could largely be met from within the local lay community. How then does this relate to the Leicester Jains in 1982? The most obvious point of divergence is the absence of ascetics in Leicester. Jain ascetics may only travel by foot, and are therefore unable to travel outside India. In East Africa—where the same absence of ascetics also prevailed—there had probably been greater contact with India, at least initially, but still the essentially ascetic system of *gaccha*s had been transmuted into the two sectarian nodes (Deravasi and Sthanakavasi). This arrangement is, in part, analogous to the more pervasive East African Hindu division into Arya Samaj (reformist, non-idolatrous, and somewhat exclusive) and the Sanatan Dharma (liberal and inclusive).

In Leicester, the leaders of the Samaj—the elected committee and the unofficial 'elders' mentioned in Chapter 6—obviously act as authority figures and decision-makers—roles that ascetics as well as laity play in India, particularly in religious matters. While ascetics in India wield a degree of unquestioned power over the laity (such as in allocating the money raised at Paryushan) the leaders of the Jain Samaj are theoretically responsible to their members and, in the case of the committee, can be refused re-election after their two-year term of office. In fact, however, the office-holders of the committee had remained largely unchanged for the previous five years or so.[1] (Prior to 1977 there were several Oswals on the committee, although the President has always been a Srimali.) In 1982 the office-holders of the committee consisted of a President, an Honorary Vice President, a General Secretary, an Assistant General Secretary, and a Treasurer and Assistant Treasurer. Routine committee meetings were generally attended by the President, the two Secretaries, and the Treasurer. The office-holders were all professionals (two doctors, a dentist, a lawyer, and an accountant) or successful business men. While these professions are not representative of the rest of the Leicester membership, they are important in maintaining the credibility of the Samaj to the non-Leicester

[1] The committee was made up of six office holders and seven ordinary members (of whom one was a woman, the representative of the Bhagini Kendra ('Women's Centre')). I restrict myself in this chapter to a discussion of the office-holding members.

membership (many of whom are business men). For this, as I hope to demonstrate in this chapter, came to be a source of tension in the Jain Samaj: the aims and expectations of the Leicester membership were potentially at odds with those of the greater membership. While the leadership had to cultivate its patrons it needed to prevent alienating its supporters—the 'laity'.

The Leicester Srimalis, as mentioned in Chapter 6, initially made a substantial contribution to the Centre (although they have had little more to give since) and make up the bulk of the numbers at any function, simply by virtue of their residence in Leicester. The patrons themselves may expect different things of the Samaj—the City Council and other official bodies expect some kind of community centre (in the standard English urban sense) to emerge, the Jains in India giving the temple wish to glorify their religion and earn themselves merit (*punya*). My concern is, however, essentially a study of the Leicester Srimalis, and hence only the Leicester part of the Samaj (the Samaj does not have regional branches, though it opened a London office in the early 1980s). But the differences in aims and expectations that I note on the wider scale were also to be found within the Leicester community, and it is to this level that I wish to devote the rest of the chapter.

In Chapter 2 I described how the Visa Srimali and Halari Visa Oswal *jati*s were divided into rural and urban sections. The distinction was absolute, if arbitrary, resting as it did on whether a person's name (or his father's name) was to be found on the urban membership list. Members of both sections theoretically had equal access to *jati* property if they lived in Jamnagar, though rural Visa Srimali Loka Gaccha members paid greater hire charges. In Leicester there are no sections of this nature, although differential access to and perceptions of property (in this case the Jain Centre) serve to emphasize the differences. Instead, it is perceptions of time and of history that serve to mark difference. While the basis of division in Jamnagar had been predicated on past experience—whether one's origins were urban or rural—divisions in Leicester arose as a result of perceptions of the present and the future—how much, and in what way, should one adapt to life in Britain, and more importantly, what was to be the role of Jainism in this adaptation?[2]

The way I choose to identify these differences is in terms of beliefs

---

[2] As mentioned in Chapter 6, Eriksson (1984) and Tambs-Lyche (1980: 39–40) among others, have claimed that a division amongst immigrant Gujarati Hindus

about Jainism. In India, significant differences in belief are articulated through the framework of sect and *gaccha*, perhaps leading to the creation of new sects, such as the Kanji Panth. I am not trying to say that differences in belief cause sectarian division, though that is often how such divisions are perceived: the Svetambara–Digambara split described in Chapter 1 is a case in point. Moreover I argued there that sectarian differences of this kind can really only be articulated within, or in the presence of, the ascetic community. In Leicester, without ascetics to control or guide, a wide variety of religious beliefs could thrive among the Srimalis.

Before going any further I should outline the characteristics of these varieties—or 'tendencies' as I shall call them—of religious belief. I have isolated three major foci, but together they form a continuum, or more accurately three points of a triangle (see Figure 8.1), rather than discrete groups. For convenience I have labelled them: orthodoxy, heterodoxy, and neo-orthodoxy. It should be stressed that these are categories of belief, not believers; an individual may at any one time espouse one or more of the viewpoints, but this is not necessarily fixed or binding. I have deliberately left the categories and their definitions somewhat vague, partly because there is not a fixed, dedicated group devoted to each of the belief types, and partly because it is my opinion that some individuals at least, who do distinguish between categories of

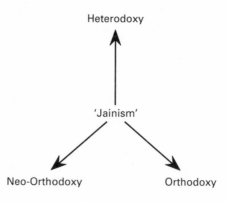

FIG. 8.1. Belief Tendencies in Leicester

predicated upon past experience can be observed: a division between those who migrated directly from India and those who came to Britain by way of East Africa. While I appreciate the argument, it is not, as I said, relevant in the Srimali case (nor, as far as I know, in the Oswal) for almost all those in Leicester came there from East Africa.

belief (and go on to make identification with certain other individuals), do not articulate their identification for fear of causing clear, opposed groups to emerge. In 1982 the status quo of the Jain Samaj was maintained, despite the tensions, if only fragilely.

Arguments, such as that described over the *arti* ceremony, did break out from time to time, but did not lead to a major cleavage of the moral community, from which both sides would stand to lose (the 'tendencies' becoming 'sections'). The model is also largely abstract given that one of the tendencies (orthodoxy) does not really have any base in Leicester, though it is thought to be the prevailing type of belief in India, and as such individuals gauge their viewpoint against it. That is to say, if I were to identify the tendencies with specific groups of people, there would only be two—heterodox and neo-orthodox. But because I identify them with categories of belief, and hold that an individual may shift between these categories, it is necessary to discuss orthodoxy. Of the other two, neo-orthodoxy is largely manifested as a self-ascribed tendency (though, of course, the label is not used) while the tendency to heterodoxy is seen in others, or noticed with regret in oneself, if it is noticed at all.

The terms are, of course, of my own coining. The Jains themselves used terms such as 'modern', 'forward-looking', 'broad-minded', and, especially, 'scientific' to describe the neo-orthodox position, and 'traditional', 'old-fashioned', and 'narrow-minded' to describe the orthodox position. Heterodoxy was less easily identifiable but was the position adopted by those who were (in their own eyes or in the eyes of others) 'simple' and 'uneducated', who had no knowledge of 'deep philosophy', and who lacked time to follow 'real' Jainism which was thought to be very demanding and difficult.[3] I also do not wish to suggest that such tendencies of belief are unique to the Leicester Srimalis, or even to Jains in general. Indeed, as I discuss in Chapter 9, following Bourdieu (1977), the analysis may extend far beyond the narrow category of 'religious belief'. I discuss the interrelationship of the tendencies in more detail below, while here I outline the characteristics of each of the tendencies.

---

[3] As I conducted my interviews in Leicester largely in English, I give the English terms my informants used. Doubtless similar, non-specialized, vocabulary would be used in Gujarati.

Orthodoxy

Orthodoxy may be considered as traditional Jainism, rooted in sectarianism and ritual. It is exemplified by the ascetics who hold knowledge and hence power. From the orthodox viewpoint Jainism is a fully revealed religion: Mahavira and the rest of the *tirthankaras* have outlined the path to salvation and no further elaboration is necessary: ascetics guide one along this path but do not propose new routes. Orthodoxy flourishes best in parochial undisturbed situations. Many of the ordinary Jains in Jamnagar, especially women, may be considered to be orthodox (and are thought so by heterodox Leicester Srimalis): unquestioningly they continue their daily round of temple-visiting, *puja*s, consultation with ascetics, and observation of all the dietary restrictions. While stress is laid on knowledge, comprehension of that knowledge is not really necessary for lay Jains, who can be guided by the ascetics. The performance of ritual is necessary, but it is not thought to please or pacify any transcendent deity. Rather it is thought to foster in one the discipline and conscientiousness which earn *punya* (merit) or shed *karma*s,[4] as well as reaffirming the religious economy of the moral community.

Examples of Orthodoxy   Because, as I said above, orthodoxy is rarely manifest in Leicester, it is difficult to give any clear or detailed examples. When individuals in Leicester did adopt an orthodox position (usually when bemoaning the lack of religious commitment in their own children) they usually ascribed it to their own upbringing: that their parents or grandparents had forced them as children to go to the temple or *upasraya*, to learn the recitations and *mantra*s, and to pay homage to the ascetics. This, for example, was the case with Ramesh and his father Rajabhai, mentioned at the end of Chapter 5. That is, religious commitment is not something which comes naturally or which is given by God, but something which one, and others on one's behalf, must toil over. Orthodoxy was generally thought to be the

---

[4] It is sometimes difficult for both observer and actor to distinguish between the two. Some, particularly the followers of the Kanji Panth, assert that to seek *punya* rather than *karma*-shedding is wrong and that one should concentrate solely on achieving liberation (*moksa*); however, they do not deny that to earn *punya* as a result of some good deed or austerity is impossible. It might be tentatively proposed that actions and prayers directed to subordinate deities (*sasana devata*s) will produce 'wholesome karma' or *punya* (P. S. Jaini 1979: 151), while selfless action and devotion to the *tirthankaras* produces a shedding of all *karma*s—good and bad—and thus leads to *moksa* (P. S. Jaini 1979: 194; Sangave 1980: 227–8).

province of women and the elderly, partly because they had more time for all the rituals, and partly because they were less subject to external influences and disruptions. For example, I was having tea one Autumn afternoon with a middle-aged woman, Kamalaben, and her daughter and son-in-law. Kamalaben lit the gas fire but, before she did so, muttered a short *mantra* which I did not catch. She was too embarrassed to tell me what she had said, but her daughter told me later that the *mantra* was one which in India would negate the violence (*himsa*) caused by the death of insects which might be residing in the firewood or cow-dung cakes. The daughter did not know the *mantra* herself and I never met anyone in India who knew a specific formula, although many people told me that lighting the butane gas commonly used for cooking was a minor act of *himsa* and I knew some who would eat cold food in the evenings rather than light a flame to which insects might be attracted.

Many of the parental generation told me that while they had to make do as best they could in England, their parents (in East Africa or India) had been 'true' Jains, if a little narrow-minded. In some respects it might be more accurate to refer to this tendency as 'orthopraxy' as it is identified with largely unquestioned adherence to a round of actions. But I retain the term orthodoxy because I am concerned with the belief about (and underlying) these actions rather than the actions themselves.

Heterodoxy

This was the position adopted by most of the Srimalis in Leicester for most of the time. One of the key features of the heterodox outlook is belief in a supreme God.

Earlier (Chapter 1), when discussing divinity in Jainism, I referred to Jain 'atheism'. The Jains do acknowledge and worship a whole variety of deities who inhabit the sixteen heavens (*urdhva loka*), the earth, and even the first hell (P. S. Jaini 1979: 129–30). Mention has already been made of some of them earlier in this book: Indra the king of the gods, for example, who ordained that the embryonic Mahavira should be transferred from his Brahman mother's womb to Trisala's. Yet particular aspects of Jain philosophy, most notably the doctrine of *karma* and the strict and absolute rules by which *karma* is supposed to operate, mean that there is no place in the Jain system for a transcendent deity who created the universe and ordains its affairs.

The *tirthankara*s and other *siddha*s in *siddha-loka* (the final resting-place of emancipated souls) are of course omniscient and omnipotent, living in perfect bliss. But for the reasons given in Chapter 1, they cannot interfere with the affairs of the world (nor in the affairs of gods and demons in other parts of the universe). All the *tirthankara*s, however, have a pair of 'guardian' deities (*sasana devata*s)—one male, one female—who are usually associated in popular mythology with helping the potential *tirthankara* to achieve omniscience. (Although as I pointed out in Chapter 1, the feature that distinguishes *tirthankara*s from other enlightened souls—*siddha*s—is their ability to attain enlightenment unaided and unprompted.) Some guardian and other deities have achieved a prominent place in Jain orthopraxy: idols of Chakreshwari and Padmavati—female deities associated with Rishabha and Parsvanath respectively—are found in many Jain temples and deities of the directions feature prominently in the rituals for consecrating idols and new temples.[5]

Although most Srimalis in Leicester were aware of these deities, few men at least had any specific knowledge of them. Several of the *sasana devata*s were known (an embroidered backdrop behind the idol in the temple room depicted Padmavati and Dharendra attending Parsvanath), but no one I questioned had incorporated them into their personal cosmology, or directed prayers or requests to them specifically. Instead I found a widespread belief in the power of the *tirthankara*s themselves to aid.

With reference to the medieval conflict between Jains and Virashaivites in the Deccan, Handiqui states: 'The Shaivas contended that the Jain conception of the Arhat [*tirthankara*] was wholly inadequate: if he was an omniscient teacher, we must ask who his teacher was, and if he was a saint devoted to austerity, there must be someone to vouchsafe the result of his efforts. In either case, it was necessary to postulate a superior Being, self-existent and without a beginning, and He was no other than Maheshvara or Shiva' (Handiqui 1949: 347).

No matter how much emphasis the Jains place on the inexorable and

---

[5] Because these gods and goddesses figure largely in iconography, temple ornamentation, and elaborate *puja*s, they seem to hold far less importance for Sthanakavasi Jains in India. When I was discussing deities with an idol-worshipping (i.e. Deravasi) ascetic in India, I was told that prayers and requests made to particular *tirthankara*s were 'intercepted' by the relevant *sasana devata*s, who, pleased that 'their' *tirthankara* was being singled out, did what they could to grant the request. Fuller details of the various deities worshipped and 'revered' by the Jains are to be found in P. S. Jaini 1979: 129–30; Kalghatgi 1969: 177–8; Buhler 1903: 66–71.

automatic functioning of the laws of *karma* there is always the opening available for one to insert a first cause, as in the example above. The involvement of gods and goddesses, many bearing the same names as, or in fact actually being, Hindu gods and goddesses, in not only the orthopraxy but also the mythology of Jainism, only serves to weaken the paramountcy of *karma* as an explanation of mankind's experience of the universe. Many of the Leicester Srimalis therefore had no difficulty in adopting a theistic outlook: some believed that the *tirthankara*s were the paramount divinity, expressing itself through a series of *avatara*s, others, such as Charandas and his companions who sang '*om jaya jagadisha hare*' every morning (a Hindu hymn to the lord of the universe) felt that the paramount deity lay behind the *tirthankara*s.

Examples of Heterodoxy The work of Gombrich (1971) and others has raised the question: what do people mean when they say 'I believe in so-and-so'—a question that is, to my mind anyway, ultimately unanswerable. Short of reducing all such beliefs and expressions of belief to the realm of personal psychology, I think the best way to approach such an issue is through a system of analogy. I, as an analyst, can use analogy by saying that certain Jains believed in a controlling, creating deity beyond the *tirthankara*s in the way that certain Hindus believe in a controlling, creating deity beyond the named deities in the Hindu pantheon. Similarly, the Jains themselves can use analogy: one Leicester Srimali, Pravinbhai, likened Mahavira to Jesus (because I, as an Englishman, was automatically thought to be a Christian). Like Mahavira, Jesus was a good man who expounded a moral code and was prepared to suffer for his beliefs. Jesus prayed to God the Father for strength and guidance; as Mahavira also needed strength and guidance, he too must have prayed to his 'father'—ergo, there is a presence beyond the *tirthankara*s. Of course, the fact that according to what we know of Mahavira's life he did not pray to anyone (in the Christian sense) is irrelevant. My informant's belief in divine immanence was such that the analogy could be drawn.

Belief in an interventive God brings with it a shift in focus in terms of the aims of religious practice and belief: no longer does one practise the religion to achieve liberation, but instead to please God—thus introducing the idea of *bhakti*. In consequence, heterodoxy is open to all forms of religious expression where *bhakti* may be found, and most of the Jains in Leicester visited the city's four Hindu temples occasionally, even frequently, and had Hindu deities in their home shrines. One or two people I spoke to had also visited a Sikh *gurduara* or a Christian church. (No one admitted to having ever visited a mosque, either in this country or abroad.) For example, Pravinbhai's wife Sushila, a woman in her early thirties with two young children, had been persuaded by her Hindu neighbours on the Rushey Mead estate to attend meetings at the Swaminarayan Centre. She told me that she preferred it to the Jain Centre as there were more people to meet, many of them with children of her own children's age, and eventually she persuaded Pravinbhai to come. However, they both continued to attend functions at the Jain Centre and seemed surprised when I queried the possible inconsistency of this. They gave me a reply which I was to hear many times in India: that God is one, only his name changes, and that it does not matter in what form he is worshipped.

Attitudes to heterodoxy were mixed: while some individuals, like Sushila and Pravinbhai, were closely involved with Hindu groups in the city and seemed to perceive no conflict between this and their membership of the Samaj, others spontaneously admitted that the Hindu beliefs and practices they followed were at variance with Jain teachings, but said either that there was no proof that the Jain path itself was correct, or that while the Jain *dharma* probably was correct it was so austere and unrewarding that they preferred to derive at least part of their religious satisfaction from other sources. In a slightly different vein was the behaviour of Ramjibhai, who lived to the south-west of the city centre, on the Narborough Road, with his wife, unmarried daughter and married son, and his son's wife and their baby boy, Jitu. Only a few hundred metres away from their front door lay the Jalaram Mandir, a terraced house converted to a temple for the worship of a nineteenth-century Saurashtran saint. Every evening, Ramjibhai would carry Jitu over to the temple and sit there proudly with him, talking with the other men (and occasionally women) who likewise had brought their grandchildren. As far as I could tell, Ramjibhai considered Jalaram to be a holy man, regardless of the fact that he was technically a Hindu saint, and he always made sure that Jitu received a taste of the *prasad* that the *pujari* offered as one left the temple. Nevertheless, Ramjibhai was a quiet but active supporter of the Jain Centre and attended all the functions—including the morning session with Charandas and the other 'elders'—as often as he was able.

Like orthodoxy, heterodoxy is concerned with knowledge. Jainism is conceived of as a religion of learning, and hence inaccessible to those with little education and no free time.[6] Most people when adopting the heterodox viewpoint bemoaned their ignorance of 'deep philosophy' but felt that if sufficient knowledge were acquired, a devotion to 'true' (orthodox) Jainism was bound to result. I myself was considered to be a case in point. I had studied Jainism through books and was due to go to India where I would meet ascetics, visit famous pilgrimage places, and perform rituals. Several people asked me—only half-seriously, I'm sure—if I was intending to become an ascetic (there are cases known of Europeans taking *diksa*). However, although the religious aspect of Jain identity was ignored or considered unimportant by those adopting a heterodox viewpoint, the social aspect certainly wasn't. People who espoused the heterodox viewpoint generally considered that their religious affiliation was just one more aspect of their *jati* identity. Manilal, who I mentioned at the end of Chapter 5, tried to convey this to me by telling me that Oswals were a 'different kind' of Jain, that beyond considerations of sect and *gaccha* the fact that they were Oswals made them different as Jains.

Neo-Orthodoxy

While orthodoxy and heterodoxy are categories of religious belief, neo-orthodoxy claims for itself the status of a science. As found in Leicester, neo-orthodox Jainism is not so much a system for achieving salvation, but a science for the individual in his or her present situation —the strict dietary restrictions are essential for a healthy body; the meditations and other austerities bring about a healthy and peaceful mind. It is also a science for society: I was told on one occasion that if everyone (Jain and non-Jain) were to adopt Mahavira's principle of 'non-violence' (*ahimsa*) all mankind's troubles would cease; on another occasion I was told that Mahavira was the first communist. Mahavira was similarly credited with making many scientific discoveries centuries before Western scientists, including the existence of bacteria, the nature of the atom, and the Theory of Relativity.[7]

[6] Britain was often characterized as a busy country where everyone works long hours, is always in a hurry, and never has any free time. Even if someone was unemployed or retired, they would still consider this 'busy-ness' a constraint.

[7] One of the important principles of Jain philosophy—*anekantavada*, the theory or doctrine of many aspects, which states that while a thing is permanent in its substance, its qualities and attributes constantly change—is often translated as the 'theory of relativity' by Jain authors (see, for example, J. Jain 1975: 68) and hence the confusion with Einstein's theory. One 'A'-level schoolboy went so far as to tell me that Einstein had taken his famous equation, $e = mc^2$, from an ancient Jain text.

Neo-orthodoxy in Leicester draws its inspiration, directly or indirectly, from two important teachers—Srimad Rajchandra and the ex-ascetic, Chitrabhanu, mentioned in the previous chapter. (The Kanji Panth shows many features of neo-orthodoxy and in India those who adopt a neo-orthodox outlook generally cite Rajchandra and Kanji Swami as their inspiration. In Leicester I rarely heard the name of Kanji Swami mentioned, perhaps because, as I mentioned in Chapter 5, the movement has become identified, in Saurashtra at least, with the Halari Visa Oswal *jati*.)

Srimad Rajchandra (1868–1901) was a lay Jain from Saurashtra, renowned for his austerities. Despite his spirituality he refused to become an ascetic and was generally anti-ascetic in his stance, largely because of his rebuttal of sectarianism. Although not denying the inspiration of Mahavira's teachings in any way, he felt his own insights (typified by the 142 stanzas known as Atma Siddhi—self realization)[8] were better suited to this present *dusama kala* (unhappy age). He also selected his own canon of Jain scriptures of those which he considered to be best suited to the needs of the modern laity. This stress on adapting Jainism to modern times (or rather, finding in the Jain writings and teachings that which is best suited to modern times) is the keynote of neo-orthodoxy and is found in the teachings and writings of Chitrabhanu also. Chitrabhanu started his career as a Svetambara Tapa Gaccha ascetic (Munishri Chandraprabhasagarji) but left his order after many years and married one of his disciples (note that all three of the neo-orthodox leader figures mentioned have rejected asceticism in their own ways). He now divides his time between India and the United States, where he has established a 'Jain Meditation Centre'. His teachings are more eclectic than those of Rajchandra and perhaps closer to those of Rajneesh (who was himself born a Jain) although his 'movement' does not in any way approach the cult status of the Rajneesh organization at its height. As mentioned in the previous chapter, Chitrabhanu came to Leicester in 1980 and was warmly approved of by all I spoke to. (He is less well thought of in India where his personal affairs, particularly his marriage and renunciation of ascetic status, are the cause of much opprobrium.)

In its rejection of traditionalism and orthodoxy, neo-orthodoxy rejects sectarian divisions and *jati* divisions (as well as making the 'scientific' adherence to Jainism an achieved, not ascriptive, status). As

---

[8] An English translation of *Atma Siddhi* is given in J. L. Jaini 1978. The only biography of Rajchandra I know of in English is by D. Mehta (n.d.).

the constitution of the Leicester Jain Samaj was drawn up by largely neo-orthodox Jains it can be said that the Samaj and the Centre are 'officially' neo-orthodox in outlook. This indeed seemed the ideal position to adopt to transcend the *jati* tensions between Srimalis and Oswals, in the initial Samaj formation, though as I outline below it has brought its own problems. There is a further outcome of adopting neo-orthodoxy: a change in the relationship between the Jains and the state. Jains in India—or, more specifically, in Jamnagar—have no significant relationship with the state as Jains.[9] Rather, they relate to the state as shopkeepers who must keep accounts, householders who must observe building regulations and pay their rates, or generally as citizens who must abide by the law of the land. The Leicester Jains too, as I described in Chapter 6, are generally perceived by the state (in this instance, Leicester City Council) as part of its 'ethnic minority' population. Generally, the only finer distinction that comes within this category is linguistic, with the Council publishing a variety of advice leaflets (on health, legal aid, etc.) in Gujarati, Urdu, Panjabi, and Hindi. However, by inviting officials of the state (such as the Mayor) to their functions, by having press articles and radio broadcasts limited in discussion only to themselves, the Leicester Jains, under their neo-orthodox leadership, seem to be attempting to forge an exclusive link for themselves, one which stresses a religious identity and which precludes discussion of the 'problems' in terms of which the local state is apt to see its 'ethnic minority' population.

Examples of Neo-Orthodoxy   Neo-orthodoxy for the most part ignores the Jain ascetics, considering them to be narrow-minded and ritualistic: with sufficient knowledge and discipline the individual has no need of ascetic guidance. Moreover, with this knowledge and discipline anyone can be a Jain, and those who are born into Jain families do not have a statutory right to salvation. The Jains in Leicester who most consistently held a neo-orthodox position often claimed to have had some kind of 'conversion' experience, or to have changed their way of thinking and come to a deeper appreciation of

---

[9] The exceptions to this statement would be the fact that Jain organizations need to alert the local police when they intend to hold a procession or block off the entire Chandi Bazaar area for a ceremony (which occasionally happens) or the fact that the various trusts administered by temples and the like are subject to India's tax and charity laws (cf. the discussion at the start of Chapter 4). Even here it could be argued that there is still no relationship between the state and the Jains as a moral community, but rather between the state and certain constituted organizations.

Jain teachings. A case in point was that of the Samaj's President, Kesu Jain. A solicitor from India (he had not been to East Africa), he claimed to have had little interest in the religion of his birth until about 1975. Prior to this he had tried to achieve personal status aggrandizement through several organizational channels: the Rotary Club, the local Conservative Party, the Indian National Club. In each case his aspirations had not been fulfilled and he had withdrawn again. Eventually, he told me, he turned to his own culture, began to read books on Jainism, realized the truth of what they were saying, and became President of the Samaj (of which he had always been a member). If such experiences were possible for people like the President (a Jain 'by birth' but not initially by conviction) then it was possible for anyone, Indian or European. Hence neo-orthodoxy is a proselytizing faith, unlike orthodoxy which is exclusive or heterodoxy which is eclectically inclusive (that is, it seeks truth in other religious systems and at the same time welcomes the adherents of those systems but does not seek to convert them to a new path).

As a professional man, it was the rational aspects of Jainism which appealed to Kesu Jain. The message and meaning of Jainism were still found to be relevant after one had discarded the ritualistic and superstitious aspects (remember that Kesu Jain did not perform *pratikramana* during Paryushan, with all its attendant ritualism (Chapter 7), preferring to meditate alone). There were others, perhaps less radical than Kesu Jain in their outlook, who espoused neo-orthodoxy. For example, it was one of the teenage sons of Ramesh, the son of the orthodox Rajabhai, who told me of the source of the Einstein equation (n. 7, above) and who frequently advocated the virtues of meditation for giving one a clear mind. He was full of admiration and respect for his father and grandfather, however, praising them for the dedication they had shown in bringing him up with feet firmly planted on the Jain path. Indeed, he was unusual in being one of the very few young men or women of his age to attend the Paryushan *pratikramana* sessions and obviously found, for the moment at least, a commitment to established forms and practices to be required and necessary. Table 8.1 summarizes some of the more important differences between the tendencies and the relationship between them.

As mentioned above, orthodoxy was not a belief pertinent to Leicester (because of the absence of ascetics) and thus we are left with two fully operational tendencies—heterodoxy and neo-orthodoxy.

TABLE 8.1. *Characteristics of Belief Categories in Leicester*

Orthodoxy	Heterodoxy	Neo-Orthodoxy
Ascetics paramount	Pro-ascetic	Anti-ascetic
Emphasis on ritual	Emphasis on faith	Emphasis on rationality
Exclusive belief structure	Inclusive belief structure	Selectively exclusive belief structure
Aim of religion is to achieve *moksa*	Aim of religion is to please God	Aim of religion is to secure individual/societal peace

Certain individuals (the President, most of the rest of the committee, and several other members of the Samaj) were committed whole-heartedly to neo-orthodoxy and had a degree of religious fervour not found in most of the Srimalis. Heterodoxy—by its nature a form of compromise and opportunism—had no fervent apologists and was in any case not always recognized by its followers: what I would describe as heterodox behaviour—belief in a creator God, or performance of Hindu ceremonies on death anniversaries—could be taken by the actor to be true and correct behaviour and not contradictory to the tenets of Jainism in any way. Neo-orthodoxy on the other hand was largely self-cognizant and its adherents perceived both the narrow-mindedness of orthodoxy and the laxness or eclecticism of heterodoxy. However, in order to discuss the structure of the contemporary Jain Samaj and to analyse its dynamics within the context of the cultural strategies adopted by other Asian groups in the city, it is necessary to impose the categories of belief—the tendencies—on to the Leicester Jain population in some way.

For the purposes of directness and clarity I discussed heterodoxy as a set of features distinct from those features which make up the other two tendencies. It is obvious, however, that one of the features of heterodoxy—the syncretism (termed 'inclusive belief structure' in Table 8.1)—enables it to encompass features of the other two tendencies. That is, that when an individual who usually adopts a heterodox viewpoint, espouses one of the other tendencies temporarily, they are able to do so because of their heterodoxy. For example, in the 'confession' of *pratikramana*, meticulous attention to performing the right motions of hands and limbs, although the actor might be ignorant of their significance, could be termed orthodox behaviour; while the use of an electric torch to read the text by—a *himsa*-less form of illumination to the modern mind, despite the ascetic injunction against electricity—could be termed neo-orthodox behaviour. Thus Figure

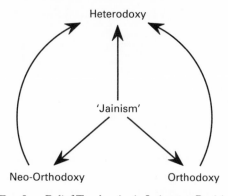

FIG. 8.2. Belief Tendencies in Leicester: Revision

8.1, which depicted the tendencies (p. 200), can be redrawn, as in Figure 8.2. That is to say, an abstract 'Jainism' gives rise to orthodox, heterodox, and neo-orthodox interpretations and, in turn, the orthodox and neo-orthodox interpretations can give rise to further heterodox interpretations.

As mentioned above, neo-orthodoxy, while expressed occasionally by many Jains, is adhered to almost exclusively by some, by virtue of the fact that some of its features are predicated upon a rejection of the other positions. Once an individual identifies and accepts these features, the paradox of returning to one of the other viewpoints becomes apparent and the individual becomes committed to the neo-orthodox viewpoint (hence the 'conversion' experiences mentioned above). Discussing the nature of ideology in general,[10] Gellner has pointed out the cognitive sovereignty that many—if not all—ideologies claim for themselves (Gellner 1979a: 122). That is, such ideologies are able to explain all aspects of the physical and social world to the believer within the terms of reference of the ideology. Adding to this, we might say that the recognition of paradox marks the beginning of ideology by bounding it and defining it in opposition to that which it is not. In this example, and the example from Chapter 4, the move is away from 'tendency' to 'section'. Yet the move is one-way, there can be no recognition of paradox from the heterodox viewpoint and therefore no transition from amorphous belief structure to ideology.

Thus it would not be accurate to say that in Leicester there are two

[10] As a brief shorthand definition, I would define ideology as a belief that can be instrumentalized or acted upon.

opposed groups of Srimali Jains. It would be true to say, however, that there is a small group which has marked itself off from the rest and which perceives its existence in terms of opposition to the rest. This group consists mainly of the committee (mostly wealthy professionals) and their supporters (mostly the retired business men I have referred to earlier as 'elders'). Moreover, it would be true to say that there are oppositions and tensions within the moral community which are articulated as though between two distinct groups. At the risk of obfuscating with further diagrams, I would say that the two 'groups' of heterodox and neo-orthodox Jains stand in relation to each other not as in Figure 8.3 (*a*), but as in Figure 8.3 (*b*).

However, while an actor from the heterodox tendency would see his opposition as opposition towards another member of his own (that is, the only) group, an actor from the neo-orthodox group would see his opposition as opposition towards a member of another group. This is essentially because the heterodox think in terms of caste (*jati*) while the neo-orthodox think in terms of religion. Informants not of the neo-orthodox group (that is, 'the heterodox') occasionally confided to me that they were unhappy about the direction the Samaj was taking, that

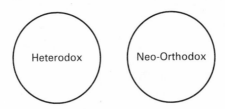

FIG. 8.3 (*a*). Heterodox and Neo-Orthodox

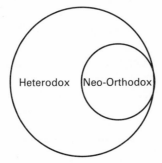

FIG. 8.3 (*b*). Neo-Orthodox in Heterodox

they saw large sums of money being spent to no apparent purpose. The basis of their unease lay in their 'communal' outlook. The Jain Samaj, in their eyes, was synonymous with the Srimali 'community' (i.e. *jati*) and thus the advancement of the Samaj should have been translated into benefits for the community—to reinforce the 'difference' (to use Pocock's (1957) term) between them and other communities. Yet the Srimali leadership did not seem aware of its communal obligations. On the other hand neo-orthodox individuals occasionally criticized 'the heterodox' to me, claiming that they had no interest in the real issues of religion, but were concerned only with their mundane social matters.

It was readily apparent that the 'religious' approach to culture—that is, emulation of the Sikh and Muslim cultural strategies—had failed when the Srimalis and Oswals ceased to maintain a joint Jain organization. However, once the Oswals and the rest of the Navnat group had removed themselves from the Samaj, and hence the Jain Centre, the bulk of the Srimalis assumed that the 'weak' cultural path of the Hindu caste associations (described in Chapter 6) would be followed, and that the Centre would become an (Indian) community centre—that is a *vadi* with religious sub-functions—in the absence of other religious property.

Both cases—the failure of the religious venture between the two Jain *jati*s, and the non-fulfilment of 'community' expectations—can be explained by the anti-caste element within neo-orthodoxy. Both the religio-cultural strategy of the Sikhs and Muslims and the caste-cultural strategy of the Hindu groups were intended to benefit only the members of the groups concerned. In contrast, the 'open' (proselytizing) aspect of neo-orthodoxy subordinated the needs of the Srimali community to the ideals of Jainism, and attempted to bring these ideals to the wider community.

My outline above and in Chapter 7 of the history of the Jain Samaj leads to a simple three-phase analysis of the development of the Srimali community in Leicester. The first phase rested on a 'religious' identity that came about through the Srimali–Oswal alliance. The second, interim phase, lasted from about 1977 to 1978, during which time the Srimalis had no alliance and no property, and religious and *jati* identities may be said to have been equally strong. The two years between 1978 and 1980 saw the purchase of the Centre, used initially by the Srimalis only but soon 'opened' to all Jains, and the modified alliance between the Srimalis and the London Oswals—leading to the creation of 'Jain Samaj (Europe), Leicester'. This initiated the third phase, again one predicated on a religious identity. This new identity differed from that of the first phase in that it recognized Jainism as a world religion and not merely the common ground between two Saurashtran *jati*s.

In the initial Samaj formation the frail Srimali–Oswal alliance was broken because the boundaries of both groups were questioned by the neo-orthodox leadership (largely Srimali) which denied Jainism as a specifically *jati* identity. Although a school was started for the second generation, it was clear that the aims of the leadership would do nothing to consolidate this alliance, nor bring about benefits for either member *jati*.[11] The uneasiness caused by this was sufficient to allow residual *jati* animosity to break up the Samaj and propel the Oswals out to establish their own, clearly communal, organization.

In the final Samaj formation, and particularly after the purchase of the Centre, the neo-orthodox leadership again made it clear that the emphasis was religious and socially inclusive. A second-generation organization, the Jain Youth, effectively ceased to function after repeated difficulties with the leadership over the use of the Centre, in which they had wished to hold dances and sports functions. Similarly, adult members of the Samaj were discouraged from holding life-cycle and other celebrations in the Centre. The discouragement was partly overt and partly structural—the Centre, as mentioned, was located in the city centre, away from the Gujarati residential areas; moreover, it was extremely expensive even for members to hire, because of heating costs.[12]

This final phase is perhaps least rooted in the desires and aspirations of the heterodox remainder. It might be fair to say that in 1982 the non-leaders were still experiencing the second phase, the 'open options' period, where they were vacillating between their religious identity and their *jati* identity. For these Srimalis Jainism was an aspect of being Srimali—in East Africa, for example, it marked them off from other *vania jati*s. In Jamnagar the Srimalis operate as a *jati* group through their property ownership: in particular they own, as

[11] For example, rotating credit schemes in this country on which individual members could draw, and the general status aggrandizement that a *jati* in India can earn through the success of its members overseas (see Michaelson 1983: 132–3, which discusses the Halari Visa Oswals doing this in East Africa).

[12] One man told me that to hire the Centre for his son's engagement function in November 1982 would have cost approximately £90. Instead he hired one of the Hindu temples, in the heart of Belgrave (Shakti Mandir), at a cost of £25.

do other *jati*s, two *vadi*s, where social and religious functions are carried out in the presence of other Srimalis. Likewise, as detailed in Chapter 4, Jain temples and other specifically religious properties are, by and large, owned by *jati*s (Srimali or Oswal) and not by sect groups or Jains as a whole.

In England, or indeed anywhere abroad, the use of Jain property needs to replicate in part the uses of Jain property in India, or for the purposes of this argument, of Jain property in Jamnagar. That is, somewhere to meet as a (religious or *jati*) group, somewhere to worship, and somewhere to perform religious observances. In Chapter 4 I noted that in Jamnagar this property was of three main types: the temple, the *vadi*, and the *upasraya*, and it was noted that the *upasraya* served two purposes: as a place of residence for the ascetics and as a place of learning and instruction for the laity. The former purpose is of course redundant in the overseas context.

It was also noted that the possible conflict between social divisions (inter- and intra-*jati*) and religious divisions (sect) was avoided through, on the one hand a proliferation of properties (thirty-nine), and on the other a structural vagueness which led to property that was divided socially (on the basis of *jati* and sub-*jati* division) to be viewed

(19)

as divided religiously (on the basis of sectarian division), thus allowing religion in its essential form to be seen as transcending mundane worldly affairs. Obviously in Leicester it was not, and will not be, possible to purchase properties to meet every religious and social need. The conflict between the religious and the social, defused in Jamnagar, appeared in Leicester in the guise of neo-orthodoxy and heterodoxy. Just as the absence of property can be detrimental to an immigrant group in Leicester, forcing it into competition with other groups to find a place to express socio-cultural solidarity, so the presence of property can cause problems, by providing a focus for internal tensions. This conflict was probably always present in the Leicester Jain community, even before the purchase of the property, although the inter-*jati* conflict was initially to the fore. At the time of my fieldwork in 1982 the potential for further conflict was still there within the mono-*jati* Samaj, and expressed in the ways I have outlined above.

9

Some Conclusions

On Comparison

In a work such as this, it would seem obvious that the conclusions should, at least in part, consist of a comparison between the Jains of Jamnagar and the Jains of Leicester. Yet how does one make comparisons? How can I say that the Jains in Jamnagar and the Jains in Leicester are like each other in these and these ways and not like each

(20)

other in those and those? Should I compare behaviour, group characteristics, analytical categories (theirs and mine)? How can I reduce the complex threads of their lives to two simple sets of coordinates which may then be mapped—one upon the other—to demonstrate areas of overlap, areas of divergence?

Certainly I am against what one might term the 'rubber ball' approach—taking some ethnographic 'fact' from one location and bouncing it off data from another, such that the angle of incidence is to be taken as a measure of how much one group diverges from the other. Such 'butterfly collecting' (as Leach termed it) is ultimately sterile, quite apart from the fallaciousness of its 'scientific' pretensions. I confess to being no more convinced by the structuralist project of stripping away the flesh of lived experience to reveal the clean white bones of the underlying structures and then comparing these. Rather, I believe that any attempt at comparison should be motivated by some purpose. In this case, I have made a number of low-level comparisons throughout the book (which the reader may locate by looking up 'Comparisons' in the index) which serve merely to give added context to certain descriptions, and in the later half of this chapter I sketch out the ground work for a much more abstract (and hence speculative) approach to comparison. Before going on to that, a review of themes is in order, to bring back together the numerous ethnographic strands that the book has followed.

A Brief Summary

I said in Chapter 1 that, in part, my problem in this book was to reconcile the extensive literature on Jainism, which presented it as a coherent religious system, with my own observations, which were largely those of division. I showed initially (in Chapters 2 and 4) that the division could be social, between different Jain groups. Later (in Chapter 8) I showed that there was the potential for division inherent within the religious ideology itself. However, I have, as far as possible, avoided the pedantic approach of saying 'this author claims the Jains do or think Y, but I observed not-Y', and tried, instead, to present the ethnographic descriptions as self-supporting and, to some extent, self-validating. The purpose of this concluding chapter is to draw together the analyses presented in each of the previous chapters and present a synthesis which simultaneously links the ideal of cohesion with the observed reality of division.

The introductory chapter outlined the ethnographic and historical subject-matter that constitutes the data of the book, and presented the argument that the use of ethnography from two locations contributed towards a greater holistic understanding, which marked an advancement on the work of earlier authors on migrant groups in Britain who simply used the 'home' ethnography to support or justify an analysis of data collected in the 'immigrant' setting. I then went on to describe in brief my view of the fundamental tenets of textual and academically construed Jainism, pointing out amongst other things, that some viewed Jainism as a science not a religion, that the Jain was essentially a man or woman alone with only willpower and diligence at his or her disposal to attain the goal of *moksa*, and that practice did not necessarily accord (to a non-believer) with doctrine. I am, of course, aware of the debate on what it means 'to believe', and particularly of the contributions made by Gombrich (1971) and Southwold (1983). Nevertheless, apart from the use of 'categories of belief' in Chapter 8, which I qualified at the time, I have tried in this book to use terms such as 'believe' in their generally accepted sense, and to let the context indicate the precise shade of meaning.[1]

Part I of the book was concerned with the ethnography of the Jamnagar Jains, and an analysis of that ethnography. Using the Visa Oswal *jati* as an example I gave an account (admittedly already presented in part by Michaelson and Zarwan) of the way in which a *jati* might begin to divide over time, and went on to compare this with other kinds of division, such as between Visa and Dasa, and between urban and rural. I then expanded the ethnography by presenting a series of communal gatherings in Jamnagar that I had witnessed or heard about (Chapter 3). These presented the obvious aspects of cohesion within the smaller groups that I had isolated, as well as relations between groups (between lay and ascetic, for example). Chapter 3 was introduced with what I called an archetype: the *samavsarana* as a symbol for coming together for salvation. But I stressed, and should perhaps stress again, that this comparison was of my own devising. A *samavsarana* was part of the 'religious furniture' at many rituals and ceremonies I observed (but not necessarily all those described in Chapter 3), but its symbolism was rarely 'mapped' on to any specific gathering, except at the *diksa* ceremony when it was made

[1] An exception is the word 'Jainism' itself. Rather than define it I have tried to qualify it each time it is used ambiguously. The basis for these qualifications will be presented at the end of this chapter.

obvious that we, the witnesses, were part of the crowd that had gathered to hear Mahavira preach and that one of our number, the *diksarthi*, had heeded his call to renounce the world and tread the path of enlightenment. I used the *samavsarana* to provide a link with the historical and mythological past described in Chapter 1; I also pointed out its attractiveness as a metaphorical fixed point for the anthropologist struggling to define some Jain 'community'. Finally, I stressed the importance of the individual in the religion, a factor not of course unique to the Jains, but a point which is in accord with the doctrinal stress on the individual soul seeking its own salvation.

At the end of Part I, in Chapter 4, I illustrated how appearances can be deceptive (a parallel example of European misconceptions of Jain behaviour can be found in Banks 1986). Here, I showed how the overt divisions into sect and *gaccha* that come from the ascetics were overridden by the laity, who divided their corporately-owned property (for the most part) by *jati*, and in accordance with the divisions I outlined in Chapter 2. I offered as a preliminary conclusion the assessment that the two forms of division (the 'overt' or 'stated' and the 'actual') represented the symbiosis between lay and ascetic.

Parts I and II were then separated by Chapter 5, which told the story of the Jains and other Gujaratis in East Africa. I noted that the relations between Srimalis and Oswals that had obtained in Jamnagar and which had been determined by a number of historical and economic factors, could now be re-negotiated. Simultaneously, the complex steps of the dance between these two partners were reworked as a new set of movements was introduced: Morris's 'communal crystallization' (1968: 34 ff.).

Part II then took up the story in England, with a discussion and analysis of the Asian groups in a new setting, Leicester. The process of 'communal crystallization' was shown to be self-reinforcing. Although Leicester City Council wished to treat its ethnic minorities equally, and, if possible, as one homogeneous group, a smaller unit—a Muslim sect, for example—granted permission by the council for a new place of worship or meeting, could call on this approval as a rallying point and means of identification. Similarly, within the 'Asian community' the actions of one group (for example, Muslim religious education provision), could galvanize other groups into action. However, for the Jains, special problems arose as a result of the ambiguity of their religious and *jati* identities. Did this conflict of identity (religious v. *jati*) arise in East Africa? Possibly it did in particular towns and has just gone undocumented. But in East Africa, the two groups (Halari Visa Oswal and Visa Srimali) were larger, and the need for inter-*jati* unity was perhaps not as great. Moreover, the 'new' ideology of Jainism as an 'open' religion, which underlay the attempts at unity in Leicester, only came to the fore towards the end of the time in East Africa, through its major exponent, Chitrabhanu. The conflict of identity for the Srimalis has its parallels at other points of Jain history and ethnography: ambiguity between pre-medieval patrons and the laity *vis-à-vis* the ascetics (discussed by R. H. B. Williams 1963: xx; see also Banks 1991: 226–7; 246–7); the nineteenth-century confusion over the Jains' status as a social and religious group, parallel to that of the Hindus (see Banks 1986); the two means of expressing solidarity through the Navnat and Navkasi feasts (see Chapter 3), and so on.

Part II continued by presenting a set of ethnographic data to parallel that given for the Jamnagar Jains in Part I. Yet the parallels were not exact: the Leicester group was smaller, newer, and less 'organic' (in that its members had come from different places at different times) than the Jamnagar groups (*jati*s, *jati* sections, sects, and *gaccha*s). This meant that events and celebrations were more arbitrary in their format, and that the Srimali Jains were more under the sway of self-appointed leader figures. Most importantly, the absence of ascetics meant an absence of traditional authority figures and doctrinal strictures. Because of this, I argued, organizational experiments in form were possible in Leicester, the most obvious being the local development of the neo-orthodox approach to Jainism discussed in Chapter 8 (although neo-orthodoxy is not unique to Leicester Jains and may be found in India).

In the last chapter of Part II, I emphasized again the different perceptions one may have of Jainism. In previous chapters I had discussed or implied the confusions that could arise when observers (including myself) viewed Jainism. In this last chapter, however, I related these perceptions to the actors alone. Not only can the observation and study of Jainism present different pictures to the historian, the theologian, and the anthropologist, but participation in the activities and beliefs of the religion can engender different perceptions in those participants. However, in this latter case I stressed that the issues that gave rise to varying perceptions were inherent within the religious corpus (history, text, ritual, doctrine) itself, which is why I insisted on calling the 'tendencies' categories of belief, not believers. There were, of course, differences between the individuals who gravitated towards different tendencies, most noticeably between the leaders and the led, but it would be crude and reductionist to imply that fixed groups developed strategies to instrumentalize specific aspects of their religion for ulterior purposes.

Up until this point I have offered little in the way of conclusions, merely drawn together a number of themes from the preceding chapters. In what follows I wish to focus on a rather grand and abstract issue—the nature of religion. It is clear that my attempts to locate the Jains in Parts I and II are continually frustrated by the fluidity and permeability of the boundaries that I and others have attempted to erect around them—they are so like their Hindu neighbours in India, so like other Gujaratis in Britain, that their internal divisions in both places seem to create intra-group differences that are far more significant than inter-group differences. Instead, somewhat hesitantly and thus briefly, I wish to consider the 'obvious' answer, the one that they themselves would automatically assume to be correct: it is Jainism that makes them Jains.

Do Religions Think Themselves?

Southwold has argued, convincingly in my view, that a religious system such as Buddhism engenders 'sapiental' strategies on the part of the believers, rather than instrumental (1983: 187 ff.). That is to say, there is a way of thinking (and believing) for ameliorating experience (the aim of all action, for Southwold) by altering the mind and the self, rather than the environing world (which is how instrumental action seeks to ameliorate experience) (ibid.: 188). Thus, if I were to paraphrase Southwold by according a spurious rationality to the religious system, it might be said that the instrumental strategy is characterized by the believer 'using' the religious system for his or her own ends, while the sapiental strategy is characterized by the religious system 'using' the believer: the 'flow' of instrumental action is reversed. But I don't credit the system with such rationality, and so instead would summarize Southwold's argument by saying that action channelled through such a system is reflexive; that is, that action on the part of a believer ultimately affects the cognitive position of the believer. In part, this is recognized by Jains with orthodox or neo-orthodox tendencies in India and Leicester, who say that they perform rituals and ceremonies not to please the absent *tirthankara*s, but to cultivate discipline and reverence in themselves. Such an explanation rests on the notion of self-awareness, and it is my belief that all adherents of major (or world, great tradition, textual) religions are self-aware. By self-aware, I mean entertaining a notion of otherness, observed within both the transcendental/mundane opposition, and the believer/non-believer opposition. I take this idea of opposites and consequent self-awareness from the work of Bourdieu (1977) and Eisenstadt (1984), which I discuss below.

Taking Bourdieu first, I wish to return for a moment to an incident I mentioned at the start of the book. At the end of Chapter 1 I related a story concerning my shopkeeper friend Jagjivandas, his daughter Hina, and the three different strategies by which they could approach the problem of her poor eyesight and low marriage prospects. In the light of the discussion in the previous chapter, we might be able to label these strategies. The approach which ascribed Hina's misfortune to bad *karma* earned in previous lives and which advocated resignation and the practice of austerities as a solution was orthodox in character; the advice to consult an astrologer and thus circumvent fate was heterodox in approach; buying contact lenses and concentrating on a 'modern' solution was a typically neo-orthodox strategy. Such labelling, by the definitions and examples I gave in the last chapter, is not perfect, but I include the example partly because, as I explained in Chapter 1, the story was narrated to me when I mentioned the varieties of belief I encountered in Leicester, and partly because I wish to discuss the principles of such division in a wider context.

Bourdieu, discussing ideology generally, rather than just religious belief, labels rather differently. He distinguishes between what he terms 'doxa', 'orthodoxy', and 'heterodoxy' (1977: 159–71). Moreover, he takes as the baseline, as the starting-point, a condition which I could not identify in the practice of Jainism in Leicester and which I suspect could not be identified in any Jain group at any time. Doxa, he says, is an 'experience', not a belief, characterized by a 'quasi-perfect correspondence between the objective order and the subjective principles of organization [such that] the natural and social world appears as self-evident' (ibid.: 164). By contrast, 'orthodox or heterodox belief implies awareness and recognition of the possibility of different or antagonistic belief' (ibid.). Doxa is only made apparent when an opposing belief is voiced (the 'universe of discourse' or 'opinion') but then doxa dissolves, for the 'quasi-perfect correspondence' is broken. Orthodoxy arises when the dominant class defends the doxa—thereby reifying it—against attack from the heterodox (ibid.: 169).

To place this more in the perspective of my own argument I turn to Gellner, who presents a more overarching view. In his article 'Notes Towards a Theory of Ideology' he proposes that ideologies are 'intellectually sovereign' and that 'from the inside, ideologies are not merely true: what is far more important is that they provide the very criterion for telling truth from falsehood. They monopolise validation' (1979*a*: 122). Although similar to Bourdieu's notion of doxa, Gellner's discussion of ideology does not presuppose such a state of primal naïvety. He goes further, too, by introducing the notions of 'offence' and 'bait' to bound the ideological system, rather than seeing the boundaries defined by conflict (Bourdieu's structural Marxism). The bait lures the would-be believer in, the offence traps him or her there and repels others, thus separating the believer from the unbeliever (ibid.: 121). In fairness, Bourdieu and Gellner are not necessarily discussing the same thing—indeed, Gellner states: 'I have endeavoured to exclude from "ideology" the very big thing, namely our total vision of reality' (ibid.: 130), which is in effect what Bourdieu labels 'doxa'. It is for this reason that I do not re-label the terms I used in Chapter 8, in such a way that 'orthodoxy' becomes 'doxa', 'neo-orthodoxy' becomes 'orthodoxy' and so on. As I said earlier, I do not consider any of the forms of Jainism I studied to be the 'original' form, something which represents the 'universe of the undiscussed (undisputed)' (Bourdieu 1977: 168). Admittedly, the picture I gave of heterodoxy in the last chapter borders on this by its eclecticism and inclusiveness, but the experience of being a member of a religious and ethnic minority is sufficient to alert an actor to otherness, to self-awareness. Bourdieu says that such self-evidence occurs only when 'the conditions of existence of which the members of a group are the product are very little differentiated' (ibid.: 167). Can such a feeling of self-evidence through minimal differentiation occur in a religious context? Any answer to such a question rests in part on the definition of religion. For example, this state of self-evidence, and thus the existence of doxa, may well be commonplace in the religion of 'tribal' and simple societies[2] but the differences between these and 'great' religions are many.

Above, I mentioned Eisenstadt who proposes that self-awareness arises from sets of oppositions. Taking his lead from Karl Jaspers' notion of the 'Axial age', Eisenstadt posits the distinction between 'pagan' civilizations, which had structured the transcendent world in a

---

[2] Note that Gellner excludes these as 'ideologies' because their doctrinal propositions lack 'independent power' (1979*a*: 130–1).

similar fashion to the mundane, a homologous perception, and the Axial and post-Axial civilizations which 'noted a sharp disjunction between the transcendental and mundane worlds, with a concomitant stress on the existence of a higher transcendental moral or metaphysical order beyond any other-worldly reality' (Eisenstadt 1984: 3–4).[3] This 'sharp disjunction' resulted in a perceived tension between the two worlds, and hence the notion of 'salvation' to bridge the gap. But while some visions of salvation focused on the need for 'the reconstruction of the human personality and behaviour in accordance with the precepts of the higher moral or physical order' (ibid.: 4), others called for total social and political reorganization and reorientation, to try and bring the mundane world to the standard of the transcendental one.

To bridge the 'tension gap', autonomous (religious) specialists arose —the Greek philosophers, Brahman priests, and the Sramanas—each of which claimed to have found the path to cross to the transcendental. Naturally, there was competition within any civilization between different groups of these élites. At any one time there might be one 'winner', a group that had gained the ear of the political powers-that-be, and a number of dissenting groups, or heterodoxies (ibid.: 5). Bourdieu says that the development of orthodoxy, a reification of the doxa, to counter a heterodoxy, is the beginning of class struggle: 'the awakening of political consciousness' (Bourdieu 1977: 169–70). Similarly, Eisenstadt states that linkages between religious heterodoxies and disenfranchised political élites could and did develop in Axial and post-Axial civilizations. These alliances led to 'a new form of civilizational dynamics, one that transformed group conflicts into potential class and ideological conflicts, and cult conflicts into struggles between the orthodox and the heterodox' (Eisenstadt 1984: 5).

However, Eisenstadt goes further and maintains that there is a difference between those civilizations where the prevailing orthodoxy was and is embodied by a central 'church' and exists as a codified and bounded doctrine (Christianity is an example, and, to a lesser extent, Islam and Judaism), and those which are 'looser', where the 'structuring and application of cognitive doctrine to mundane matters has never been a matter of paramount importance' (ibid.: 6). In this

---

[3] The 'Axial age' concept is a more refined version of Rhys Davids' 'leap forward in speculative thought' (the second of Deo's 'reasonable views' to explain the rise of the Sramana movements, including Jainism; 1956: 49), the period in the first millenium BC when the world's great civilizations (Greece, China, India) were consolidated.

second type, typical of Hindu and Buddhist civilizations, any opposition towards these prevailing orthodoxies is organized through a set of sects, while in the former type, opposition is articulated through heterodoxies. The difference, for Eisenstadt, rests on the fact that heterodoxies aim to change the political and cultural bases of the civilization, while sects merely seek to expand 'the institutional scope and diversity' of society (ibid.: 8). Hence Hindu sectarianism 'played an important role . . . in changing the processes of caste mobility and [in] crystallizing new castes' (ibid.: 7). It also helped to integrate the tribal groups and to establish trade centres based around temple complexes (ibid.).

The point of Eisenstadt's argument is to demonstrate that the oriental heterodoxies operated in a totally different way from those of Christendom (particularly Calvinism) and hence the absence of radical social upheavals, akin to capitalism, in these civilizations can be explained. However, even given the 'looseness' of Hindu civilization and doctrine, Eisenstadt fails to realize the radical break with the prevailing world view that Jainism—and more especially, Buddhism—presented. What Eisenstadt does not explain is why Buddhism, for him a sect of (or more accurately, a sect in relation to) Hinduism, should itself become a religion, an orthodoxy. Two related questions spring from this. First, what is a religion? Secondly, what is the difference between a religion and a sect?

Religions or Sects?

With regard to religion, Southwold has pointed out that Buddhism sits uneasily with most definitions because it is neither concerned with superhuman or god-like beings, nor do Buddhists contrast radically the Durkheimian 'sacred' with the 'profane' (Southwold 1978: 365 n. 7). Both these points are equally well true of Jainism, especially the sacred/profane contrast: as I said in Chapter 1, the universe for the Jain authors is essentially mundane: gods, men, *tirthankaras*, and demons are all subject to the same natural laws. However, I could not state, with the conviction that Southwold does for the Buddha (1978: 366), that my informants all knew perfectly well that Mahavira was not a transcendental god, or the expression of such a god. In fact, in Chapter 8 I stated that some people clearly thought that he was. I have, however, no desire to try and explain this in the way that Southwold (1983), and more especially Gombrich (1971), do. I am not trying to substitute my picture of 'true' Jainism for the prevailing one, nor do I think there is a 'true' picture of the religion. The intellectual satisfaction of the quest to find such a picture is undoubtedly attractive, hence the nineteenth-century search for the historical Jesus and the historical Buddha (see Southwold 1983: Chapter 10), but it is illusory.

Southwold, following Needham (1975), describes the category 'religion' as a polythetic class. That is, a class which has certain features, some of which are shared by some members of that class (the religions of the world) but none of which are shared by all members (1978: 370 and *passim*). Could we go further and say that all the varieties of a particular religion constitute a polythetic class, one in which all the varieties exhibit—but may not share—some of the features? There would be both longitudinal and latitudinal perspectives to this: the Jainism practised in the fifth century BC (probably) has little in common with the Jainism practised in and around the same region of Bihar today. Similarly, the varieties of Jain belief in Leicester that I have described in Chapter 8 are clearly not mirror-images of Jamnagar Jainism. But all these, and many other 'Jainisms' I have not described, bear certain marks, certain distinguishing features, that legitimates a common identity (which brings us back to a monothetic class). For the analyst, these features include the use of the historical and mythological person of Mahavira as a focal point, the concept of *ahimsa*, the existence of an ascetic order with certain codes of dress and other behaviour and so on. For the Jains, too, a level of identification with other Jains, predicated on a sense of common core features, is a taken-for-granted feature. The point is, that just as academics and theoreticians search for 'Real Definitions' and monothetic classes (classes in which all members share all the same features) so do the ordinary people.

There is the idea—met in India at least—that all religions are fundamentally the same, but there is also the idea that sects within a religion can be 'better' or 'worse', hierarchically ranked because some match up to the required component of features necessary for admission to the class better than others. The outside observer may have a supposedly objective idea of a prototype or an exemplar—one member of a class or category that best typifies the features that make up that class or category. For the insider, on the other hand, there are or may be both moral and political subjectivities which rank the class member to which one is affiliated as the exemplary one: thus we have the idea of hierarchical or ranked monotheticism.

This is the origin of religious 'corruption'—a charge often levelled at one aspect of religious practice (or belief) by proponents of another (see Gombrich 1971: 45–52). Differing subjective criteria of evaluation, however, may promote non-hierarchical 'difference'; this brings about the idea of cohesion, that for those who do not wish to see the differences, there are no differences—members of a monothetic class must all be the same. Jains of the heterodox tendency in Leicester perceived differences, but not cleavages, between themselves and those who espoused neo-orthodoxy. And, as I pointed out, some who perceived these differences only mentioned them to me in private, fearing that a public declaration would result in fission. It is here, I think, that the ideological differences between a religion and a sect lie. Perceived monothetic classes are 'stretched' as much as possible to reconcile differences between varieties of a religion, often by introducing the idea of hierarchy, or by the use of the 'lineage perspective' (see Chapter 1) which relates sects more or less closely to an original and full member of the class, thus providing a common core. But too much stretching and the differences become irreconcilable, a sect becomes a religion, a member of another, ideally monothetic, class (though both continue to be members of the same polythetic class, 'religion'). In actuality, of course, sects become religions for other reasons, most importantly the provision of state patronage.

Buddhism died out in India yet became a religion elsewhere, while Jainism stayed, and although it did become a state religion at various points in its history there are some today who would consider it no more than an adjunct to the prevailing Hindu ethos. I suggested in Chapter 1 that Jainism was able to survive in medieval India when Buddhism could not because the Jain ascetics might have been more astute in shifting their attention from their waning or fickle patrons to their increasingly wealthy laity. In a short paper on the subject P. S. Jaini (1980) offers a further explanation. Considering a variety of causes advanced by other scholars for the decline of Indian Buddhism, he accepts only one, 'insufficient cultivation of the laity', as able to explain both Buddhism's disappearance and Jainism's survival (ibid.: 84) (all the other arguments advanced are equally applicable to Jainism and thus cannot explain its continued existence apart from Buddhism). Yet even this he sets aside as insufficient and looks instead to non-sociological explanations. He concludes by claiming that Buddhism, with its conception of *bodhisattva*s as heavenly mediators, was more prone to (doctrinal) encroachment by the Hindu majority, than the atheistic Jainism. These *bodhisattva*s became 'virtual gods, who dispensed worldly boons and even spiritual grace in a manner not unlike that of the Hindu deities' (ibid.: 86). Eventually, the *bodhisattva*s 'functionally usurped' the historical Buddha, leaving Buddhism as a simple polytheistic system (ibid.). Hindus took over Buddhist temples and easily made them their own through iconographical shifts (ibid.: 86–7). Conversely, by sticking dogmatically to their 'unexciting' but unique doctrines, the Jains ensured their own survival (ibid.: 88). In some respects, Jaini's explanation implicitly rests on that which he partially rejects: that survival was possible through the strength of lay–ascetic ties. The adherence to such unique and fortifying doctrines was only possible because of the closeness of ascetics and laity. But the argument is important because in this implicit link between his own theory and the one he rejects lies the notion of cultural cohesion—that because ascetics and lay were united in doctrine they ensured their communal stability and survival. Structure and culture combine to support and reify.[4]

Together and Apart

What then of the cohesion and division I mentioned at the beginning of this chapter? Clearly, there are two levels we must consider: the cohesion of the Jain 'community'—the groups of people calling themselves Jain—which at the same time features a large number of divisions, while on the other level there is the cohesion of religious doctrine, which, as I showed in Chapter 8, also exhibits cleavages. The cohesion of doctrine is doxa in Bourdieu's usage: the empirical 'reality' of its existence, like the reality of a 'Real Definition' (Southwold 1978: 370) is unimportant to the observer, what matters is its reality as perceived by the actors. It is my opinion that the perceived reality of doxa is that which mitigates against the tendency for fission within the 'community' (and thus allows us, once aware of this, to remove the inverted commas around the word).

Throughout the book I have presented a series of oppositions, in both the religious and the social spheres: lay/ascetic; neo-orthodox/ heterodox; Digambara/Svetambara; Mahajan/other Oswal; Oswal/ Srimali. All these are transformations of the basic orthodox/heterodox

---

[4] Southwold uses a similar argument to explain that 'empirically indeterminate doctrines' (such as rebirth) can, by a process of cultural reification, become 'important and indubitably true to members of a cultural community' and thus form a rallying point for a society (1978: 374–5).

opposition which arises when the illusion of doxa is broken. They are a series of power relations, even confrontations, within the Jain doctrinal corpus and within the Jain community. But the ideal of a monothetic class, the ideal of cohesive ideology, is that which attaches significance to these oppositions. The notion of 'difference' is predicated on a concept of 'sameness'.

This idea, that the potential for sameness bridges the gap between differences, thus enabling social processes to continue, is by no means novel or startling. As I said in the beginning, I set out to write a descriptive work, and I hope that the analysis and theoretical abstractions presented in this final chapter are largely self-evident from the rest of the text. Moreover, such a conclusion, which supports a 'common sense' view, is one that I feel will be most satisfying to my informants and to Jains elsewhere, as well as being the one that I, the anthropologist, endorse.

REFERENCES

ADAMS, C. J. (1977) (ed.), *A Reader's Guide to the Great Religions*, 2nd edn. (New York: Free Press).

BAIRD, R. D. (1976), 'Religion and the Secular: Categories for Religious Conflict and Religious Change in Independent India', in Smith (1976), 47–63.

BALLHATCHET, KENNETH, and HARRISON, JOHN (1980) (eds.), *The City in South Asia: Pre-modern and Modern* (London: Curzon).

BANKS, MARCUS (1986), 'Defining Division: An Historical Overview of Jain Social Organisation', *Modern Asian Studies*, 20/3: 447–60.

—— (1989a), 'The Narrative of Lived Experience: Some Jains of India and England (Photographic essay)', *Critique of Anthropology*, 9/2: 65–76.

—— (1989b), 'Review of: Judith Thomson and Paul Heelas, *The Way of the Heart: the Rajneesh Movement* (Aquarian Press 1986)', *JASO* 20/1: 88–9.

—— (1991), 'Competing to Give, Competing to Get: Gujarati Jains in Britain', in Werbner and Anwar (1991), 226–50.

—— (forthcoming), 'Why Move? Regional and Long Distance Migrations of Gujarati Jains', in Foot (forthcoming).

BAROT, ROHIT (1973), 'A Swaminarayan Sect as a Community', *New Community*, 2: 34–7.

BAYLY, CHRISTOPHER (1978), 'Indian merchants in a "Traditional" Setting: Benares 1780–1830', in Dewey and Hopkins (1978), 171–93.

—— (1983), *Rulers, Townsmen and Bazaars: North Indian Society in the Age of British Expansion, 1770–1870* (Cambridge: Cambridge University Press).

BECHERT, HEINTZ (1983), 'A Remark on the Problem of the Date of Mahavira', *Indologica Taurinensia*, 11: 287–90.

BHACHU, PARMINDER (1985), *Twice Migrants: East African Sikh Settlers in Britain* (London: Tavistock Publications).

BHADRAGUPTAVIJAYJI, MUNI (1976), *Life of Children* (Mehsana (Gujarat): Shri Vishva Kalyan Prakashan Trust).

BHAGAVAN MAHAVIRA 2,500th Nirvana Mahotsava Samiti (1977) (ed.), *Mahavira and his Teachings* (chief ed., A. N. Upadhye) (Bombay: Bhagavan Mahavira 2,500th Nirvana Mahotsava Samiti).

BHARATI, AGEHANANDA [Leopold Fischer] (1965), 'A Social Survey', in Ghai (1965), 13–63.

—— (1972), *The Asians in East Africa: Jayhind and Uhuru* (Chicago: Nelson Hall).

BHATTACHARYA, J. N. (1973), *Hindu Castes and Sects* (Calcutta: Editions Indian) (First published 1896).

BHATTACHARYA, N. N. (1976), *Jain Philosophy in Historical Outline* (Delhi: Munshiram Manoharlal Publishers Pvt. Ltd.).

BHATTACHARYA, S. (1973), 'The Rise of the Vaisyas in the Post-Vedic Period', *South Asian Review*, 7: 43–53.

BOURDIEU, PIERRE (1977), *Outline of a Theory of Practice* (Cambridge: Cambridge University Press) (First published 1972).

BRIGGS, H. G. (1849), *The Cities of Gujarashtra: Their Topography and History, Illustrated in the Journal of a Recent Tour* (Bombay: James Chesson).

BUHLER, J. G. (1903), *On the Indian Sect of the Jainas* (London: Luzac and Co.) (First published 1887).

BURGESS, JAMES (1869), *The Temples of Satrunjaya: The Celebrated Jaina Place of Pilgrimage near Palitana in Kathiawad* (Bombay: Sykes and Dwyer).

—— (1876), *Report on the Antiquities of Kathiawad and Kachh*, Archaeological Survey of Western India, ii (London: W. H. Allen).

BURGHART, RICHARD (1983), 'Wandering Ascetics of the Ramanandi Sect', *History of Religions*, 22: 361–80.

—— (1987) (ed.), *Hinduism in Great Britain: The Perpetuation of Religion in an Alien Cultural Milieu* (London: Tavistock Press).

CARRITHERS, MICHAEL (1988), 'Passions of Nation and Community in the Bahubali Affair', *Modern Asian Studies*, 22/4: 815–44.

—— and HUMPHREY, CAROLINE (1991) (eds.), *The Assembly of Listeners: Jains in Society* (Cambridge: Cambridge University Press).

CATER, J., and JONES, T. (1978), 'Asians in Bradford', *New Society*, 44: 81–2.

CHATTERJEE, A. K. (1978), *A Comprehensive History of Jainism* (Calcutta: Firma Klm Private Ltd.).

COLEMAN, DAVID A. (1982) (ed.), *Demography of Immigrants and Minority Groups in the United Kingdom* (London: Academic Press).

COMMISSARIAT, M. S. (1938), *A History of Gujarat: Including a Survey of its Chief Architectural Monuments and Inscriptions*, i, AD 1297–AD 1573 (Bombay: Longmans, Green and Co.).

COTTAM, CHRISTINE (1980), 'City, Town and Village: The Continuum Reconsidered', in Ballhatchet and Harrison (1980), 324–42.

DEO, S. B. (1956), *History of Jaina Monachism: From Inscriptions and Literature* (Poona (Pune): Deccan College).

—— (1974), 'The Expansion of Jainism', in Ghosh (1974), 22–34.

DERRETT, J. M. D. (1968), *Religion, Law and the State in India* (London: Faber and Faber).

DESHPANDE, PANDURANG GANESH (1978), *Gujarati–English Dictionary* (Ahmedabad: University Book Production Board).

DEWEY, C. and HOPKINS, A. G. (1978) (eds.), *The Imperial Impact: Studies in the Economic History of Africa and India*, Institute of Commonwealth Studies, Commonwealth Papers No. 21 (London: Athlone Press).

DUMASIA, NAOROJI K. (1927), *Jamnagar: A Sketch of its Ruler and its Administration* (Bombay: The Times Press).

DUMONT, LOUIS (1980), *Homo Hierarchicus: The Caste System and its Implications*, 2nd edn. (Chicago: University of Chicago Press) (First published 1966).

DUNDAS, PAUL (1985), 'Food and Freedom: The Jaina Sectarian Debate on the Nature of the Kevalin', *Religion*, 15: 161–98.

EISENSTADT, SAMUEL N. (1984), 'Dissent, Heterodoxy and Civilizational Dynamics: Some Analytical and Comparative Indications', in Eisenstadt, Kahave, and Shulman (1984), 1–9.

—— KAHAVE, R., and SHULMAN, D. (1984) (eds.), *Orthodoxy, Heterodoxy and Dissent in India* (Berlin: Mouton).

ERIKSSON, ROLF (1984), ' "Indians" and "Africans" in a Hindu Gujarati Context', unpublished paper presented at a symposium on Gujarati ethnicity (organizer: Maureen Michaelson).

FISCHER, EBEHARDT, and JAIN, JYOTINDRA (1977), *Art and Rituals: 2,500 Years of Jainism in India* (Delhi: Sterling Publishers Private Ltd.).

FOOT, ROSEMARY, and BROWN, JUDITH (forthcoming) (eds.), *Migration: The Asian Experience* (London: Macmillan).

FORBES, A. K. (1924), *Ras Mala: Hindu Annals of the Province of Goozerat in Western India*, 2 vols. (London: Oxford University Press) (First published 1856).

FORESTER, TOM (1978), 'Asians in Business', *New Society*, 43: 420–3.

FOX, RICHARD G. (1969a), *From Zamindar to Ballot Box: Community Change in a North Indian Market Town* (New York: Cornell University Press).

—— (1969b), 'Varna Schemes and Ideological Integration in Indian Society', *Comparative Studies in Society and History*, 11: 27–45.

—— (1973), 'Pariah Capitalism and Traditional Indian Merchants, Past and Present', in Singer (1973), 16–36.

GALEY, JEAN-CLAUDE (1985) (ed.), *L'Espace du temple: Espaces, itinéraires, médiations*, Collection Purusartha No. 8 (Paris: Éditions de l'École des Hautes Études en Sciences Sociales).

—— (1986) (ed.), *L'Espace du temple II: Les sanctuaires dans le royaume*, Collection Purusartha No. 10 (Paris: Éditions de l'École des Hautes Études en Sciences Sociales).

Gazetteer (1884), *Gazetteer of the Bombay Presidency*, viii, *Kathiawar* (Bombay: Government Central Press).

—— (1970), *Gazetteer of Jamnagar District* (Ahmedabad: Government of Gujarat).

GELLNER, ERNEST (1979a), 'Notes Towards a Theory of Ideology', in Gellner (1979b), 117–32.

—— (1979b) (ed.), *Spectacles and Predicaments* (Cambridge: Cambridge University Press).

GHAI, D. P. (1965) (ed.), *Portrait of a Minority: Asians in East Africa* (Nairobi: Oxford University Press).

GHAI, Y. P., and GHAI, D. P. (1971), *The Asian Minorites of East and Central Africa*, Minority Right Group Paper No. 4 (London: Minority Rights Group).

GHOSH, A. (1974) (ed.), *Jaina Art and Architecture*, i (Delhi: Bharatiya Jnanpith).

GOMBRICH, RICHARD F. (1971), *Precept and Practice: Traditional Buddhism in the Rural Highlands of Ceylon* (Oxford: Oxford University Press).

GUPTA, A. (1975), 'India and the Asians in East Africa', in Twaddle (1975), 125–39.

GUPTA, G. R. (1971) (ed.), *Family and Social Change in Modern India* (Durham, NC: Carolina Academic Press).

GUSEVA, N. R. (1971), *Jainism* (Bombay: Sindhu Publications Private Ltd.).

HANDIQUI, K. K. (1949), *Yasastilaka and Indian Culture* (Sholapur (India): Jaina Samskrti Samrakshaka Sangha).

HASTINGS, J. (1914) (ed.), *Encyclopedia of Religion and Ethics*, vii (Edinburgh: T. and T. Clark).

HOCKINGS, PAUL (1987) (ed.), *Dimensions of Social Life: Essays in Honor of David G. Mandelbaum* (Berlin: Mouton de Gruyter).

HOLLINGSWORTH, L. W. (1960), *The Asians of East Africa* (London: Macmillan).

HOLY, LADISLAV, and STUCHLIK, MILAN (1981) (eds.), *The Structure of Folk Models* (London: Academic Press).

HORSCH, PAUL (1966), *Die Indische Gathe- und Sloka-Literatur* (Berne: Francke Verlag).

HUMPHREY, CAROLINE (1982), 'A Conversation with Jain Nuns', *The Jain*, 6/3: 6–7.

—— (1985), 'Some Aspects of the Jain Puja: The Idea of "God" and the Symbolism of Offerings', *Cambridge Anthropology*, 9/3: 1–19.

HUSBAND, C. (1982) (ed.), *'Race' in Britain: Continuity and Change* (London: Hutchinson and Co.).

ILIFFE, JOHN (1979), *A Modern History of Tanganyika* (Cambridge: Cambridge University Press).

INDEN, RONALD (1986), 'Orientalist Constructions of India', *Modern Asian Studies*, 20/3: 401–66.

India Today (International Edition) (1981), *Bahubali: A Spectacular Celebration*.

—— (1984), *Battle for Bahubali*.

JACKSON, P., and SMITH, S. J. (1981) (eds.), *Social Interaction and Ethnic Segregation* (London: Academic Press).

JACKSON, ROBERT (1976), 'Holi in North India and in an English City', *New Community*, 5: 203–10.

JACOBI, H. (1914), 'Jainism', in Hastings (1914), 465–74.

JAIN, J. (1975), *Religion and Culture of the Jains* (Delhi: Bharatiya Jnanpith).

JAIN, J. C. (1947), *Life in Ancient India as Depicted in the Jaina Canons* (Bombay: New Book Company).

JAIN, K. P. (1930), 'A Further Note on the Svetambara and Digambara Sects', *Indian Antiquary*, 59: 151–4.

JAINI, J. L. (1916), *Outlines of Jainism* (Cambridge: Cambridge University Press).

—— (1978), *The Self-Realization: Being the Translation of Atma-Siddhi of Shrimad Rajchandra* (Ahmedabad: Shrimad Rajchandra Gyan Pracharak Trust) (First published 1923).

JAINI, PADMANABH S. (1977), 'Bhavyatva and Abhavyatva: A Jain Doctrine of "Predestination"', in Bhagavan Mahavira 2,500th Nirvana Mahotsava Samiti (1977), 95–111.

—— (1979), *The Jaina Path of Purification* (Belmont: University of California Press).

—— (1980), 'The Disappearance of Buddhism and the Survival of Jainism: A Study in Contrast', in Narain (1980), 81–91.

JHAVERI, M. B. (1949), *Jain Views Regarding Religious and Charitable Trusts* (Bombay: Shri Jain Swetambar Conference).

JOSHI, HARKISAN (1988), *Nagar, Navanagar, Jamnagar* (in Gujarati) (Jamnagar (India): Jamnagar District Cooperative Publishing and Printing House Ltd.).

KALGHATGI, T. G. (1969), *Jaina View of Life* (Sholapur: Lalchand Hirachand Doshi).

KAPFERER, BRUCE (1976) (ed.), *Transaction and Meaning: Directions in the Anthropology of Exchange and Symbolic Behaviour* (Philadelphia: Institute for the Study of Human Issues).

KAPLINSKY, R. (1978) (ed.), *Readings on the Multinational Corporation in Kenya* (Nairobi: Oxford University Press).

KHAKHAR, D. P. (1876), 'Castes and Tribes in Kachh', *Indian Antiquary*, 5: 167–74.

KINCAID, CHARLES A. (1931), *The Land of Ranji and Duleep* (Edinburgh: William Blackwood and Sons Ltd.).

KNOTT, KIM (1986), *My Sweet Lord: The Hare Krishna Movement* (Wellingborough: Aquarian Press).

LCC (1981), *Key Facts about Leicester. No. 1: Population* (Leicester: Leicester City Council, City Planning Office).

—— (n.d.*a*), *Places of Worship in Leicester* (Leicester: Leicester City Council, City Planning Office).

—— (n.d.*b*), *Places of Worship in Leicester: Advice Notes for Prospective Developers* (Leicester: Leicester City Council, City Planning Office).

LCCR (1982*a*), *Distribution of Ethnic Minorities in Leicester* (Leicester: Leicester Council for Community Relations).

—— (1982*b*), *The Ethnic Minority Population of Leicester* (Leicester: Leicester Council for Community Relations).

LEVINE, N., and NAYAR, T. (1975), 'Modes of Adaption by Asian Immigrants in Slough', *New Community*, 4: 356–65.

LODRICK, D. O. (1981), *Sacred Cows, Sacred Places: Origins and Survivals of Animal Houses in India* (Berkeley: University of California Press).

MAHIAS, MARIE-CLAUDE (1985), *Délivrance et Convivialité: Le Système culinaire des Jaina* (Paris: Éditions de la Maison des Sciences de l'Homme).

MAJMUDAR, M. R. (1965), *Cultural History of Gujarat* (Bombay: Popular Prakashan).

MAJUMDAR, R. C., RAYCHAUDURI, H. L., and DATTA, K. (1963), *An Advanced History of India* (London: Macmillan).

MANGAT, JAGJIT SINGH (1969), *A History of the Asians in East Africa: 1886–1945* (Oxford: Clarendon Press).

MANKAD, DOLARRAY R. (1972), *Jamnagarno Itihas* [History of Jamnagar (in Gujarati)] (Aliabada (Jamnagar): Haribhai Research House).

MARRIOT, McKIM (1976), 'Hindu Transactions: Diversity without Dualism', in Kapferer (1976), 109–42.

MAYER, PHILIP (1961), *Townsmen or Tribesmen: Conservatism and the Process of Urbanisation in a South African City* (Cape Town: Oxford University Press).

MEHTA, D. (n.d.), *Shrimad Rajchandra: A Life* (Ahmedabad: Shrimad Rajchandra Janma Shatabdi Mandal).

MEHTA, M. J. (1927?), *The Jains and Palitana* (Ahmedabad: (LD Institute Library, No. 3808)).

MICHAELSON, MAUREEN (1983), 'Caste, Kinship and Marriage: A Study of Two Gujarati Trading Castes in England', unpublished Ph.D. thesis: University of London.

MORRIS, H. STEPHEN (1957), 'Communal Rivalry among Indians in Uganda', *British Journal of Sociology*, 8: 306–17.

—— (1968), *Indians in Uganda: Caste and Sect in a Plural Society* (London: Weidenfeld & Nicolson).

MURRAY, R. (1978), 'The Chandarias: The Development of a Kenyan Multinational', in Kaplinsky (1978), 283–307.

NAHAR, P. C. (1929), 'A Note on the Svetambar and Digambar Sects', *Indian Antiquary*, 58: 167–8.

—— (1932), 'Antiquity of the Jain Sects', *Indian Antiquary*, 61: 121–6.

NARAIN, A. K. (1980) (ed.), *Studies in the History of Buddhism* (Delhi: BR Publishing Corporation).

NEEDHAM, R. (1975), 'Polythetic Classification: Convergence & Consequences', *Man*, NS 10/3 : 349–69.

NEVASKAR, B. (1971), *Capitalists Without Capitalism: The Jains of India and the Quakers of the West* (Westport, Conn.: Greenwood Publishing Corporation).

NOBLE, WILLIAM A. (1987), 'Houses with Centered Courtyards in Kerala and Elsewhere in India', in Hockings (1987), 215–62.

PANDE, G. C. (1978*a*), 'Introduction', in Pande (1978*b*), 3–9.

—— (1978*b*) (ed.), *Sramana Tradition: Its Contribution to Indian Culture* (Ahmedabad: LD Institute of Indology).

—— (1978*c*), 'Sramanism as a Weltanshauung and its Relationship to the Tradition', in G. C. Pande (1978*b*), 1–26.

PATEL, NARSI (1971), 'Hinduism outside India: Selective Retention in Gujarati Families', in Gupta (1971), 233–56.

PHILLIPS, DEBORAH (1981), 'The Social and Spatial Segregation of Asians in Leicester', in Jackson and Smith (1981), 101–21.

—— (1983), 'The Socio-Cultural Implications of Asian Patterns of Settlement', unpublished Ph.D. thesis: University of Cambridge.

POCOCK, DAVID F. (1955), 'The Movement of Castes', *Man: Proceedings of the Royal Anthropological Institute*, 55: 71–2.

—— (1957), ' "Difference" in East Africa: A Study of Caste and Religion in Modern Indian Society', *Southwestern Journal of Anthropology*, 13: 289–300.

QUIGLEY, DECLAN (1988), 'Is Caste a Pure Figment, the Invention of Orientalists for their own Glorification?', *Cambridge Anthropology* 13/1: 20–36.

REES, T. (1982), 'Immigration Policies in the United Kingdom', in Husband (1982), 75–96.

RENOU, LOUIS (1953), *Religions of Ancient India* (London: Athlone Press).

REYNELL, JOSEPHINE (1985*a*), 'Honour, Nurture and Festivity: Aspects of Female Religiosity among Jain Women in Jaipur', unpublished Ph.D. thesis: University of Cambridge.

—— (1985*b*), 'Renunciation and Ostentation: A Jain Paradox', *Cambridge Anthropology*, 9/3: 20–33.

—— (1991), 'Women and the Reproduction of the Jain Community', in Carrithers and Humphrey (1991), 41–65.

ROBINSON, VAUGHAN (1982), 'The Assimilation of South and East African Asian Immigrants in Britain', in Coleman (1982), 143–68.

ROWE, WILLIAM L. (1973), 'Caste, Kinship and Association in Urban India', in Southall (1973), 211–49.

RUBY, JAY (1980), 'Exposing Yourself: Reflexivity, Film and Anthropology', *Semiotica* 3/1–2: 153–79.

RUSSELL, ROBERT VANE (1916), *The Tribes and Castes of the Central Provinces of India* (London: Macmillan and Co).

SAHLINS, MARSHALL (1987), *Islands of History* (London: Tavistock Social Science Paperbacks) (First published 1985).

SANGAVE, VILAS A. (1980), *Jaina Community: A Social Survey* (Bombay: Popular Book Depot) (First published 1959).

SAPSFORD, JOAN (1980), 'A Study of the Following in Leicester of Jalaram Bapa', unpublished B.A. thesis: University of Leicester.

SCHERMERHORN, RICHARD A. (1978), *Ethnic Plurality in India* (Tucson: University of Arizona Press).

SHAH, A. M. (1982), 'Division and Hierarchy: An Overview of Caste in Gujarat', *Contributions to Indian Sociology*, NS, 16: 1–33.

—— (1988), 'The Rural–Urban Networks in India', *South Asia*, 11/2: 1–27.

—— and SHROFF, RAMESH G. (1959), 'The Vahivanca Barots of Gujarat: A Caste of Genealogists and Mythographers', in Singer (1959), 40–73.

SHAH, SNEH (1979), 'Who are the Jains?', *New Community*, 7: 369–75.

SHETH, C. B. (1953), *Jainism in Gujarat: AD 1100–1600* (Bombay: Shree Vijay Devsur Sangh Gnan Samiti for the Managing Trustees of the Godiji Jain Temple and Charities).

SINGER, MILTON (1959) (ed.), *Traditional India: Structure and Change* (Philadelphia: The American Folklore Society).

—— (1973) (ed.), *Entrepreneurship and Modernization of Occupational Cultures in South Asia* (Durham, NC: Duke University Press).

SMITH, B. L. (1976) (ed.), *Religion and Social Conflict in South Asia* (Leiden: E. J. Brill).

SOMPURA, K. F. (1968), *The Structural Temples of Gujarat (up to 1600 AD)* (Ahmedabad: Gujarat University).

SOUTHALL, AIDEN (1973) (ed.), *Urban Anthropology: Cross-Cultural Studies of Urbanization* (New York: Oxford University Press).

SOUTHWOLD, MARTIN (1978), 'Buddhism and the Definition of Religion', *Man*, NS 13: 362–79.

—— (1983), *Buddhism in Life: The Anthropological Study of Religion and the Sinhalese Practice of Buddhism* (Manchester: Manchester University Press).

STEVENSON, A. M. (1910), *Notes on Modern Jainism* (Oxford: Basil Blackwell).

—— (1915), *The Heart of Jainism* (Oxford: Oxford University Press).

TAMBIAH, STANLEY J. (1984), *The Buddhist Saints of the Forest and the Cult of Amulets* (Cambridge: Cambridge University Press).

TAMBS-LYCHE, HARALD (1975), 'A Comparison of Gujarati Communities in London and the Midlands', *New Community*, 4: 349–55.

—— (1980), *London Patidars: A Case Study in Urban Ethnicity* (London: Routledge and Kegan Paul).

TATIA, N., and KUMAR, MUNI M. (1981), *Aspects of Jaina Monasticism* (Delhi: Today and Tomorrow's Printers and Publishers).

THOMPSON, JUDITH, and HEELAS, PAUL (1986), *The Way of the Heart: the Rajneesh Movement* (Wellingborough: The Aquarian Press).

TIMBERG, T. A. (1971), 'A North Indian Business Firm as Seen through its Business Records, 1860–1914', *Indian Economic and Social History Review*, 8: 264–283.

—— (1978), *The Marwaris: From Traders to Industrialists* (Delhi: Vikas Publishing House PVT Ltd.).

TINKER, HUGH (1975), 'Indians Abroad: Emigration, Restriction and Rejection', in Twaddle (1975), 15–29.

TOD, JAMES (1920), *Annals and Antiquities of Rajasthan*, 3 vols. (London: Oxford University Press).

TSUJ, N. (1970), 'Review of: Die Indische Gathe- und Sloka-Literatur (Paul Horsche)', *Indo-Iranian Journal*, 12: 27–34.

TWADDLE, MICHAEL (1975) (ed.), *Expulsion of a Minority: Essays on Ugandan Asians* (London: Athlone Press).

UGANDA RESETTLEMENT BOARD (1973), *Interim Report* (London: HMSO).

VINAYASAGAR, MAHOPADHYAYA, and LATH, MUKUND (1977), *Kalpa Sutra* (Jaipur, India: D. R. Mehta, Prakrit Bharati).

WARD, ROBIN, and JENKINS, RICHARD (1984) (eds.), *Ethnic Communities in Business* (Cambridge: Cambridge University Press).

WATSON, JAMES C. (1977) (ed.), *Between Two Cultures: Migrants and Minorities in Britain* (Oxford: Basil Blackwell).

WEBER, MAX (1958), *The Religion of India: The Sociology of Hinduism and Buddhism* (New York: The Free Press) (First published 1920).

WERBNER, PNINA (1990), *The Migration Process: Capital, Gifts and Offerings among British Pakistanis* (Oxford: Berg).

—— and ANWAR, MUHAMED (1991) (eds.), *Black and Ethnic Leaderships in Britain: The Cultural Dimensions of Political Action* (London: Routledge).

WESTWOOD, SALLIE, and BHACHU, PARMINDER (1988) (eds.), *Enterprising Women: Ethnicity, Economy and Gender Relations* (London: Routledge).

WILBERFORCE-BELL, H. (1916), *The History of Kathiawad: From the Earliest Times* (London: Heinemann).

WILLIAMS, RAYMOND B. (1984), *A New Face of Hinduism: The Swaminarayan Religion* (Cambridge: Cambridge University Press).

WILLIAMS, R. H. B. (1963), *Jaina Yoga: A Study of the Mediaeval Sravakacaras* (London: Oxford University Press).

YANCEY, W. C., ERICKSEN, E. P., and JULIANA, R. N. (1976), 'Emergent Ethnicity: A Review and Reformulation', *American Sociological Review*, 41: 391–403.

ZARWAN, J. (1974), 'The Social Evolution of the Jains in Kenya', *Hadith* [Special issue: *History and Social Change in East Africa*, ed. B. A. Ogot], 6: 134–44.

—— (1975), 'The Social and Economic Network of an Indian Family Business in Kenya, 1920–1970', *Kroniek van Afrika*, 3: 219–236.

GLOSSARY

The glossary lists all the terms used in the text with their correct diacritical marks. I pointed out in the Preface that local pronunciation does not always accord with the textual bias of the metropolis (wherever and whenever that is located). The reader should thus be aware that the diacritical marks give a guide to one particular form of pronunciation and spelling, that used by standard dictionaries and glossaries. On the whole, the meaning or definition of a word accords with its use in the text and thus derives from the context from which it is drawn (either abstract or textual Jain discourse, or contemporary usage among Gujarati Jains).

A line over a vowel (e.g. ā) indicates a lengthening of that vowel; ś and ṣ are aspirated, ś being close to 'sh'; 'c' is always pronounced 'ch'; an 'h' after a consonant indicates aspiration, so 'th' is never pronounced as in 'theatre', but as in 'pithead—that native speakers of standard English regularly aspirate initial consonants; ṭ, ḍ, ḷ, and ṇ are retroflex consonants pronounced with the tongue far back in the mouth; ṅ (Gujarati terms) or ñ indicates nasalisation, as does ṃ (Sanskrit and Prakrit terms).

ācārya	the (male) head or leader of a group of ascetics 29, 46, 47, 81, 82, 83 n., 88, 97, 106 n., 118
*āgama*s	the canonical scriptures; it consists of some sixty texts but some of them are no longer in existence and the status of the remainder varies between the different sects 20, 110
ahiṃsā	the desire not to cause violence or harm 5, 18–20, 94, 107, 109, 207, 228
ailak	a grade of Digambara asceticism, midway between layman and full ascetic 30, 119
ajīva	non-living 16
anekāntavāda	the principle of 'relativity', of looking at an issue from several viewpoints 186, 207 n.
aṅga	literally, 'limb'; a branch of the scriptures 21
aṅga pūjā	worship of an idol of the *tīrthaṅkara* during which the limbs and other parts of the body are anointed with sandalwood paste 172
āṅgī	body-cladding of ornamented silver which is placed on the normally bare idol of a *tīrthaṅkara* at certain festivals 114
*aṇuvrata*s	minor vows (*vrata*s) which may be taken by lay people 46

arihant	someone worthy of worship, a synonym for *tīrthaṅkara* 83 n.
ārti	act of worship in which a small oil lamp on a *thālī* is waved in front of an idol (of a *tīrthaṅkara* or some other being worthy of devotion); the *stavan* which accompanies *ārti* praises the first *tīrthaṅkara* Rishabha (under his name Adinath) and each verse is sung while the *thālī* is slowly circled round clockwise 83, 114, 136, 172–3, 175, 177, 182–4, 188, 192, 194, 197, 201
aticār	breaches of *ahiṃsā* that one commits accidentally 177
aṭṭhāī	a total fast of eight days 176
avasarpiṇī	one-half of the the time-cycle of the universe during which things gradually get worse (physically and morally) 23
āyambīl	a restricted diet in which most flavourings are eschewed and food is taken only once a day 91–4, 95, 97, 175, 189
āyambīl olī	a special period of fasting—see *āyambīl*
āyambīlśālā	a hall where people gather to observe *āyambīl* 95
bāldīkṣā	*dīkṣā* taken by a child 95–6
bāndhaṇī	a tie-and-dye fabric found especially in Gujarat and Rajasthan; Jamnagar is renowned as a local centre of production 42
bāṇia	trader or merchant (see also *vāṇia*) 5
bāvangāmī	the fifty-two—the villages around Jamnagar in which Halari Visa Oswals are to be found 49, 59 n., 129–31, 133
bhajan	a religious or devotional song 114, 116, 172, 175
bhajiyā	small pellets of deep-fried chick-pea flour paste 97
bhakti	religious devotion; term used of a number of Hindu movements which stress devotion to God over learning or the correct performance of rituals 27, 149, 185, 205
bhandāro	a communal feast for all the Brahmins in some small area 96
bhāvanā	a religious or devotional song 175
bhojansālā	a hall for eating, usually attached to a *dharmaśālā* or *upāśraya* 92, 105, 189

bodhisattva	A Buddhist who vows to attain Buddhahood but 'postpones' doing so and enters heaven in order to help other creatures 229–30
caṅdan	sandalwood, an auspicious substance used in offerings 88
cāndī	silver 44
cattāri mangalaṃ	the auspicious four—four persons and things that enshrine the Jain path, part of one's daily prayers and intoned as a communal prayer at functions in Leicester 192, 193
cevḍo	a snack of small fried items—split peas, peanuts, chick-pea flour, vermicelli, etc. 172
comāsuṅ	the monsoon or rainy period, during which ascetics should remain in one place 176
corāsī	the eighty-four *jātis* or 'orders' of Brahmans in Gujarat; a feast at which all Brahmans in a wide area come together 96
covīsī khaṃbhāḷio	the Khambhalia twenty-four—the villages near to Jamnagar where the Halari Visa Oswals claim to have orginally settled 49
dahiṅ	yoghurt 92
dāḷ	split pea or lentil; a watery or stiff preparation of cooked split peas or lentils 93, 97
dalāl	dealer or middleman 65
dān	gift 26, 82
darśana	a system of philosophy 26; (as used by contemporary Jains) the 'beholding' of an idol; this is thought to be an active process of worship not a passive one 32, 83, 113, 114, 117
derāsar	a (Jain) temple 44, 45, 83–4, 102, 112–14, 117–24
deśī	of the countryside 58
devadravya	god's money—that class of gifts which can only be used for the purposes of worship 105–6, 122
dharma	religious duty or law; that which dictates the correct way to behave for a person in a particular situation 26, 206
dharmaśālā	a rest house, usually for religious pilgrims 13, 105
dhārmik	religious 91

dhotī	man's long loin-cloth; worn by older men daily but by younger men only for religious ceremonies and festivals 79, 83, 113, 178, 180
dīkṣā	religious initiation 28–9, 78, 80–2, 88–90, 95, 97, 99, 100, 115, 123, 207, 220
dīkṣārthī	a (female) religious initiant 80–2, 88–90, 97, 108, 221
diśā	direction or quarter 51
divyadhvani	the divine sound uttered by a *tīrthaṅkara* (according to Digambaras) at a *samavasaraṇa* which can be understood by all 77
dukā	(from *dukān*—shop) name used of Asian merchants' stores in parts of East Africa 126
duṣamā	unhappy; the name of a section of the *avasarpiṇī* half of the universe's time cycle 16, 22–3, 118, 208
duṣamā suṣamā	unhappy–happy; the name of another section of the *avasarpiṇī* half of the universe's time cycle 22
gaccha	an order of ascetics; a division within the Jamnagar Jain *jāti*s 33–4, 55-6, 58, 60–1, 79, 81, 89, 90, 100, 102, 108, 110–12, 117–24, 138, 174, 176, 180, 195, 198, 200, 207, 221, 222 (see also *gaccha* names in main index)
galī	a small, narrow residential street 70–1, 108
gaṇa	a small band of ascetics who travel together 90
gaṇdharas	the group of disciples who first follow a *tīrthaṅkara* when he begins preaching 22, 25
gāṇṭhiyā	a dry snack made of deep-fried chick-pea flour paste 172
garbha gṛha	the inner sanctuary of a temple 83
ghar derāsar	'house temple'; a temple containing consecrated idols located in a private house to which the public is allowed access 112–13, 120
goḷ	unrefined cane sugar molasses 92
gulāb jāṃbu	deep-fried sweet, like a small doughnut, soaked in sugar syrup 91
gurduārā	Sikh place of worship 144, 148, 150, 206
guru	(religious) teacher 29, 88–9, 108, 110, 118, 181 n.
guru–cela	'teacher–student'—a very special relationship in Indian religious systems 138

hiṃsā	the desire to cause violence or harm 18–20, 61, 83, 182, 203, 211 (see also *ahiṃsā*)
hiṅg	asafoetida, an acrid smelling and tasting spice 93
īśat prāgbhārābhūmi	the slightly bending place—term used to describe the crescent-shaped heaven at the top of the universe where the *tīrthaṅkara*s and other liberated souls reside 17, 20–1
jalebī	a sweetmeat made by dribbling batter into hot oil in spirals and then soaking in sugar syrup 172
jām	title of the rulers of Jamnagar 39
jāti	'caste' 4–5, 44, 45, 48–59, 61–4, 73, 76–8, 80, 82, 88, 90–1, 94, 96, 98, 99, 100, 108–12, 117–24, 127–9, 133, 136, 151, 156, 163–6, 167, 170, 174, 197, 199, 207, 213–17, 220–2
jilla	sub-district, one of the administrative regions of modern India 40, 44, 45
jina	spiritual conqueror—a synonym for *tīrthaṅkara* and the origin of 'Jain' 15, 46, 77, 83, 184 (see also *tīrthaṅkara*)
jina āgama	the corpus of Jain scriptures 105
jina bhavana	Jain temple 105
jina bimba	Jain image or idol of a *jina* 105
jīva	soul; life-form 16, 19, 20, 83
jīvadyā	compassion for life; giving money or other gifts to aid this cause is one of the many ways to earn *puṇya* 190
jīvat-khāna	life store—room where Jains are said to deposit household sweepings so that any insects accidentally swept up can live in safety 19 n.
jñāti	'caste'; also sometimes used to describe a group in the process of becoming endogamous and thus forming a new *jāti* 5 n., 53, 61
kaḍhī	a thin sauce of yoghurt and chick-pea flour used to moisten rice 93
kāla	a segment or era of the universe's time-cycle 18, 118, 208
kaṅku	red turmeric powder used for making an auspicious mark on the forehead (the red dot worn between the eyes by married women is known as *bindī* or *bīnkī*) 89

kariyātuṅ-nu pāṇī	a medicinal drink made by boiling a bitter herb (ophelia chirata) 93
karma	generally 'action', but used by Jains to describe minute particles of matter that cling to the soul through action and weigh it down 16–19, 23, 30 n., 34–5, 86, 100, 122, 176, 187–8, 202, 203–4, 205, 224
kevalajñāna	omniscience; the state of the soul after it has shed all *karma* and has total perception 16, 22, 23, 46, 113
khākharā	a dry biscuit made by dry-roasting *roṭlī* 93
khāṅd	refined sugar 93
khes	cloth worn by men over the shoulders and teamed with a *dhotī* 79, 83, 178, 180
khicaḍi	a substantial dish of rice and split peas or lentils cooked together 60, 93
khorāk	substantial food such as rice and *dāl*, a meal 91
kṣullak	the lowest grade of Digambara ascetic 30, 119
lāḍu	a sweet ball, made of pellets of fried chick-pea paste 160
loṭī	a small metal water pot 86
loṭo	a large metal water pot 82
mad	pride 84
madh	honey; some Jains maintain a lifelong prohibition on honey in their diet justifying it by one or more of three reasons: honey gathering entails the loss of the bee lavae's lives; honey ferments easily and causes countless tiny beings to come into existence and then die; fermenting honey could contain alcohol which—if consumed—might lead to a loss of self-control and possible *hiṃsā* 93
mag-nu pāṇī	water in which *mag* (mung or moong in English) beans have been cooked 93
mahāvīra janma vāncan	the reading of Mahavira's birthday (from the Kalpa Sutra) 178
mākhaṇ	butter 92
mālā	a rosary made up of 108 beads (an auspicious number) 121 n., 181, 186
mālājāpa	'telling' the *mālā*, often by reciting the Naukār *mantra* once for every bead 179

mamrā	puffed rice eaten as a snack 93, 172
mān	respect 84
maṇḍap	an often highly decorated awning supported on four poles under which ceremonies, such as marriage, are conducted 116
maṅgaldīvo	similar to *ārti* but performed with a five-branched light 114, 172–3, 175, 183–4, 188, 192, 194, 197
mantra	sometimes a spell or a secret and talismanic phrase, but usually used by the Jains to describe short 'prayers', versed stanzas of veneration to describe praiseworthy beings 15, 94, 116, 136, 161, 172, 179, 186, 188, 202, 203
marī	black pepper 93
melā	a fair—agricultural or recreational 104
micchāmi dukkaḍam	a phrase asking pardon (of a *guru* or of a fellow Jain) for any thoughtless act which caused harm 181, 182
mīṭhāī	collective term for sweetmeats of all kinds 97
mokṣa	salvation, emancipation; the *karma*-free soul finally gaining release from the body and ascending to *siddha loka* 15, 90, 101, 105, 109, 202 n., 211, 220
muh patti	mouth covering, either specially constructed (Sthanakavasi laity and ascetics) or simply a piece of cloth or a handkerchief knotted around the face (Deravasi ascetics and laity), used by the laity when in close proximity to an idol, reciting a *mantra*, speaking to an ascetic, or reading scriptures or *sutra*s; the common explanation given is that one's hot and perhaps malodorous breath harms or kills small air creatures—while this cannot be avoided on a daily basis (although Sthanakavasi ascetics wear them permanently) it is a precaution that can be taken in the above situations 83, 118, 181
mūlasūtra	one of the canonical scriptures—a text of lectures, *mantras* and stories all of which are claimed to make up Mahavira's last sermon 21
mūlnāyak	original hero—the principal idol or *mūrti* in a *derāsar*; the *derāsar* may often be named or known locally by the name of the *tīrthaṅkara* represented 112

mumukṣā	*mokṣa*-seeking—a term often associated with the Kanji Panth as they place the striving for *mokṣa* over the perceived goals of other sects, such as gaining *puṇya* through performing elaborate rituals or ostentatious charity in the form of *jīvadayā* 101
mūrti	idol or statue 112
namaskār	salutation or greeting 15, 182, 191
nānā jīva	small lives/souls—see *jīva*
nāsto	a snack (often translated, inappropriately, as 'breakfast'), food which is not *khorāk* 91, 172
nāt	local pronunciation of *jñāti* 5 n., 53, 54, 94–6, 133
naukār (mantra)	a nine-line *mantra* which salutes (i.e. *namaskār*) five worthy classes of beings—*tīrthaṅkaras*, other liberated souls, *ācāryas*, teaching ascetics, and all other ascetics 15, 94, 97, 173, 186, 193
nav	nine 15 n.
navnāt	nine *nāts*—a federation of *jātis* brought together for business and sometimes marriage purposes 54
nigoda	tiny, one-sensed creatures which exist everywhere; the very lowest form of life into which a soul can be born 83, 94
pad	rank, grade 97
padmāsana	a seated posture, the legs crossed, the hands in the lap; this is a posture of meditation and Svetambara *mūrtis* of the *tīrthaṅkaras* are usually depicted like this 118
pādukā	footprint; the presence of a being worthy of worship at a particular site is often marked by *pādukā* 118
pāghaḍī	turban 96
pajusaṇ	a period of ten days of fasting and penance during *comāsuṅ*, culminating in *saṃvatsarī* 177 (*see* Paryushan)
pakṣ	party or grouping 54
pañcāṅg	printed calendar 33, 122–3, 177, 178
pañca parameṣthin	the five beings worthy of worship for a Jain (see *naukār (mantra)*) 83 n.
pañcāyat	'caste' council or executive body; also a form of local level government in post-independent India 116

panth	way or path, hence its metaphorical use to mean (religious) sect 54, 67, 138
pāpaḍ	crisp savoury biscuit of rice and *dāl* flours, usually known as poppadam in English 93
pāraṇa	fast breaking, also the meal or food used to break the fast 86–8, 91, 192
Paryushan = *paryūṣaṇa*	Sanskrit form of the Prakrit *pajusaṇ* 77 n., 176–84, 191–2
pāthraṇuṅ	small mat 180
pāṭhśālā	teaching hall; a large room often attached to an *upāśraya* where formal instruction in Jain principles and practices is given 58, 71, 84, 86–7, 94, 96, 107, 161, 178 n., 188
peṇḍa	sweet made of coagulated milk 172
prasād	the returned offering—the sweet, coconut, or other food item that one takes away from a Hindu temple after it has first been offered to the god 206
pratikramaṇa	a daily recitation—obligatory for ascetics, recommended for the laity—during which the day's sins are confessed to a *guru* 161, 176–84, 186, 189, 192, 197, 209, 210, 211
pūjā	worship; usually taken to mean an act of ritual worship, such as anointing the idols 30, 32, 77, 83, 105, 107, 113–14, 117, 148, 171–2, 175, 202, 204 n.
pūjārī	priest; for the Jains *pūjārī*s are simply technicians, they generally only officiate at weddings and funerals while those employed in *derāsar*s are little more than sweepers and cleaners 113, 206
puṇya	merit; good *karma* 30 n., 108, 199, 202
puṇya-kṣetra (sāt)	the (seven) 'fields' of merit in which the laity can 'sow' their good deeds and 'reap' the reward of *puṇya* 30, 105–6
rajoharaṇa	small broom of soft fibres, looking a little like a large dish-mop, used to gently sweep away insects one might sit on; ascetics carry these all the time, the laity only on certain occasions, such as visiting ascetics or when performing *pratikramaṇa* 180
roṭlī	small, thin unleavened bread 93, 97
roṭlo	larger and coarser form of *roṭlī*, often made from millet 93, 97

sādhāraṇa	general, ordinary (funds); gifts to *derāsar*s and other religious organizations which are specifically not marked as *devdravya* 105, 122
sādhu	male ascetic 28, 30, 69, 79 n., 82, 87, 88, 90, 97, 105, 108, 136
sādhvī	female ascetic 28, 30, 69, 79 n., 80, 81, 83, 87, 88, 105, 108, 136
sākar	sugar candy, coarse lumps of crystallized sugar 192
sallekhanā	ritual fasting to death; this is the final austerity which can only be undertaken with the permission of one's *guru* 88 n.
samavasaraṇa	sacred assembly; the gathering of all living things to hear the message of salvation preached by the *tīrthaṅkara* 22, 76, 77–8, 81, 99–101, 184–5, 220–1
sampradāya	religious sect 54
saṃsāra	worldly life; the cycle of death and rebirth 15, 21
saṃskāras	(Hindu) life-cycle rituals such as those for birth, marriage, death, etc. 27, 78 n.
saṃvatsarī	the annual ceremony of public confession (see *pratikramaṇa*) which occurs at the end of Paryushan; also the name for the day on which it occurs 58 n., 88, 110, 112, 127, 171, 176–7, 182–4, 191
sāṃvatsarīk kṣamāpanā	apology letters; pre-printed or handwritten letters are sent to friends and relatives one could not see in person at *saṃvatsarī* in order to say *micchāmi dukkaḍam* to them 182
saṅgha	(entire) religious community; for the Jains this means *sādhu*s, *sādhvī*s, *śrāvak*s, and *śrāvikā*s 25, 26, 28, 123
saṅgharo	a sub-order of ascetics; some *gaccha*s—such as the Tapa Gaccha—are very large and are split into smaller sub-sections for administrative and practical purposes 90
sarpiṇī	one-half of the universe's time-cycle 18
*śāsana devī*s	female guardian deities associated with the *tīrthaṅkara*s 32
*śāsana devatā*s	male guardian deities associated with the *tīrthaṅkara*s 202 n., 204
satsaṅg	(religious) association or gathering 76, 172–3, 175, 182, 188

śeraḍī-no ras	sugar-cane juice 86
śibir	a camp; series of meetings held under canvas 77, 187 n., 188
siddha	emancipated soul; used to refer to those men (and possibly women) who have achieved liberation but have not preached the message of salvation 15 n., 83 n., 184, 204
siddhacakra	wheel of the *siddha*s—a diagrammatic representation of beings and qualities worthy of worship for a Jain, found in *derāsar*s incised upon brass or copper plates and constructed temporarily out of fruit, rice, etc. on the floor of the *derāsar* for certain rituals 83, 92, 117, 184
siddha loka	place or abode of the *siddha*s; a more common name for *īśat prāgbhārābhūmi* 17, 204
snātra pūjā	bathing worship; a small metal idol of a *tīrthaṅkara* is bathed in a stream of milk and water, in memory of the holy bath given to the infant *tīrthaṅkara*s by the gods of heaven 79 n., 175
śrāvak	layman 28, 105
*śrāvakācāra*s	texts of lay doctrine and practice written between the fifth and thirteenth centuries AD 25–8, 181
śrāvikā	lay woman 28, 105
śrī mālā	holy garland 51
stavan	religious song 116, 136, 172–3, 182–3, 184, 188
śud	the bright half of the lunar month 82, 86, 91
sūṇṭh	dry ginger 93
suṣamā	happiness 16, 22
sūtra	scripture or holy text 181
talāv	small lake 42
tāluka	district, one of the administrative regions of modern India 40, 44, 59
tapas	austerity 83 n.
tapascaryā	penance, the effect of *tapas* 93
tapasvī/tapasī	woman/man who performs *tapas* 86–8, 93–4, 97, 190, 191–2
tapasyā	austerity—mental or physical 35, 86
tel	oil 92
thāḷī	flat stainless steel (or, formerly, brass) dish with raised sides used as a plate for eating and for many other purposes 86, 87, 91, 92, 93, 192
tilak	auspicious mark on the forehead 89–90

tīrtha	literally, 'ford' or 'crossing place'; used to denote a pilgrimage site, particularly one associated with the liberation of a *tīrthaṅkara* 103
tīrthaṅkara	ford-builder, one who has crossed the ocean of worldly life; there have been twenty-four *tīrthaṅkara*s in our era (starting with Rishabha and ending with Mahavira), but Jain texts speak of earlier and later series, as well as *tīrthaṅkara*s who are currently preaching on other continents of the earth 15–18, 21–3, 30, 32, 46, 78, 79, 82, 83 n., 84, 86, 90, 100, 101, 103, 105, 109, 112–14, 117, 118, 154, 172, 179, 185–6, 195, 202, 204–5, 223, 227
tithi	auspicious day of the lunar month, variously calculated 33–4, 107, 110, 122
upādhyāya	preceptor or ascetic teacher 83 n.
upāśraya	monastery, a place where ascetics stay and to which the laity may retreat for short periods of prayer and meditation 58, 60, 73, 74, 81, 84, 87, 88, 90, 92, 103, 107–8, 110–11, 112, 115–16, 117–24, 138–9, 180, 183, 188, 190, 191, 216, 202
upvās	a fast, total abstinence from food (and sometimes water) 86, 191
vad	the dark half of the lunar month 177
vādī	large building with open or covered courtyard for *jāti* functions 59, 62, 87, 91, 97, 112, 116–17, 117–24, 136, 214, 216
vāḍkī	small dish 91, 93, 192
vāṇia	trader or merchant (see also *bāṇia*) 5, 44, 51, 53, 54, 75, 76, 94, 95, 110, 133, 161, 215
varghoḍo	procession 78
varṇa	'caste'; one of the four classes of humankind 4, 48, 53
varṣī dān	yearly giving or year of giving 80–2, 88
varṣītap	year's austerity, the name given to a particular kind of fasting 85, 86–7, 190
vastīpatrak	register of a census—a directory listing all registered members of a *jāti* 49 n., 79 n., 90
videśī	foreigner; outsider 51
vidiśā	outside or beyond some region 51

AUTHOR INDEX

SUBJECT INDEX